Ian W. Shaw is the author of five books including *The Bloodbath* (2006), *On Radji Beach* (2010), *Glenrowan* (2012) and *The Ghosts of Roebuck Bay* (2014). *The Bloodbath* was nominated for a Victorian Premier's Literary Award and was shortlisted in the Local History category. Ian is a graduate of the University of Melbourne and holds postgraduate degrees from Monash University and the University of Michigan. After ten years as a secondary school teacher, Ian worked in the Commonwealth public service and private enterprise for three decades, and is an expert on security issues. He lives in Canberra.

THE
RAG TAG
FLEET

IAN W. SHAW

hachette
AUSTRALIA

Published in Australia and New Zealand in 2017
by Hachette Australia
(an imprint of Hachette Australia Pty Limited)
Level 17, 207 Kent Street, Sydney NSW 2000
www.hachette.com.au

10 9 8 7 6 5 4 3 2 1

National Library of Australia
Cataloguing-in-Publication data:

Shaw, Ian W., author.
The rag tag fleet/Ian W. Shaw.

ISBN: 978 0 7336 3729 2 (paperback)

United States. Army, Pacific.
World War, 1939-1945 – Equipment and supplies.
World War, 1939-1945 – War work – Australia.
World War, 1939-1945 – Campaigns – Pacific Area.
Fishing boats – War use – Australia.
Fishing boats – War use – Pacific Area.
Civilians in war – Australia – Biography.
Military service, Voluntary – Australia – History.
Military supplies.
Military sealift – Australia – History.
Pacific Area – History, Military – 20th century.

Cover design by Luke Causby, Blue Cork Design
Cover photographs courtesy of Australian War Memorial/Colin Thomas Halmarick
    (AWM 054583/054582)
Maps by Kinart
Text design by Bookhouse, Sydney
Typeset in 12/17.25 pt Simoncini Garamond by Bookhouse, Sydney
Printed and bound in Australia by McPherson's Printing Group

The paper this book is printed on is certified against the
Forest Stewardship Council® Standards. McPherson's Printing
Group holds FSC® chain of custody certification SA-COC-005379.
FSC® promotes environmentally responsible, socially beneficial
and economically viable management of the world's forests.

For all those who went down to the sea in ships.

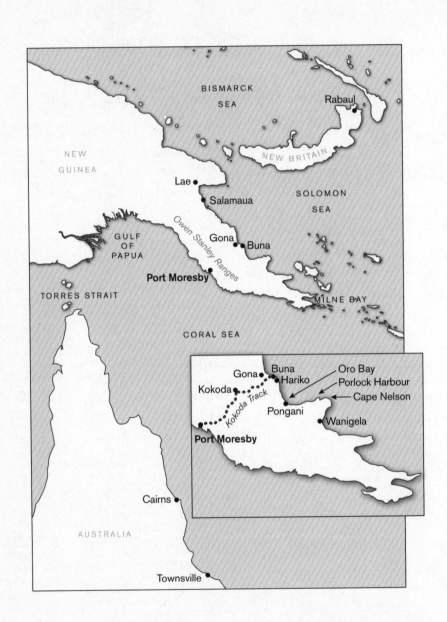

CONTENTS

PROLOGUE

SAILING THE SOUTH SEAS 1934–41

For young men who would never want for anything, the Fahnestock brothers certainly had a way of putting themselves into places where they could easily lose everything. Their family's wealth and connections could potentially have turned them into the type of New York playboys that had spawned countless books and movies in post-Depression America, but someone somewhere had encouraged them to look beyond themselves and their privileged existence to make something of their youth and talents, to live a life that mattered, a life that made a positive difference for others. Like many others in those years, Bruce and Sheridan Fahnestock turned their eyes to the South Seas and the East Indies, the thousands of islands dotted across the Pacific and into the Indian Ocean, places that had only recently been exposed to the West. They would learn what they could in that vast region and they would bring that knowledge home and share it with whoever was interested. It wasn't public service and it wasn't charity; it was an opportunity to learn more for themselves and to then pass on to others what they had learned.

Just what those learnings would be was uncertain to both of them when the planning began.

•

Adam Bruce Fahnestock was born in 1910, and his younger brother, John Sheridan Fahnestock, was born in 1912. Despite their given names, the oldest brother was only called Bruce, and the younger was known as Sheridan, though even this was usually reduced to 'Sher'. The brothers had both been born in Washington, DC, sons of a successful inventor and businessman, also named Bruce Fahnestock. Their father was interested in just about everything that moved and that could be built. By the time Sheridan was born, Bruce Fahnestock senior held patents on early motion picture projectors, the Lanston monotype, a telegraphic machine for the transmission of pictures over telegraph lines, an automatic locomotive stoker and the dynamometer car, a travelling laboratory for testing railroads and track equipment.

Bruce and Sheridan Fahnestock both inherited their father's love of inventions and new ideas, as well as his love of sailing, especially blue water sailing. When the boys were still young, Bruce senior moved the family back to his native New York, into a large property at Manhasset on Long Island, where he and his wife Mary renewed friendships with many of the prominent New York families.

It was a major stretch to go from sailing the waters of Long Island Sound and coastal New England to making a major exploratory voyage to and through the South Seas, but that is what Bruce and Sheridan planned to do during 1933 and 1934. Bruce had recently graduated from Brown University, where he had developed interests in both the natural world and writing, and he saw the voyage as an opportunity to work in both areas while doing something he loved. His somewhat fractious temper ruled him out as the expedition's leader, and he was more than happy to hand that role, and the responsibilities that went with it, over to Sheridan. Finance for the project would not be a problem either as the brothers had received a small inheritance from a cousin, John Hubbard, which was more than enough to cover the cost of a boat and provisions for what would be an extended period of time away from home.

It would be a scientific expedition, with clear goals and expectations, even though it might look like a pleasure cruise. While the brothers commenced a search for a suitable vessel for the expedition, they also began to look for suitable crewmates. They would eventually settle on four other young men for the voyage; the first three were Dennis Puleston, Wilson Glass and George Harris – all twenty-two or twenty-three years old, well educated and capable sailors. The last crewman, and the oldest of the lot at twenty-five years of age, was Hugh Davis, director of the Mohawk Zoo in Tulsa, Oklahoma, selected in part because of his qualifications and in part because his zoo would underwrite some of the trip's expenses in return for specimens.

The major sponsor of the expedition was the American Museum of Natural History in New York City. As part of that sponsorship, the Fahnestock brothers spent as much time as they could spare over a twelve-month period working as unpaid interns at the museum, honing their skills across a range of natural sciences. While Sheridan concentrated on broader areas, like history and anthropology, Bruce spent most of his time there studying entomology. When they weren't at the museum or busy with their normal lives, the brothers would drive to the ports and harbours of New England looking for the ship that would carry the expedition.

They eventually found her, a short distance to the north, anchored off City Island at the end of Long Island Sound. She was a forty-metre, three-masted schooner named *Director*, recently retired after long service as a pilot schooner for the harbourmaster at Portland, Maine. She was in relatively good condition and fell within the price range they were prepared to offer. After buying the boat, the brothers sailed the *Director* down the sound and around to Manhasset, where they lovingly and painstakingly renovated and equipped her for the voyage to follow. It would be a long voyage too, as the Fahnestocks had decided that when their work in the South Seas was done, they would continue on to circumnavigate the world and sail all the way back to New York.

Everything went according to plan and the Fahnestocks and their crew made their final farewells before a departure scheduled on the best tide that fell around 17 December 1934. The night before the scheduled departure, Bruce Fahnestock senior told Mary that he felt ill and was having trouble breathing. He took to bed and died soon afterwards.

Mary Fahnestock immediately contacted her sons. Bruce had never been sick for a single day in his life, she told her sons, and his passing had been sudden and without pain. He would have been extremely disappointed if he thought they would cancel their expedition because of an event like this. They should therefore go ahead with their plans and, if possible, she would join them as soon as she could.

•

The *Director* sailed from New York some days after Bruce and Sheridan buried their father. From New York, the schooner made its way down the east coast of America and across the

Caribbean to Panama where Mary Fahnestock was waiting for them; she had sailed directly there on a steamer after making arrangements for the maintenance of the family home. Clearing the Panama Canal and entering the Pacific Ocean, the expedition made stops at the Galapagos Islands and the Marquesas Islands before heading down and across to French Polynesia. From there, they sailed across to Samoa and Tonga before heading due west to the New Hebrides and the islands of Melanesia beyond. Wherever they stopped, they stayed for as long as it took to collect and document specimens for the Museum of Natural History. Hugh Davis was the expedition's herpetologist and photographer, capturing everything they saw and everywhere they went on film and in writing.

The expedition ran into trouble while sailing among the islands that stretched from the Solomon Islands to New Britain. Bruce Fahnestock fell extremely ill with malaria and several of the others were also suffering from a variety of illnesses. A decision was made to terminate the expedition early and to sail directly to the Philippines where American assistance would be available.

Bruce became extremely ill soon after they docked at Manila. As well as malaria, he was diagnosed with a strangulated hernia, which was fixed by an operation at the American hospital in Manila. To add to their woes, Sheridan then went down with an attack of Blackwater fever, but fortunately survived.

The expeditioners agreed that they had achieved as much as could reasonably be expected and declared the expedition over in mid-1937. The *Director* was sold to local interests in Manila while the specimens they had collected were packed carefully into three large chests and despatched to the Museum of Natural History. All but the Fahnestocks booked passage home aboard one of the Dollar Line Steamships which operated between

Manila and San Francisco. The three Fahnestocks decided to take the opportunity to visit Beijing, then a remote and exotic location.

Shortly before they arrived in the city in July 1937, Japanese militarists had staged an incident, later known as the Marco Polo Bridge Incident, during which Chinese and Japanese troops clashed. The Japanese militarists used this clash as an excuse to begin a full-scale invasion of China, and the Fahnestocks had front row seats when it began.

Sheridan was filming the ceremonial entry of Japanese troops into Beijing when a Japanese officer approached him and punched him in the head, twice, while he was peering through the lens of his camera. Sheridan, who was much larger than the Japanese, considered punching him back, but realised that hundreds of Japanese troops were watching, so he simply stopped filming and stepped back. Had the cameraman been Bruce, who was even bigger and had a fiery temperament, the outcome might have been different.

The incident served as a disquieting coda to what had been a more than interesting and quite successful cruise. It was also enough to convince the Fahnestock brothers to return home to plan what they would do next.

•

Back home in Manhasset, Bruce and Sheridan both wrote extensively of their adventures for the New York *Herald Tribune* and for magazines such as *Harper's* and *Esquire*. They also collaborated on a book they called *Stars to Windward* and found themselves in considerable demand as occasional speakers and guest lecturers. Their mother, not to be outdone, wrote her own book, which she entitled, *I Ran Away to Sea at 50*; she dedicated it to 'Daddy

Bruce'. Mary Fahnestock, too, found herself in some demand as a public speaker, particularly at women's clubs.

Based on the success of their first expedition, Bruce and Sheridan threw themselves into planning a second, larger expedition to the South Seas. Again, they were fortunate to find a benefactor to underwrite their expedition, which promised to be a lot larger and more expensive than their first. That benefactor was John Hubbard's widow, Helen Hubbard (nee Fahnestock), who was both wealthy and extremely fond of her young cousins. One of the objectives of the second expedition, scheduled to depart sometime in 1940, was to record the music of the Pacific Islands and East Indies, which was believed to be rapidly disappearing; it was a project very close to Helen Hubbard's heart.

Helen Hubbard's first contribution was to purchase the vessel on which the second expedition would sail. It was a beautiful, three-masted schooner some forty metres in length, which the Fahnestocks promptly named *Director II.* Helen Hubbard also furnished Bruce and Sheridan with elaborate (and expensive) state-of-the-art recording equipment to record the music of the islands they visited, as well as birdsongs from the South Seas. The equipment included on-board disc cutters and cables to attach to the microphones they would take ashore to make their recordings. Finally, she bought the brothers a Piper Cub aircraft, which would be delivered to the *Director II* just days before its departure.

Once again the expedition was sponsored in part by the Museum of Natural History, and the brothers also negotiated a number of other sponsors based on the success of their first expedition. Early on, they agreed to broadcast a number of programs for the National Broadcasting Corporation (NBC) network over their shortwave radio. The outbreak of war in

Europe in September 1939 put paid to the plan for a regular schedule of broadcasts, but it was agreed the expedition would provide occasional broadcasts for the network to air. Another plan to chart Pacific Ocean currents for the US Hydrographic Bureau also fell through because of the changed conditions brought by the European war. Implicit in the voyage was the desire of all three Fahnestocks to collect material for future articles and books.

They planned, as well, to use their Piper Cub aircraft to chart routes through the tropical reefs they would encounter and to reconnoitre the principal harbours in the region. This was partly to make their travels safer; it was also tied up in a meeting the brothers had no wish to advertise.

•

At 11.30 a.m. on 20 November 1939, Bruce and Sheridan Fahnestock paid an official visit to President Franklin Delano Roosevelt, meeting the president in the Oval Office of the White House. The brothers already knew the president through family and social connections, but this meeting was not to discuss mutual friends or society scandals. Roosevelt was well aware of the brothers' plans for a second South Seas expedition and he asked them to keep their eyes open while they were sailing through the Pacific and among the islands of the East Indies. The United States was preparing to do whatever it could to prevent the war that had just broken out in Europe from spreading. With that in mind, Roosevelt asked the Fahnestocks to evaluate French, Dutch and British defence preparations in their colonies and dependencies, as the United States could be expected to underwrite some of them. As well, Roosevelt and his advisers were interested in any observations the Fahnestocks might have on what Japan and Japanese interests were doing in those areas.

Sheridan Fahnestock, as the formal leader of the expedition, would carry an American passport annotated by Secretary of State Cordell Hull, which would describe him as being on 'special duties'. With a good luck wish and a handshake, the meeting was over.

•

Given the significance of what the Fahnestocks hoped to achieve on this second expedition, they were as meticulous as ever in their planning, and even more meticulous in the selection of their crew. Sheridan would again command the expedition with Bruce as his deputy. Bruce would also act as scientific director, and he chose and appointed George Folster as his deputy. Folster, a graduate of the Harvard Business School, was thirty-four years of age and had worked in executive positions at a number of department stores. Dawson Coleman Glover, 'Gubby', was the crewman responsible for all radio communications. An impressive figure, Gubby Glover was dark-haired, well over 190 centimetres in height and had what all who knew him would describe as an 'engaging' personality.

Glover was studying at Yale alongside two other crewmen and friends, Bob Wilson and Phil Farley. The remainder of the crew were Ladislaw (Laddie) Reday, an engineer and recent graduate from the Massachusetts Institute of Technology; George Paterson and Rollin Grant. Edward Dair, in civilian life a portrait artist, would serve as first officer and official photographer for the expedition. With the exception of Folster, all were twenty-five years of age or less, recent graduates of Ivy League universities and keen for adventure.

There would also be several supernumeraries on the expedition. Mary Fahnestock would again accompany her sons, and had spent several months studying the calorific and vitamin contents of various foods before ordering supplies for a voyage expected to last up to two years. She wouldn't have to worry about cooking those foodstuffs though, as the ship would have its own cook, an African American named James Cole who had studied with some of the great chefs of Paris. There was also a steward named Julio Brenes to assist with the catering. Nor would Mary Fahnestock be the only woman aboard. In May 1939, Sheridan and Margaret Steele had announced their engagement and had married later that year. Margaret would accompany her husband, as would Helen Folster, the wife of George Folster. Bruce Fahnestock had also married between expeditions but his wife, Betty, and their young son would remain behind at their new home in Hartford, Connecticut.

The *Director II*, its crew and passengers departed New York on 1 February 1940, farewelled by Mayor Fiorello La Guardia and carrying the personal bon voyage of President Franklin Roosevelt. The Fahnestocks expected to be away for at least two years, during which they would sail some 65,000 kilometres before returning home with enough material to fill a small museum. They would spend the bulk of that time in the South Pacific and among the islands of the Indonesian Archipelago, and would studiously avoid possible areas of conflict. After passing through the Panama Canal at the end of February, they set out across the vast emptiness of the Pacific Ocean.

In the main, the second expedition travelled very much along the path pioneered by the first. After visiting the Galapagos Islands, where they picked up a young turtle as a ship's pet, the voyage continued to the Marquesas Islands, where they had what they all believed to be an unusual, even quite haunting, experience. In those islands, it was common for the elders of the various clans to sing what they called 'Prediction Songs' and the Fahnestocks were anxious to record some of these. As they were doing so, they learned that one of the songs was actually about them, or at least about their ship. The song referred to the visit by the original *Director* some five years earlier. The song explained how the *Director II* was just that previous ship now grown to adulthood but, when it departed, that would be the last they would ever see of it for the ship was fated to never return.

The fact that a large part of the Western world was at war came home to them in French Polynesia. Calling in at Tahiti, French authorities there pointed to the Piper Cub aircraft and said that it would probably be considered as part of an espionage operation if it were flown anywhere near sensitive ports and harbours in the western Pacific. Rather than draw any unwanted attention to themselves, the Fahnestocks offloaded the aircraft for sale.

From Polynesia, the *Director II* sailed to Pago Pago in American Samoa before heading down to the Fiji Islands where they discovered undecipherable writing on several ancient monoliths and started a debate which has yet to be concluded. By then, several of those aboard were heartily sick and tired of cruising the endless ocean and visiting islands which seemed to be only marginally different from the islands they had just visited. Somewhere in the South Pacific a decision was made to sail to Australia, where everyone could take a break from the expedition and – possibly – from each other.

The *Director II* sailed to Brisbane and docked in the Brisbane River on 8 October 1940. The boat and its passengers became instant celebrities. They were so different, so American and such a breath of fresh air for a country at war. Various newspapers in the nation's capital cities devoted many columns, and many photographs, to telling readers what they should know about the expedition. Helen Folster, for instance, was described as 'the attractive young wife of George Folster', who had already painted several appealing watercolours on the trip. Mary Fahnestock was also taking notes for a book she was thinking of writing, while her daughter-in-law, Margaret, and Helen Folster were both keeping diaries of their voyage.

Some reports mentioned that the *Director II* would be having some mechanical reconditioning and a general overhaul while tied up in Brisbane, but the newspapers were more interested in the ship's pets, the Galapagos turtle, a Siamese cat and a Manchu Spaniel named 'Siege'. Readers were also regaled with the fact that James Cole, the cook, had collected recipes at every port they called into and that by the time they docked in Brisbane, he had filled 100 pages of his notebook with them.

The crew all took the opportunity to go shopping in Brisbane, with European-style foods and meals being high on their list. The men also spent time in local museums seeking additional information, particularly on Pacific natives' songs, and flora and fauna. The Fahnestocks also wanted to purchase charts of Queensland's coastal waters, although that was something of a problem. At the outbreak of hostilities in Europe in 1939, the British Admiralty had ordered that all recent shipping charts be removed from sale so they didn't find their way to the enemy. The charts the Fahnestocks eventually purchased to plot their course were well out of date.

The Fahnestocks and their crew and passengers also developed a new strategy for the expedition. The *Director II* would sail from Brisbane to Townsville, where the two younger women would temporarily depart for a holiday in Sydney. From Townsville, the *Director II* would sail up through the Torres Strait and across the Coral Sea to the Solomon Islands before skirting the north coast of New Guinea and sailing into the Netherlands East Indies. Margaret Fahnestock and Helen Folster would rejoin the expedition somewhere there. That was the plan, anyway.

They departed Brisbane on the evening of 16 October and two days later, navigating on the basis of their dated charts, the *Director II* ran aground on a shoal off Port Curtis, some twenty-five kilometres from Gladstone.

At first the crew thought they were not in any real distress and that they would either sail off the shoal at high tide or be pulled off by other boats. A radio message was sent out describing what had happened, and the men went to work to repair and restore the damage. But the longer they were stuck, the more water the *Director II* took on, and after several hours it was obvious that the ship could not be saved. By then, several boats had sailed out from Gladstone to offer assistance and the exercise became one of saving as much of what was aboard as possible. As well as valuable personal items, they made sure all the recordings that had been made on the voyage were safe. Those recordings would soon be described by the *Townsville Daily Bulletin* as 'the largest mass of raw material musicologists and anthropologists have ever recorded in the South Seas'. Ten hours after it had run aground, the *Director II* slid off the shoal and disappeared into the deeper water that surrounded it; the second expedition was over.

•

The loss of the *Director II* was a disaster for the Fahnestocks – insurance estimates placed the vessel's worth at around US$125,000 – but they seemed to take some solace in the fact that their precious recordings had been saved.

They were temporarily stranded in Gladstone where the locals took them to heart. From Gladstone, they made their way back to Brisbane where they caught the mail train down to Sydney. The Fahnestocks – Bruce, Sheridan, Margaret and Mary – departed Sydney aboard the *Monterey* on 22 November 1940, nine days after Laddie Reday and several others had sailed aboard the *Sea Witch*. The Fahnestocks returned directly to New York with their precious recordings, and began to make preliminary plans for a further voyage. Julio Brenes would follow them the following January while Ned Dair stayed on in Sydney where he was gainfully employed painting the portraits of a number of local socialites.

●

When they arrived back in New York at the end of 1940, the Fahnestock brothers collaborated on an article for *Harper's Magazine* in which they reflected on one of the changes they had observed on their second voyage to the Pacific. Entitled 'South Seas War Baby', it described in some detail, and with some sensitivity, how French involvement in the European war had thrown the isolated French colonies in the Pacific back to their traditional ways. The particular area they described was the valley of Atuona, on the island of Hiva Oa in the Marquesas Islands group. It was a place they had visited five years previously, so they were able to compare how the war was affecting life there. They detailed in sympathetic terms how the families who lived in the valley slowly lost their reliance on imported French goods and fell back into their traditional lifestyle. They suggested, too, that those families may have been much better off without all the 'benefits' of civilisation.

Bruce and Sheridan Fahnestock met with President Franklin Roosevelt again on 25 January 1941, in the Oval Room at the White

House, a meeting that lasted from 12.45 p.m. until 1.25 p.m. No minutes or notes from that meeting are available but it involved a third South Seas expedition, one that would have as its cover the recording of songs from throughout the Indonesian Archipelago. While making those recordings, the expedition would also take careful note of Japanese infiltration through the area and the defensive preparedness of both the Netherlands East Indies and the British colonies of Malaya and Singapore.

Unlike their first two South Seas expeditions, this third attempt would not be a major enterprise, but rather a small and focused effort. Bruce and Sheridan sailed directly to the East Indies where they chartered a yacht and hired a professional photographer named Howard Kincheloe whom they met in Java shortly after arriving there. The three men sailed to Bali and the islands at the eastern end of the archipelago, recording the music and photographing the musicians they found there. They then travelled west, all the way to Singapore, where their expedition ended and the brothers farewelled Kincheloe before returning to the United States.

•

In early September 1941, a covering letter and detailed report were brought to the desk of President Roosevelt. The package was described as 'Letter from A. Bruce Fahnestock, 12 Chelsea Lane, West Hartford, Connecticut, and Sheridan Fahnestock, Glen Mary Farm, Great Mills, Maryland, undated, to General Watson, with enclosed letter to the President from Messrs. Fahnestock, giving their impression in connection with their trip to the Indies, Java, Madoera, Kangean, Bali, Singapore and Biliton'. On 6 September, after reading the Fahnestock report, Roosevelt put the letters and envelopes together again and added a brief note of his own before passing the bundle to Captain Beardall, his naval aide. The annotation read, 'What do you think we should do?'

•

There was no immediate action taken by either man, and the report – and the circumstances under which it was compiled and written – remained a secret to all but a few in the Washington hierarchy. While they were pondering what to do, the world moved closer and closer to a world war, and those military authorities who might have taken more than a passing interest in the Fahnestock report had far weightier things to consider.

Bruce and Sheridan also moved on with their lives. Once again, they spoke publicly and wrote about much of what they had observed on their three expeditions to the South Seas. One of the hypotheses they advanced was that their recordings showed that at one time there were migrations from the western and northern regions of the Indian subcontinent down as far as New Zealand and out as far as Hawaii. Musicologists who had listened to their recordings said that this was indeed possible, and that a preliminary study of the music showed overlapping musical themes in island groups separated by several thousands of kilometres of ocean.

In January 1942, Bruce and Sheridan Fahnestock presented a talk on what they had collected in their three South Seas expeditions to a sold-out crowd at the Town Hall in New York City. It would be the first and only time they played segments of their musical recordings to the general public. The event, though, was something of an anti-climax. The United States was now at war following the Japanese attack on Pearl Harbor. Most in the crowd were concerned about what the war would mean for them. The Fahnestocks were concerned about how they could contribute to the war effort.

1.

MISSION X

The fact that Japan entered the war in December 1941 was not a surprise to many Americans, especially those who had watched Japanese expansionism during the previous few years and who knew that the Japanese military had even more grandiose plans for their country. The way they entered, though, came as a complete surprise to all but a few at the top of the military and political hierarchies, and even they were astounded at the sheer audacity of the Japanese attack at Pearl Harbor.

The attack was one of a series of coordinated strikes, and even before the dive-bombers struck at Battleship Row in Pearl Harbor, high-level bombers had attacked Singapore and Manila, and Japanese troops had stormed ashore in northern Malaya and across the border into the British territory of Hong Kong. Within a few days, the Allies were under pressure and wilting all the way across Asia and into what would become known as the South West Pacific Area (SWPA). As those days became weeks, the Japanese gains grew at an alarming rate. The British were forced down the Malay Peninsula and into the 'impregnable bastion' of Singapore; American forces in the Philippines were slowly pushed back onto the Bataan Peninsula and Dutch forces in the East Indies, particularly their naval and air forces, were almost completely destroyed in a series of clashes with technically and numerically superior Japanese forces.

Within the United States, years of pursuing a policy of isolationism disappeared overnight and the country clamoured for revenge. Throughout the country, volunteers rushed to enlist in the armed forces, to do their bit, and in Washington and elsewhere, those who thought they could contribute in other ways tried to push themselves and their ideas to the forefront. Among that crowd were the Fahnestock brothers. Their president had asked them to assess the defences of the islands of the South Pacific and now many of those islands were in harm's way, directly in front of an advancing Japanese horde. Bruce and Sheridan stepped forward and asked whether they could assist in the great national effort.

•

The Fahnestock brothers' connections to President Roosevelt may not have given them access to the Oval Office at this time of national crisis, but they were certainly given a hearing in Washington. Sheridan was debriefed by the Office of Strategic Security (OSS) – the forerunner to the Central Intelligence Agency – on what he and Bruce had seen and learned during their most recent South Seas expedition. The Fahnestocks also let it be known that they had a plan to assist the US forces that were under such pressure in the Philippines.

It was a simple plan. During their expeditions through the South Pacific and East Indies, the Fahnestocks had learned a lot about navigation in that part of the world and a lot more about boats and shipping movements there. The seas in the South

Pacific were often shallow and full of reefs and shoals that made the use of large vessels almost impossible. The Fahnestocks had noted that the overwhelming majority of inter-island trade and travel was undertaken in small ships, many of less than 100 tons, and that a large proportion of these were either sailboats with auxiliary engines or larger fishing boats that also carried general freight. They were used because they were the best, and sometimes the only, ships that could safely navigate the waters.

The Fahnestocks believed that it would be possible to support American forces in the Philippines – and elsewhere if necessary – through the use of these small non-naval vessels. The small ships would blend in to the local scene in a way that US Navy ships never could. While their payload might be limited, if enough of them were brought into use they could carry a lot of ammunition and supplies from bases in safe areas to positions where the troops were under pressure. If guerrilla operations were envisaged, the small ships would be ideal for inserting and extracting such troops, and they could also be used to carry military experts and specialised equipment. The Philippines comprised some 16,000 islands, and Japanese forces could not watch all of them or check on who was sailing between them. It was an area the Fahnestocks knew and it was a style of operation with which they were familiar.

In January 1942, as the Fahnestock brothers were preparing and delivering their presentation to a sold-out crowd at the New York Town Hall, a regular US Army colonel named Arthur Wilson was promoted to brigadier-general and made quartermaster for all the US forces that had been, and would be, despatched to Australia and beyond to confront the Japanese forces still sweeping through Asia towards Australia. Wilson knew President Roosevelt, and it may have been through him that he first learned of the Fahnestock brothers and their plan, although it is more likely that it came from sources within the OSS. Either way, he thought it was an idea that needed further exploration, especially given the situation unfolding in the Philippines.

•

One day in late January, Sheridan Fahnestock received a cryptic invitation to a meeting backstage at the Washington Auditorium. There, he found a US Army major sitting behind a plain desk. The man invited Sheridan to sit in the chair in front of the desk and then proceeded to question him on his knowledge of the Pacific, as well as his background and general thoughts on the war now raging in the Far East.

Seemingly satisfied with the answers, the major introduced himself as Arthur Wilson and said that he had been 'made responsible' for Australia, but didn't provide any context for the statement. Wilson then proceeded to ask Sheridan if he would be interested in commanding a small boats operation. Before he could answer, though, Wilson continued that he – Sheridan – would have to source the boats and crews, adding that certain specialists would be given priority for the operation. Wilson concluded by saying that if Sheridan wanted to take the task on, he should assemble a small team to assist and await further instructions. Oh, and the name of the operation was 'Mission X'.

•

Neither Sheridan Fahnestock nor the broader American public were privy to the truth about the fighting in the Philippines. Newsreels and newspapers depicted a brave and stubborn defence, led by the inspirational General Douglas MacArthur who, when reinforced sufficiently, would return to the offensive and push the Japanese back out of the islands. Nothing could have been further from the truth.

Prior to mid-1941, US Army and US Defence Department doctrine saw the Philippines as being indefensible. Should war with Japan commence, a possibility that had influenced military policy for several years, US forces in the Philippines would delay, not deny, a Japanese occupation of the islands. The time bought by those forces would be used to build up the main US Pacific forces then based in the Hawaiian Islands. At the beginning of 1941, the forces available in the Philippines to carry out this delaying action numbered around 20,000 US and local troops.

The Japanese occupation of southern Indochina on 21 July 1941 prompted a major rethink of the Philippine defence orthodoxy. In the following months, substantial reinforcements in men, equipment and aircraft were despatched to the Philippines to act as a deterrent to possible Japanese designs on the islands. Even that reinforcement was not without its critics. The Philippines was scheduled to be granted its independence in 1946, and there were those who said the Filipinos might side with their fellow Asians rather than with their colonial overlords, in which case any supplies sent there might ultimately be turned on American soldiers. In the end, though, the reinforcement of forces in the Philippines simply provided the Japanese military with one more obstacle to overcome.

On 8 December 1941, Japanese bombs rained down on recently arrived US Army aircraft lined up neatly alongside the runways at Clark Field outside Manila. The American forces were immediately on the back foot. The loss of so many US Navy vessels at Pearl Harbor accentuated the potential problems in supplying the Philippine forces with the supplies they would need to continue the fight when the Japanese invaded, which they soon did. Consequently, on 16 December, US Command in Australia was authorised to take any actions necessary to supply MacArthur's forces.

To do that, General George Brett, then in command of US forces in the South West Pacific, was instructed to build up a supply base through local purchases of relevant materials and foodstuffs. The highest priority was to be given to those supplies specifically requested by MacArthur. Brett was also told that the forces then available to him were to handle the transportation requirements necessary to commence and continue supply operations to US forces in the Philippines. Both to cover the supplies to be delivered and for the lease or purchase of suitable vessels to carry those supplies, US$10 million was made available.

As early as the first week of January 1942, army command in the United States recognised that the relief of its forces in the Philippines was impractical, although this fact was not relayed to either MacArthur or the general public. Instead of sending a substantial relief force, a decision was made to resupply the defenders there with what were described as 'small quantities of key items necessary to prolong the defence and improve morale'.

US Army Colonel John Robenson was to become a key part of the proposed operation. Robenson's convoy was heading to Manila but had been redirected to Darwin. On 19 January 1942, Robenson was ordered to travel to Java to acquire boats and crews to run supplies through the Japanese blockade to US forces in the Philippines. Robenson, six other officers and one enlisted man immediately flew from Darwin to Java to begin that process.

Unfortunately, there were a number of problems with this plan. To begin with, the local boat owners were unwilling to either lease or sell their vessels for payment in anything but US dollars. When this was relayed back to Washington, US$2 million in notes of various denominations, and in eight bundles of US$250,000, were placed on separate aircraft which flew out of Tampa, Florida, on 24 January, headed halfway around the world to Java.

A more serious problem was the inability of Robenson's team to find crews for the vessels they were hoping to acquire. Unsurprisingly, no one seemed to want to sail a small, unarmed or lightly armed boat into waters controlled by the Japanese. Most Javanese and Chinese sailors simply refused point-blank, no matter how much money they were offered.

Robenson's team finally managed to acquire a single vessel, a small Chinese freighter named the *Taiyuan*, on 8 February. It was the team's only acquisition, and it was ultimately a waste of time and money. The *Taiyuan* would be scuttled at Surabaya in early March, shortly before that city fell to the Japanese.

The Robenson mission was just one of a number of schemes the US Army tried to develop to get supplies through to its beleaguered forces. A number of American and Philippine freighters were scattered across the Pacific when the Japanese struck at Pearl Harbor and elsewhere. Several of them were taken over by the US Army, loaded with supplies and despatched for the Philippines as blockade runners; the army had only mixed success with them, however. One of those ships made it through to the US bastion at Corregidor, where the last American forces were holding out, while two others reached Cebu in the southern Philippines. Another two were sunk by Japanese aircraft en route to bomb Darwin on 19 February 1942. Several other missions were cancelled or abandoned when the crew threatened to walk off the ship when informed of their destination.

Finally, there were plans to use ships that were, literally, banana boats to try to reach the troops. Six decommissioned World War I US Navy destroyers had been sold off to the United Fruit Company in the early 1930s. Before their sale, they were completely stripped of armaments and were even sold without engines. United Fruit had four of the old destroyers equipped with diesel engines, which gave them a top speed of around sixteen knots, and then used them to transport cargoes of fruit between Central America and the major ports of North America.

One of those four vessels was lost at sea in 1933; the other three were chartered by the US Army at the outbreak of hostilities in the Pacific. One of those three, the *Masaya* (ex-USS *Dale*), was available almost immediately while the others would not be available for some time because they required repairs. The plan was to provision all three ships in New Orleans and then sail them to Hawaii, from where they would make a direct run to the southern Philippine island of Mindanao. It was an operation that would be run independently of the other blockade-running operations, but it too failed to eventuate. The *Masaya* eventually made it to the South Pacific, but no further. By then, the American position in the Philippines was beyond salvation.

•

Thankfully unaware of the US Army's attempts to provide a steady supply line to the Philippines, Sheridan Fahnestock concentrated on putting a team together to implement Mission X, irrespective of how obscure the actual mission's objectives may have been. His first recruit for the team was his brother Bruce, whose main interest at that time was producing a weekly world affairs program for his local radio station, WTIC, in Hartford. The brothers quickly agreed that the ideal team for their new mission would be the one that had sailed the *Director II* across the Pacific, and they set about tracking down their crew.

Phil Farley and Bob Wilson were easy to find. Both had returned to Yale where they were in the final year of their studies. Coincidentally, both were also completing officer training with the US Navy Reserve. Laddie Reday had already followed his brother Joe into the army and as Lieutenant Ladislaw Reday was attending the Coastal Artillery School not too far away at Fort Monroe in Virginia. Reassignment orders with a large 'SECRET' stamp on them quickly brought him back to Washington.

Gubby Glover was harder to trace, as he had been expelled from Yale, but he was in occasional contact with mutual friends and was tracked down because of this. Glover was in New York with his new bride, but immediately said he'd be in Washington the next day. The only crewman they missed was George Folster, who had already signed on as NBC's South West Pacific correspondent for the duration of the war. Fortunately, there was a ready-made replacement in Sheridan's brother-in-law, Heath Steele, who was already in the army and who was completing cavalry training with his National Guard unit at Fort Wheeler in Georgia. He, too, was quickly summoned to Washington.

Two days later, in a small office in a nondescript building in Washington, the members of the Mission X team were sworn in as soldiers in the army of the United States. The authorities recognised that Bruce Fahnestock, tall and gangly, courageous and humorous, was not the best leader for the group as he also possessed a mercurial temperament. Sheridan Fahnestock was the obvious choice as team leader; short, even stocky, he exuded an air of confidence in himself and in those who worked for him. Sheridan was made a captain and Bruce a first lieutenant, with the others from the *Director II* given the rank of second lieutenant. Heath Steele was made a sergeant, as was Frank Sheridan, a cousin of the Fahnestocks and the last recruit to their team.

Two days later, they received their orders and travel warrants, and almost immediately flew from Washington, DC across the country to San Francisco, where they were picked up and driven to Fort Mason, a large military base on the shoreline of San Francisco Bay. On their third day at the fort, they were issued with uniforms and all sorts of military accoutrements. Soon after that, a fleet of taxis transported the group and their new belongings to the docks, where they boarded the liner *President Monroe*. Seven days later, they walked off the ship in Hawaii.

The team was put up in a hotel on Oahu for a week and then travelled as passengers on a number of new B-26s, Martin Marauder bombers that were being flown to Australia for further deployment against the Japanese. That flight was a challenge. The aircraft flew at a height of about 500 metres and it emerged that few of the aircraft's crews had made overwater flights before. As well, the aircraft's maximum range was just 950 kilometres, so the journey was undertaken in a series of island hops.

The end of their trans-Pacific flight was anything but an anti-climax. The first three B-26s to touch down at Brisbane's Archerfield airfield all overshot the runway and finished up in the market gardens beyond. The three aircraft were all written off but fortunately there were no injuries to either crew or passengers. Again, the Mission X team waited for a couple of days in Brisbane before being flown, without any adventures, down to Melbourne.

There they were given a number of rooms in what had been a bank building in the heart of the city and accommodation in a nearby hotel, and told to continue their planning for a small ships supply operation. It was by now early March and they were told that General MacArthur was on his way to Melbourne as well. With very little in the way of strategic or tactical knowledge, they put their heads together and began to sketch out what they thought they should do, and balanced that against what they knew they could do. There was practically no difference between the two so, metaphorically speaking, they all rolled up their sleeves and got down to business in a new role, in a new country and at the start of a new war.

•

One of the most important decisions the Mission X team would make was also one of their earliest. Their knowledge of sailing, especially for recreation or exploration, far exceeded their know-ledge of boats. Previously, they had identified where they wanted to go and which vessel they thought was best suited to take them there. Now the requirement was to build up a fleet of small boats that could undertake a number of wartime tasks in foreign waters somewhere to the north and west of Australia. It highlighted their collective lack of knowledge of boats and sailing in this part of the world.

Sheridan Fahnestock first approached the Melbourne repres-entative of Lloyd's Register of Shipping and asked him about finding a good marine surveyor who could evaluate and advise his team on which boats were best suited for the tasks they had in mind. Lloyd's said that they were short-staffed but recom-mended that Sheridan contact the Jack Savages, both senior and junior, saying that either one of them would be the best they would find in Australia.

Sheridan made some enquiries about the Savages and liked what he learned. The senior, John Joseph 'Jack' Savage, had commenced building boats in 1898 at Middle Park, just outside Melbourne and on Port Phillip Bay. His yard there could build boats up to thirty metres in length, and he soon gained a reputation for producing vessels of great quality and style. By the 1920s, Jack Savage was able to open a second boatbuilding shed on the Yarra River near Scotch College to produce primarily smaller recreational and sporting craft. His business continued to grow to the point where it was relocated to a major shipyard at Nelson Place in Williamstown in 1934.

Sheridan and Laddie Reday went to Williamstown to meet Jack Savage, who impressed both men. They found him, 'white-haired, red-cheeked and jolly'. He was scaling back his own involvement in boatbuilding, handing the company over to his two sons, John – also known as Jack or Young Jack – and Tom. If the older Jack was unable to commit to assisting the Americans, the younger Jack was more than keen. At twenty-five, he was of a similar age to most of the members of Mission X and he shared their passion for sailing. Even more importantly, he was an expert marine surveyor and wanted to be involved in war work where he could apply both his skills and knowledge and, with these, make a positive contribution to the prosecution of the war.

A job was offered and agreed on a handshake, and on 5 April 1942 Jack Savage became the first Australian to be employed as part of the Mission X operation. That handshake was good enough for both sides and, even when contracts were introduced shortly afterwards, neither Jack nor Sheridan ever felt the need for one to be either offered or signed. Young Jack was given the responsibility of inspecting and then approving or rejecting the boats that were to be commandeered, purchased or leased by the US Army. In reality, and because it was work that he loved and at which he excelled, he also assumed responsibility for supervising the repair and reconstruction of the ships brought into their fleet as well as the conduct of salvage operations. Jack Savage was the person the team needed most at that point, as they simply did not have the expertise he possessed.

Sheridan and the others in Mission X had work to do, and quickly, as the tide of war swept down upon Australia. The approach of the Japanese army was one of a number of coincidental events that would shape Mission X and its contributions to the war. Those events, military politics in particular, swirling around the small Mission X operation would combine to make it a key factor in the broader struggle to the north of Australia.

•

There is always inter-service rivalry between the various elements of the armed services in any given country, and the outbreak of war is no guarantee that the rivalry will be shelved. When Douglas MacArthur arrived at Melbourne's Spencer Street Station on 21 March 1942 after being ordered to leave the Philippines, a crowd of thousands was there to greet him as both a hero and a saviour. MacArthur clearly foresaw a major, if not primary, role for himself and the US Army troops he would command in the destruction of the Japanese thrust south. He also realised that he would need a lot more than his own personal standing and a well-heeled phalanx of media advisers to reach the supreme command he so coveted. While Pearl Harbor had decimated some elements of the US Navy, its aircraft carriers were at sea during the attack. The Navy, stung badly by Pearl Harbor, saw in those aircraft carriers and in its Marine Corps the ideal tools to stop and turn back the Japanese.

There was some degree of ill-will between MacArthur and his navy counterpart, Chester Nimitz, and to forestall that ill-will from growing into a counterproductive rivalry, a decision was made at the top level of US military command to divide the Pacific area into two theatres of war. One, the Central Pacific, would be allotted to the navy and marines. The other, the South West Pacific Area, would fall under MacArthur's command. The decision was agreed in Washington on 30 March 1942 and the Australian government was informed of it soon afterwards; it was formally endorsed by the Australian government on 14 April.

While significant parts of the effort against the Japanese flowed directly from that decision, other parts flowed from what had occurred at and before Pearl Harbor. One was that what remained of the US Pacific Fleet would be engaged in either seeking out the main Japanese battle fleet or in supporting the marines in their efforts to wrest back islands occupied by Japanese forces. An additional complication, if one was needed, was that Roosevelt had agreed with the European Allies – primarily Churchill and Joseph Stalin – that he would support a Europe First strategy, pushing both the Central and South West Pacific theatres a little bit further down priority lists. Against this background, US Army strategic planners estimated that there would not be enough resources available from the United States to support offensive operations in the South West Pacific until the middle of 1943. This was a prospect that MacArthur would not and could not countenance.

With the division of the Pacific theatre into two components, New Guinea became the responsibility of the American and Australian armies, as were the islands to the immediate north and west of New Guinea. Many of those islands, including New Britain just to the north of New Guinea, and the islands of the

Indonesian Archipelago to the west, were already in Japanese hands, and those Japanese would have to be forced out and back if the Allies were to take the war all the way back to Japan.

MacArthur was committed to following this strategy, which would require a series of amphibious assaults on Japanese positions. Unfortunately, there were no dedicated landing craft to undertake or support such assaults. The US Army Transportation Service, the arm responsible for the movement of US Army troops, simply had no ships available in the South West Pacific. The Royal Australian Navy had a number of corvettes available to assist and protect landing craft, should they become available, but the corvettes would be constrained because of the shallow water and coral reefs that covered much of the area where the fighting was most likely to take place.

The idea behind Mission X, the thought that small, shallow draught ships could operate in waters inaccessible to larger vessels, and thereby supply and support US troops in the Philippines, had come almost full circle. The Philippines themselves were all but lost – the final US forces at Corregidor would surrender on 9 April – but the concept of a small ships operation was the one idea which could sustain US Army operations in the South West Pacific until the full industrial might of the United States kicked in some time in mid-1943. Sheridan and Bruce Fahnestock did not know it, but their original proposal was about to assume a significance far greater than they could ever have foreseen.

•

One of the many assets the Americans brought to the war was a tradition of industrial organisation, the ability to bring together the various parts of an enterprise in a way that optimised the output (and the profits) of that enterprise. The idea behind

Mission X was for it to be a small, irregular contributor to the war, but the circumstances facing the Allies in the South West Pacific from the middle of 1942 demanded more than that. The professionals were brought in to give shape and substance to the Fahnestocks' ideas.

Mission X was first given a new name; it became the Small Ships Supply Command, a notionally standalone operation, but that was soon superseded as well. On 29 May, it became the Small Ships Section of the Water Branch of the US Army's Transportation Service and then ultimately the Small Ships Division of the Transportation Service of the US Army Forces in Australia, or USAFIA. It was also given a formal mission: 'to deliver ammunition, medical supplies and perishable food to outlying bases that could not be reached by deep draught ships, and to assist in tactical operations when required'. Finally, on 14 July, it was formally designated as simply the Small Ships Section, the name it would proudly carry for the rest of the war.

It was also given a new structure and a new chain of command composed largely of officers personally selected by Arthur Wilson, who by 21 March had become Chief Quartermaster and Assistant Chief of Staff of the USAFIA. As head of the Water Branch, he appointed Colonel Thomas Plant, in civilian life the vice-president of the American-Hawaiian Steamship Line. Colonel Thomas Wilson (no relation), formerly of the Alaska Steamship Corporation and Greyhound Bus Lines, was flown to Australia to take up the position of Chief of the Transportation Division and Deputy Chief Quartermaster of the USAFIA. An army major named Jack McKinstry was appointed as an assistant to Thomas Wilson and within weeks a formal transportation structure was up and running in Australia.

Within the larger USAFIA transportation umbrella, the Small Ships Section was also restructured. A commanding officer was appointed to the section, a Colonel Harry Cullins, who was recalled to active service specifically to head up the Small Ships. He, too, was given an assistant, Major Reford 'Mike' Shea, who in civilian life had been a road contractor. Neither knew very much about ships and shipping but both knew an awful lot about the US Army and military administrative procedures. Finally, Major Gordon Evans was posted to the Small Ships Section as its personnel officer. He was from the Deep South and his unmistakable accent and courtly Southern manners made him popular with everyone in the section.

Coincidental with this restructure was a more formalised set of requirements for the section, which would now 'assemble and operate coastal vessels; man, equip, provision and repair and maintain their small boat fleet, and coordinate small boat operations with larger US-operated vessels'.

The changes in the administrative arrangements had little immediate effect on the original Mission X men, and even less effect on the way they organised their lives. While continuing to use army protocols only when absolutely necessary, they worked hard during the day and partied hard at night, at least until that workload started to catch up with them. A lot of their work involved talking to and with Jack Savage and other marine surveyors about what kinds of ships would be most suitable for their purposes and where those ships might be available. They also kept an eye out for whatever they could use on the ships they were planning to acquire, and in doing just that they made a significant discovery.

One of the contacts they had developed in the military bureaucracy that had sprung up in Melbourne told them of two goods carriages loaded with American machine guns, both .30 and .50 calibre, which were packed in boxes stacked high in the carriages, now in a rail yard not far from the centre of Melbourne. The machine guns had originally been intended for US forces in the Philippines, but had been diverted to Melbourne where consideration had been given to sending them to Australian forces based in Singapore. The fall of the 'impregnable fortress' on 15 February 1942 had made that plan irrelevant and the current thinking was that they would be sent up to Darwin and placed in storage there until they were needed.

The Small Ships' personnel believed they had a greater need for them in the here and now, as they could be mounted on the ships they were to acquire and thereby provide at least a rudimentary defence for those ships. A set of official-looking orders was drawn up, and a copy of those orders placed in the consignment box attached to the railway wagons, snuck in late at night and after a few drinks. The next morning, in their officers' uniforms, Sheridan Fahnestock and Laddie Reday showed another set of orders to the guard at the rail yard gate, checked with him that they matched the orders on the freight cars and then organised for the machine guns to be forwarded to the Small Ships' own freight storage area.

•

At the end of May 1942, a number of decisions about the status and role of the Small Ships Section were put into action. The most obvious was the relocation of its headquarters from Melbourne to Sydney, a process that took place over several weeks. The site chosen for the new headquarters was the Grace Building on the corner of York and King Streets in the heart of Sydney's CBD. The move was made because Sydney was Australia's largest port, and moreover a port where both the procurement and refitting of the small ships selected for service could occur. The Grace Building was close to Walsh Bay, which was to become a critical part of the Small Ships' operations. The new headquarters would stay in place until well after the war.

Some personnel changes were also implemented. Harry Cullins was replaced as Commanding Officer of the Small Ships Section by Major George Bradford. Part of Harry Cullins' brief had (allegedly) been to introduce a more military air to the section, so presumably he had either succeeded in this or, more likely, had given up on the attempt to turn civilians into soldiers and sought more rewarding work elsewhere. George Bradford proved to be an inspired choice for the role. Before the war, he had been president of the Everett Steamship Company, whose head office was in Shanghai but whose main facilities were in Manila where Bradford and his family had lived. He knew a lot about sea transportation and sailors, and he moved effortlessly into his role at the head of the Small Ships Section.

At the same time, Mike Shea became the section's executive officer and Sheridan Fahnestock its operations officer. The structure was completed with the arrival of Lieutenant Ken Cantrell, an Englishman and a member of the Royal Navy Volunteer Reserve. Cantrell, who adopted quite a diffident attitude towards many of the colonials with whom he had contact, was appointed as liaison officer to the Australian authorities, guaranteeing some heated clashes. Cantrell loved the Small Ships, though, and his free-wheeling ways endeared him to the others.

Japanese forces were moving closer and closer to Australian soil. A number of northern outposts, including Darwin and Broome, had been bombed, while a midget submarine attack in Sydney Harbour seemed to signal the opening of the real battle for Australia. The Japanese would have to be stopped in battle, somewhere and some time soon, and there was no doubt that the Small Ships would have a role in that battle.

The only question was whether the ships and crews they could find would be up to the daunting task, and whether the ships and crews could be found and prepared for their role in whatever time they might now have.

2.

FORMING A FLEET

The Pacific War provided a constantly changing background against which the work of the Small Ships Section continued at a frantic pace. By the middle of 1942, Japanese forces were almost literally on Australia's doorstep, and there was no doubt that their determination to sever the supply line between the United States and Australia would see them attempt to seize a strategic foothold in New Guinea at some point. There was an understanding that the Allies could not allow that attempt to succeed, suggesting an increasing likelihood of a decisive battle somewhere in Papua, the eastern end of the island of New Guinea.

It was an area unsuitable for modern naval forces any larger than gunboats. There were only a few deep-water ports, and where they existed, there was usually little in the way of port facilities. US resources, in the form of specialised vessels designed for use in such waters, would ultimately become available, and in significant numbers, but that would not be until some time around the middle of 1943, a year away, and an awful lot could happen in that year.

So it would be the Small Ships Section, and what it could cobble together at short notice, bearing the brunt of the responsibility and the action until those vessels were ready to be brought into action.

•

There were a number of constraints on where the Small Ships Section could source its vessels. When the war broke out in Europe in September 1939, the Australian government almost immediately assumed control of all Australian shipping, establishing the Australian Shipping Control Board to oversee all matters relating to shipping in and from Australian waters. The board then requisitioned any vessels that military authorities deemed necessary for defensive and/or offensive operations, leaving the companies that ran the important coastal trade to continue to do just that. Smaller vessels were acquired on a needs basis, with the smaller coastal vessels being requisitioned early for supply runs between the northern Australian ports and the defence outposts being established across the top of the continent.

Australia, like the rest of the British Empire, also received supplies under the United States' Lend Lease scheme, which generated monetary credits for the United States. Once the structure and functions of the Small Ships Section had been formalised in June 1942, and the operation had been moved to Sydney, those credits were used by the Small Ships to buy the vessels it needed for its operations. If a suitable vessel could not be purchased for an agreed price, the threat of compulsory acquisition always sat in the background. The requisitions – whether purchased, leased or compulsorily acquired – were to be submitted to the Australian Shipping Control Board, which would assess any competing needs; it seems to have approved every one of the Small Ships' acquisitions. The Australian government also formally granted to the United States Army the authority to lease, purchase or commandeer any private vessel deemed suitable for wartime service.

With this authorisation, and against this background, the Small Ships' officers and Jack Savage set out at the beginning of June 1942 to acquire suitable vessels for the flotilla they hoped to despatch to northern Australia preparatory to deployment somewhere in the islands beyond Cape York. It was quite a monumental undertaking and, to make it easier for all involved, Australia was divided into regions with one or more officers assigned to each area to select appropriate vessels and begin the process of acquiring them. That search eventually would include all of eastern Australia from Cairns to Hobart and across to Adelaide, and later across the Tasman Sea to New Zealand.

Bob Wilson was sent to Adelaide to assess and acquire suitable ships operating in South Australian waters or out of South Australian ports. Sheridan and Laddie Reday went down to Hobart for the same purpose; they were joined there by Gubby Glover, who remained in Tasmania after Sheridan and Reday were recalled to Sydney to help with the increasing workload there. Bruce Fahnestock had originally remained in Sydney, but increasingly spent more time searching coastal New South Wales for suitable vessels. Phil Farley had also been based in Sydney, but was soon sent across to New Zealand to search for ships there; he was replaced by a US Army lieutenant named Unander. Melbourne and southern Victoria were left to Jack Savage, who would be joined by other officers when the opportunity arose. Royal Australian Navy (RAN) officers could also be seconded to the Small Ships to assist with the process if required.

The Fahnestocks and the others from the *Director II* expedition, now known with some affection as 'The Originals', possessed
quite a depth of knowledge of sailing but they had little knowledge of just what might be required in supporting a combat
mission in such waters. So, without any pretence at expertise,
they sought out and listened to those who might be able to
contribute to increasing that limited knowledge.

Through their questioning, and with Jack Savage's guidance,
they were increasingly inclined to base the flotilla they were
building around a core group of one specific type of boat: vessels
then called seine trawlers, fishing boats specifically designed for
fishing in Australian waters, particularly the sometimes rough
waters of Bass Strait and the Tasman Sea. They were heavily and
solidly built, mostly between fifteen and twenty metres in length
and with a relatively deep draught for a small boat. Powered by
diesel engines, they had solid bows to withstand the pounding
of the seas and were often sheathed with Kauri Pine, which
would withstand the marine termites and worms that attacked
wooden hulls in the tropics.

More importantly, they carried heavy duty winches to haul in
the seine nets the trawlers carried. Known as coiling winches,
these would serve two important purposes when used in a
military capacity. They could be used to winch the boat closer
to primitive port facilities and they would enable the boats to
be run up onto beaches where there were no port facilities of
any kind. The trawler would be run up onto the beach at low
tide and there unloaded directly onto the sand. Anchors would
be attached to the winches and carried by the ship's dinghy to
deeper water. At high tide, a process known as 'fishtailing', using
the winches on alternate anchors, would drag the trawlers back
into the deeper water.

Due to the war, there was a sense of urgency attached to the process of acquiring suitable vessels and then getting them ready for army service. Wherever possible, haggling over the price was avoided and, as soon as the acquisition papers had been signed and approved, the vessel would be given a designation – a sequential number with an 'S' prefix – and an American flag would be run up the flagpole.

There were few problems beyond the pace of the work. Laddie Reday was sent to Melbourne for a period of time to assist Jack Savage there, and soon found that 'we worked, sometimes without sleep, averaging eighteen to twenty hours a day inspecting, planning, bullying shipyards, making changes and repairs and arming the ships'. Many of the vessels they sought out and assessed were either idle or working minimal hours because of a lack of crew or markets due to the war. Only once was Jack Savage offered a bribe to upgrade a vessel that was being inspected for sale to the Small Ships. After the bribe was offered, Savage told the owner that he would, indeed, have to reassess the boat. The owner was delighted until Jack told him that he had now found some defects and would have to reduce the offer by 20 per cent; he was never again offered a bribe.

This is not to say that the process always went smoothly or was seen as satisfactory by all parties concerned. Mike Richards, a northern New South Wales fisherman, witnessed several acquisitions and recalled one that went very differently.

'The American ways of direct action,' he recollected, 'applied to shipping requisitions just as they did in any other field. Their method was simple and effective but was not appreciated by shipowners. A Marine (sic) sergeant simply walked up the gangway, accompanied by a private armed with an American flag. The ship's national flag was hauled down (often against the captain's protest), and the Stars and Stripes raised in its place. The sergeant then informed the captain that his ship was now the property of the US Army and he was not to do anything without their approval. He would proceed on his way leaving an armed sentry on the gangway to see that his orders were obeyed.'

While acquisitions like this may have occurred, they were the exception rather than the rule, and what Mike Richards described was more likely to be the end of a process that began with someone like Jack Savage assessing the vessel's suitability.

•

When the Small Ships assessment and acquisition teams went out, its members occasionally found little pockets of boats and crews that so perfectly fitted their requirements that they could almost believe that Providence was smiling down on them. One of those pockets was Greenwell Point, just to the east of Nowra on the New South Wales South Coast.

There they met the skipper of the trawler *Bonwin*, Bill Priest, a character described by Laddie Reday as 'burly, tough . . . Priest had twinkling blue eyes and an easy grin.' As well as some outstanding personal qualities, the 42-year-old fisherman brought a wealth of experience to his work. Priest was born on the island of Unst in the Shetland Islands to the north of Scotland. Raised in a large family by his mother after his father and oldest brother enlisted for service in World War I, Bill went to sea soon after that war ended and sailed around the world. He rejoined his family when they all migrated to New Zealand in 1923. There he became a fisherman and married. At the height of the Great Depression, in 1934, he crossed the Tasman with his family to try his luck in Australia. Settling at Greenwell Point, he met and became close friends with Bert Evans, also working in the fishing industry as a marine engineer.

Bert Evans had a background that was almost as exotic as Bill Priest's. Seven years younger than his friend, Evans had been born at the Bellinger Heads Pilot Station in northern New South Wales, where his father was the ship's pilot. When Bert was still a child, the family relocated to the Crookhaven Heads Pilot Station, from which all the Evans children were rowed across the river to attend school at Greenwell Point. Later, in Sydney as an apprentice telephone technician, Bert became another casualty of the Depression, but fortunately found alternative work as a deckhand on the Sydney Harbour ferries.

Evans was drawn back to the South Coast and became the assistant lighthouse keeper and launch man at the Crookhaven Heads Pilot Station, closing one loop in his life. There, he also became involved in both fishing and boatbuilding, and found a kindred spirit in Bill Priest. The two men entered a partnership of sorts, becoming co-owners of the *Zoie*, a trawler that Bert built himself at Orient Point on the Crookhaven River. When he finished the *Zoie*, he turned right around and built a second trawler, which the partners named the *Darwin*.

In June 1942, a Small Ships acquisition party visited Greenwell Point and found four suitable vessels in the boat harbour there: the *Zoie* and the *Darwin* (paying 1600 pounds for the former); the *Bonwin*, then skippered by Bill Priest; and another trawler, the *Black Fin*, skippered by Tommy Nielsen, who was a good friend of both Bill Priest and Bert Evans and was also married to one of Bert Evans' sisters. The acquisition papers for all four vessels were dated 12 June 1942. Finding them-selves suddenly without boats, the three fishermen discussed employment options with the Small Ships team. The next day, all three signed contracts with the US Army's Small Ships Section.

The acquisition party noted that *Black Fin* was owned by a fisherman who was based at Eden, further down the coast to the south. There, they had even more success, finding no fewer than seven suitable boats, most of them seine trawlers. Over a period of several days, the team inspected and acquired the *Willyama II*, *Kelton*, *Minston Brae*, *Two Freddies*, *Margaret Twaits*, *Helen Dawn* and *San Cristoforo*. They also acquired several new recruits for the Small Ships Section, including the skipper and part-owner of the *Willyama II*, Ralph Andrews.

Andrews joined almost by accident – which, coincidentally, was how he became a fisherman in the first place. Ralph had been born across the Tasman Sea, at Dunedin on New Zealand's South Island, in 1911 while his father, also Ralph, was the representative of an English tea company. That occupation then took the Andrews family to Auckland, where Ralph and his two brothers, Frank and John, learned to sail on Auckland Harbour. It also brought the Andrews family to Sydney in 1919 when Ralph senior was appointed Australasian manager for Lipton's Tea. The family moved into a lovely house at Bellevue Hill in Sydney's eastern suburbs and the boys were enrolled in a school just down the road, Scots College.

It was an idyll truncated by bad news. Ralph senior was diagnosed with tuberculosis and the family moved to Wagga Wagga in 1927 in the hope that the drier air in the interior of the country would help his condition. Unfortunately, the disease had taken too great a hold and Ralph Andrews senior died there in 1928. Shortly afterwards, the family returned to Sydney to an apartment overlooking Rushcutters Bay. They also took out a long lease on a holiday house at Newport. The three Andrews boys took every opportunity they had to spend as much time sailing as they possibly could.

Ralph junior had left school when the family had lived in Wagga Wagga and for a decade had worked as a commercial traveller, most recently for Johnson & Johnson, saving as much money as he could. Eventually, he and a friend, who agreed to become his business partner, had saved enough to finance the construction of a fishing trawler, which Ralph named the *Willyama II*. The boat was completed in June 1941 and Ralph went straight from commercial traveller to commercial fisherman. Early in his sailing career, Ralph had learned celestial navigation, which he now put to good use to fish out beyond the fifty fathom mark, ranging from Bass Strait to as far north as the Queensland border.

Ralph's career as a fisherman came to a sudden halt after just twelve months. Around the middle of June 1942, Ralph was visited in Eden by two Americans who said they were there to assess the *Willyama II* with a view to acquiring it for the US Army. In discussions with them, Ralph learned about the Small Ships Section and also gathered that they did not know a lot about the waters off the South Coast. As conversationally as possible, Ralph said to them, 'Hop in, and we'll go over to New Zealand for lunch.' Equally conversationally, one of the Americans thanked Ralph for his kind offer, and said they were very busy at the moment, but perhaps at another time . . .

Just a few days later, Ralph received some more visitors, this time an Australian naval officer and a civilian who said the *Willyama II* had been acquired – they used the term 'impressed' – by the Australian government. They also asked Ralph whether he would sail the *Willyama II* to Sydney, which he agreed to do. A few days later, Ralph steered his trawler into Sydney Harbour and tied up alongside several other vessels at Number 10 Wharf, Walsh Bay.

Ashore, a number of propositions were put to him. The *Willyama II* would be refitted for maritime service with the US Army, and after that refit would be sailed to a northern Australian port to commence wartime duties delivering supplies to isolated bases. If Ralph was prepared to sign on with the Small Ships Section, he could sail north with his boat. Ralph had been a member of the RAN Reserve, his brother John was currently serving with the RAN while his other brother, Frank, was in the United Kingdom serving there with the Royal Navy. In those circumstances, and now without his boat, it was not all that difficult a decision. Plus, as Ralph signed and dated the employment contract, he noted the date: it was 4 July 1942.

•

In all, seventeen seine trawlers would be selected for acquisition, all relatively new, including some with less than two years' service. They were all taken to Sydney, where they were stripped and reinforced if necessary, painted battleship grey and outfitted with what they would need for war service, a process that included the mounting of machine guns, generally placed either on each side of the wheelhouse or at the bow and stern of the vessel. They weren't much but they did provide a feeling of reassurance.

While all this was going on, the acquisition teams kept working. They sought out sailboats – ketches, yawls and even schooners – which they knew could be invaluable in carrying larger loads without appearing to be military vessels. In deeper water, they could also be used as lighters to transfer supplies from larger to smaller vessels. Finally, the teams sought out punts and scows – large, flat-bottomed vessels with extremely shallow draughts which, either under their own power or under tow, could safely sail in waters far too shallow for other boats. Most were sourced from either Tasmania or New Zealand.

While the seine trawlers would provide the immediate backbone of the Small Ships flotilla, other vessels were acquired for what they could already do or for what they might become. Thus it was that the team acquired the *Argosy Lemal* – referred to by many who came to know her well as the *Agony Remorse* – a postcard picturesque steel-hulled and triple-masted 280-ton schooner acquired from the Adelaide Steamship Company. Before the war, she had carried barley between Adelaide and Melbourne. Now she was earmarked to be a floating mobile command post. After being packed full of the latest radio equipment, she would sail to wherever the US Army was operating, cruising offshore and serving as the communications hub between MacArthur's headquarters and the forward command posts on the ground. The theory was that the *Argosy Lemal* was identical to the hundreds of old schooners that carried trade goods between the various island groups and that, if she behaved as they did, she would not draw attention to herself.

Equally attractive, at least in the eyes of some fishermen, was the *Hilda Norling*, built at Queenscliff in Victoria, and coming in at twenty metres long, six metres wide and with a displacement of 100 tons. She was a two-masted ketch, fitted with a sixty-two horsepower diesel engine, but that wasn't what made her special. The *Hilda Norling* was built specifically for cray fishing in Victorian and Tasmanian waters and was believed to have the largest crayfish well (hold) of any vessel built for that trade; when full, it would hold 400 dozen crayfish. A well that size would also hold a lot of vital military supplies and, because of this, she was acquired in July 1942.

The Small Ships Section also acquired a deep-sea trawler, but one that had been specially modified. She was the *Minnamurra*, built as a trawler but spotted before she went into service by Captain P.G. Taylor, the co-pilot on many of Sir Charles Kingsford-Smith's most famous flights. Taylor had the *Minnamurra* refitted as a luxury cruiser, and she was still in that configuration when acquired by the Small Ships. Ominously to some, the *Minnamurra* had refused to leave her slipway when launched, considered a bad omen in sailing circles.

A second luxury boat was acquired around the same time. The *Shangri-La* had been built and outfitted to specifications laid down by its owner, the great-grandson of the founder of the Howard Smith Limited Shipping Company, one of Australia's largest commercial enterprises in its heyday. The *Shangri-La* was bought outright with a specific purpose in mind; she was to be the command vessel for the Small Ships Section.

•

The fall of the Philippines and the Japanese advance down into the Malay Peninsula, Singapore, the Netherlands East Indies and out into the Central Pacific pushed a lot of boats and people ahead of them and some of both – ships and people – found their way to the Small Ships Section, often by a circuitous route. One of the larger windfalls was the arrival of the *Mactan*.

The *Mactan* was an old ship, a medium-sized freighter of some 2000 tons, built in 1899 and for many years plying her trade in both Far Eastern and Australian waters, most recently for the Manila-based Compagnia Maritima. Hurriedly converted to a hospital ship in Manila in December 1941, she was loaded up with 200 wounded American and Filipino soldiers and sailed from Manila in January 1942, one of the last ships to escape before the city fell to the Japanese.

Although bombed early in the voyage, the *Mactan* avoided significant damage and eventually made it all the way to Sydney. There, she was initially requisitioned by the RAN for use as a stores ship but was subsequently handed over to the Small Ships Section. The *Mactan* was a welcome addition to the growing flotilla, but equally welcome was the crew she carried. That crew were predominantly Filipinos, some sixty of them, under the command of Major Rafaelo Cisneros, assisted by Lieutenant Ireneo Ames, both of the Philippine Offshore Patrol, an army unit with naval responsibilities. Both Cisneros and Ames were offered positions with the Small Ships, with their current ranks, and both accepted. Most of the Filipino crewmen transferred across with them. However, because many of them didn't speak English, they would be formed into crews led by an English-speaking officer.

While not directly part of the Small Ships, the section's fortunes would also be in part dependent on a number of ships that fled to Australia from the Netherlands East Indies (NEI) to prevent their destruction or capture by the advancing Japanese. These freighters were part of a state-owned freight line in the East Indies known by its initials, KPM. When it became obvious that Java was about to fall, all KPM ships were ordered to sail for the nearest Allied safe port.

In all, twenty-nine ships, displacing between 500 and 6000 tons, made it to Australian waters, some of them after being redirected from India. In Australia, those ships, with their Dutch masters and crews, were placed under charter to the British Ministry of Transport, which immediately allocated them to the US Army, specifically the USAFIA. They were a windfall for the Americans, and would become a key part of the supply line supporting US forces.

Sometimes, ships and crews simply appeared on the scene, and no one was quite sure just when and how they came to be Small Ships. One such example was the wooden auxiliary ketch, the *Melanesia*, built in 1917, sixteen metres long and just thirty-one tons. The boat had formerly been owned by the Seventh Day Adventist Church and had been used to support missionary work in New Guinea and the Pacific Islands.

Finally, Small Ships had another windfall when the *Kurimarau* sailed down from northern waters just ahead of the Japanese. Owned by the Lever Brothers (Lever & Lever), the *Kurimarau* had been used for transferring cargo and stores from the various Lever Brothers plantations in the Solomon Islands. Her entire crew came across to the Small Ships when she was acquired soon after arriving in Sydney. That crew comprised eighteen Solomon Islanders, most of whom were from the island of Malaita, three European engineers, a radio officer and a mate, Jack Gaskell.

•

In 1940, Clarrie Dawes was a fourteen-year-old boy, living in a broken home and dreaming of going to sea. Clarrie's home was in Thevenard, the port area of Ceduna on the far west coast of South Australia, where he would watch the grain carriers and other ships come and go while wondering what would happen when they reached the other end of their voyage. The world was at war and the great navies had put to sea but Clarrie knew – sadly – that he was too young for the navy, even in wartime. So most days he would wander down to the wharves to watch the boats, big and small, and to wait until he, too, would be old enough to sail away.

There was one small ship whose arrival Clarrie always looked forward to. The *Coorabie* was a frequent visitor as it collected wheat from the smaller, shallower ports along the coast and brought it back to Ceduna, where it was transferred to larger vessels for carriage to Port Adelaide. Clarrie was always assured of a job, and some pocket money, when the *Coorabie* docked. He repaired wheat bags that had a tear in them or had split along the seam. Those bags would be placed in high stacks in the holds of the bigger ships, and a leaking bag could cause an entire stack to fall over.

On one of those visits in the latter part of 1940, the first mate asked Clarrie whether he would be interested in joining the ship as a 'peggie', a junior hand who brought the sailors their meals from the galley, cleaned up afterwards and did other odd jobs. The mate said that the *Coorabie* would be sailing at 5 p.m. that afternoon and if Clarrie was there with his gear, he would be signed on as a crewman. Clarrie was there on time, even a little early, with his small bag of belongings; an hour later, he was a sailor.

Clarrie soon learned that a sailor's life was hard, but easy to love. The hardest part was when the *Coorabie* was in port, as he was expected to help with the loading and unloading as well as undertaking his assigned tasks as the ship's peggie. In what spare time he had, Clarrie learned from Bill Webster, the first mate, how to become a real sailor, how to read a compass and steer a ship as well as a hundred and one more mundane tasks.

When the *Coorabie* arrived back at Port Adelaide at the end of one trip around the middle of 1942, it was met by representatives of the ship's owners and an American army officer. The crew members were informed that their ship had been acquired by the US Army. The American officer then asked them whether they would be prepared to sail the ship to Sydney, where it was to be refitted and armed. Those who sailed to Sydney, he added, would be given accommodation and a train ticket for the return trip to Adelaide. Clarrie was one of those who opted to stay with the ship.

When they arrived in Sydney, another American officer addressed the crew, saying there would be employment for anyone who wanted to sign up. Bill Webster took Clarrie aside and told him that he had been offered the command of another ship, one that was currently in dry dock and being refitted. Webster had accepted that offer, and he wanted Clarrie to sign on with the Americans and become part of the crew of Webster's new ship. When Clarrie said he would be happy to sign on, Bill Webster said that he would now be signing on as an able seaman rather than as an ordinary seaman. It was unexpected but welcome as it meant that the sixteen-year-old's wages had just been doubled to fifty pounds a month.

Two others from the *Coorabie*'s crew also joined Webster, and the three young men collected their belongings and followed their new captain to where his new command was waiting in dry dock; her name was the *Leprena*.

•

The early Small Ships crews came from two main sources. The first were those who, like Clarrie Dawes, were already employed aboard the boats acquired by the Small Ships Section. Most of those sailors were faced with immediate unemployment should they opt not to sign on with the US Army. Those among them eligible for armed service knew that, sooner or later, their choice for employment would be taken away from them. The second source was the general public, and in particular those men and boys who were not considered eligible for service in the Australian armed forces for reasons of age or disability. Eventually that source would provide hundreds of sailors whose ages ranged from fifteen to seventy years of age.

The hiring of all those sailors was the subject of an agreement struck between the US Army and Australian authorities. The agreement allowed the US Army to employ Australian crews, with certain conditions. To begin with, if the sailor was Australian, he had to be a male aged either over forty-five years or between fifteen and seventeen years old. Any who fell between those ages had to be unsuitable for service with the Australian armed forces because of either those age restrictions or medical impairment. They also had to be issued with clearance papers by the Australian manpower authorities.

Those crews were offered six-month contracts which stipulated a number of conditions, including that the sailors must be prepared to sail their ships in New Guinea waters. The contracts also included a clause stating that, if the sailor's work was deemed satisfactory, the contract would be extended for a further six months. The contracts could only be renewed in Australian territory, meaning a return home was guaranteed for those with ongoing employment. The exact legal status of those who would be overseas at the expiration of their contract, and whose contracts were not renewed was put in the too-hard basket at that time.

Both sources of manpower resulted in the recruitment of some outstanding sailors from all around the world. One of these was a young man named Neil Sandery, who had previously worked as a Sydney Harbour tugboat captain and who was well-known in both yachting and fishing circles. He was usually described as tall, rangy and quiet, and his mother, Elizabeth Powell, was a well-known Victorian writer, adventurer and social activist. He may have inherited a number of those qualities because, at eighteen years of age, Neil circumnavigated Australia on a small yacht and later made several extended voyages into the Pacific, all before he turned twenty-one. Whenever he could, Sandery would sail north to the Great Barrier Reef on fishing expeditions, sometimes accompanied by his young wife, Isabel.

Some of the recruits were larger than life characters, such as Ray Parer, whose job description could justifiably be 'adventurer'. Parer had been a soldier and then an airman with the Australian Flying Corps during World War I, had won the Air Force Cross and had been one of the first aviators to fly from England to Australia. His adventures in early aviation in Australia seemed to almost always end in either crashes or financial difficulties, and he sought his fortune elsewhere. When the war broke out, Parer was in New Guinea, working with one of his brothers on a gold lease near Wau. He proposed sailing from Lae to Singapore to enlist in the RAF there, but was advised against doing so by the Department of Civil Aviation. Instead, he returned to Australia and joined the RAAF. However, health problems – he was deaf in one ear – saw him transferred from the RAAF's Active List to its Reserve List. Parer promptly resigned and then equally promptly joined the Small Ships.

Laddie Reday would later recall that 'there would be many crooks, soldiers of fortune, derelicts, bums and ne'er-do-wells who would come forward and talk their way into our Small Ships', but that catalogue of rogues were primarily those who joined later in the war when rank opportunism was more powerful than patriotism. The majority of the early volunteers for the Small Ships came from diverse backgrounds, but all joined primarily because it would give them the opportunity to contribute directly to the war effort, something that might otherwise have been denied to many of them.

However, it is also fair to say that the sailors recruited in mid-1942 were a mixed bunch. There were several men with just one arm, and two who possessed one leg each; one of them, a man named Horace Drape, was apparently never called anything but 'Hoppy' Drape. There was also one woman, for a while at least. Her name was Vi Miller and she joined as the cook and deckhand on her husband's fishing boat, *Sunshine*, after it was acquired in Mackay in July 1942. After serving happily for several weeks, she was dismissed before the *Sunshine* departed Australian waters later that year. There were several sets of brothers, many itinerants and at least one father and son in Small Ships uniform before the end of the war.

Like the Filipinos who escaped capture by sailing to Australia aboard the *Mactan*, the Small Ships attracted others who had fled from the Japanese. Two were Australian residents who fled New Britain after the Japanese landed on the island in January 1942. One was A.D. Hallam, a sailor in World War I who had subsequently built up a successful timber, trading and shipping business in New Britain. For three months after the Japanese occupied key points on the island, Hallam remained there, rescuing what he could of his property while hiding and being warned of approaching Japanese by friendly natives. When the Japanese seemed to be closing in, he escaped in his motor launch, the *Malahuka*, which he had hidden in a tidal river inlet and which carried him to Port Moresby. From there, he made his way to Sydney and the Small Ships.

Another was the English-born Jack Gilmore. He and his wife were well-known to Australian expatriates in New Britain as the proprietors of the Rabaul Hotel. Walking away from their hotel shortly before the Japanese landed, the Gilmores also escaped aboard a small boat, and when they too arrived in Sydney, Jack volunteered for service with the Small Ships.

Two Chinese also signed on after having considerable adventures in just getting to Australia. One was Chang Keng, who escaped from Hong Kong by boat just prior to that colony's fall to the Japanese in December 1941. The boat he was on was torpedoed by a Japanese submarine off the coast of Java, with Chang being one of the survivors rescued by a Dutch vessel also fleeing the Japanese. Chang landed in Perth, and from there made his own way across to Sydney, where he joined the Small Ships. Chang was joined in the service by Tai Fu Sung from Shanghai, who also escaped that city just ahead of the Japanese. He sailed off on a small boat that was eventually found some distance out at sea by a Royal Navy warship based in Singapore. Taken back there, Tai decided to keep going and made his way to Sydney and the Small Ships.

There were at least twenty Aboriginal men and Torres Strait Islanders who volunteered for service with the Small Ships, and they came from all across the Top End to sign up. Among the first were Willy George, original from Murray Island, and Kamuel Abednego, who would serve with distinction as first mate aboard the *Two Freddies*.

Six Singapore Docks policemen fled on a sampan the day before the island was surrendered to the Japanese in February 1942. The group was led by Norm Byrne, a forty-five-year-old New Zealander who had served with distinction as an infantryman during World War I, winning the Military Medal during the final days of that conflict. Norm led the others safely through Japanese-controlled waters to Australia, where they then followed him into the Small Ships.

The most exotic of them all, though, was probably Peter Dyez, a former lieutenant in the French Foreign Legion. Dyez was one of ten Legionnaires who chose to flee Indochina when it was occupied by Japanese forces in 1941. The group stole a yacht and sailed it all the way to New Caledonia where they were promptly arrested by the local authorities and charged with desertion. The men organised another escape, which included the theft of a yacht, and this time sailed to Townsville. Not really knowing what to do, the Australian authorities allowed the men to travel to Sydney to join the Small Ships Section there.

•

Regardless of their background, or where they had travelled from to sign up, when the employment contracts were signed, the Small Ships crews were all issued two sets of khakis – trousers, shirts and jacket – plus regulation shoes and a US Army Transportation Service cap. Most would wear ordinary civilian clothes when working aboard ship, and only used their billed cap with its impressive gold and blue insignia for going ashore and when they wanted to impress an audience. They were paid at US Army rates, which were well in excess of their Australian equivalents; they were, though, required to pay tax on their earnings. And, despite the sometimes malicious rumours to the contrary, the Australian soldiers who joined the Small Ships were never required to swear an oath of allegiance to the United States.

All the Small Ship sailors, a number that would include citizens of a dozen or more nations, sailed under the US flag. This was technically illegal, as only US-registered vessels were entitled to fly the US flag and, for the first twelve months at least, there were few, if any, US-registered vessels in the Small

Ships fleet. In that period, the overwhelming majority of the vessels employed were Australian. However, as there was no Australian registration in 1942, those ships remained, legally, British-registered vessels flying a foreign flag. It made for some very interesting hypothetical questions.

Those questions were put to one side during that period, though, as there were issues of far greater import to consider. The months of June and July 1942 were a period of almost non-stop and furious activity. The nineteen vessels and 100 sailors that the Small Ships Section claimed at the end of June were trebled by the end of July.

To outsiders, it would have seemed as if the section was in some kind of race against time, and that was precisely how the organisers felt. They were racing against the time it would take the Japanese forces in the north to organise themselves.

3.

NORTH

Whether or not Japanese planners ever envisioned a landing on the Australian mainland is a moot point, but there is no doubt of their intention to sever the supply line between the United States and Australia. The Japanese lost several capital ships in the Battle of the Coral Sea in May 1942 – the first major naval battle carried out by aircraft rather than surface vessels – and their loss severely impinged on their capacity to use elements of the Imperial Japanese Navy to interdict that supply line. If a naval-based solution was now impractical, Japan would take land and use that land as a permanent and unsinkable base for its aircraft. Thus, it looked firstly towards Port Moresby and, soon after, towards the Solomon Islands. Success in seizing and holding land there would enable the Japanese to establish satellites to their main South Pacific base at Rabaul. That success would also mean their aircraft could control the seas well to the east, out towards Fiji, Tonga and Samoa. If that didn't break the Allies' supply line, it would certainly stretch it very thin.

•

In March 1943, a year after his arrival in Melbourne, Douglas MacArthur publicly revealed that he had no sooner reached Australia than he concluded that the key to its defence lay not on the Australian mainland but in New Guinea. Within weeks, he was looking to establish a significant air force presence somewhere towards the eastern tip of the island. The air presence would protect the eastern approaches to Port Moresby, the only significant town and port in the eastern half of the island; it would also avoid the necessity for Allied aircraft to fly over the high Owen Stanley Ranges on every mission against the Japanese to the north, and it would provide a base from which an advance along New Guinea's north coast and the islands beyond could be launched.

Within the larger strategy that MacArthur and his staff were developing, New Guinea's northern coast was a vital part of Allied operations in the foreseeable future. Control of it would firstly remove any possible threat of a direct attack on the Australian mainland and all but end the threat of a Japanese interdiction of the Pacific supply routes. Establishing a series of air bases along the coast would both threaten and then neutralise the main Japanese stronghold at Rabaul while providing bases for the Allies to leapfrog Japanese positions all the way back to the Philippines, whose liberation was always central to MacArthur's plans.

MacArthur identified Abau-Mullins Harbour, on the far south-eastern coast of New Guinea, as a potential base, and it was promptly given the codename 'Boston'. Boston was never developed as a base because reconnaissance showed that Milne Bay, at the extreme eastern tip of the island, was a far better prospect; it was given the codename 'Fall River'. On 25 June, the former KPM freighter *Karsik* disembarked an advance party of Australians there.

Looking further afield, a joint Australian–US reconnaissance party was sent to a point about halfway along the northern coast between Milne Bay and the main north coast town in Papua, the settlement of Lae. There were only two real European outposts along that long stretch of coast: Buna Government Station, near the native village of Buna; and the Anglican mission at Gona, some fifteen kilometres to the north. One of the main attractions of the area was a small airfield hacked out of kunai grass alongside the government buildings at Buna.

The reconnaissance party sent to Buna in early July found the existing airfield there in urgent need of a major upgrade, and even then it would be problematic for military use. However, the party also found an eminently suitable site for an airfield at Dobodura, some twenty-five kilometres south of Buna. A plan was developed for the seizure of Buna, after which an all-weather airfield would be constructed at Dobodura. The area would be taken over by Allied troops on 10 August, with some of the US troops to be used – it was primarily an American operation – marching over the mountains on a little-used track and the remainder being despatched by sea. Critical to the plan was the creation of a sea supply line to bring in supplies and equipment from what would be the main Allied base at Milne Bay. The nature of the coastal waters between Buna and Milne Bay mandated that small ships would provide the most important link in that supply line.

As the planning continued at the hectic pace that MacArthur demanded, it suddenly became irrelevant; the Japanese had beaten MacArthur to the punch.

•

Japan's New Guinea campaign stepped up on 21 July 1942 when 8000 troops from its South Seas Force landed on the north coast of the island. The troops splashed ashore on several beaches along a twenty-kilometre stretch of coast from Gona Mission in the north to the small government station at Buna in the south. Ironically, the Japanese had chosen the same location as MacArthur's planners and for essentially the same reasons: several areas of flat coastal plain, clearly defined tracks and, of course, the presence of an airfield at Buna. They had beaten the Allies by a good three weeks.

Apart from the beaches, coastal plains and airfield, the Japanese planners had selected the area for a more important purpose. From their new Buna–Sanananda–Gona bridgehead, the Japanese intention was to push south in an overland reconnaissance in strength, to test the feasibility of establishing an overland route through the Owen Stanley Ranges, which would firstly threaten Port Moresby and, if sustainable, enable them to capture that key point without the risks attached to an amphibious assault. This reconnaissance soon developed into a substantial offensive when the Australian forces defending the route chosen, the Kokoda Track, were pushed back with relative ease.

If all went according to the plan they were developing, the Japanese troops expected to push through the mountains to the coastal plains on the other side and there push the Allied troops back into the sea, capturing Port Moresby in the process. Its capture would give them a major base opposite the Australian mainland, thereby threatening a large part of northern Australia. As well, it would protect the southern approaches to their main base at Rabaul and also offer them new opportunities to the east.

Meanwhile, as the frontline troops were pushing the Australians back along the track, Japanese engineers and rear echelon troops worked hard to make their new bridgehead on the north coast as impregnable as possible.

•

The landing of Japanese troops at Buna, and their subsequent push towards Port Moresby along the Kokoda Track, represented a temporary glitch to MacArthur and his planning staff. Confident that they would be stopped by the Australian troops being rushed to New Guinea, however, MacArthur and his staff continued to plan for the first Allied offensive operation against the Japanese since Pearl Harbor. Planning was one thing; putting those plans into operation was something else entirely. When queried by Washington about his operational plans for New Guinea, MacArthur replied on 2 August that those plans had been greatly hampered by a critical shortage of transportation, especially sea transport. He was still preparing for an offensive, though, and was confident of achieving a remarkable victory.

•

Against this background, the work of the Small Ships Section proceeded at a hectic pace. At the Grace Building, a thousand and one loose ends were being tied up. To support the new ships and crews, a whole new structure had to be brought together, and this was where the expertise of the Americans who had worked for years in transportation proved its worth. The Small Ships needed a range of skilled tradesmen to support the on-water operations, and so orders went out to hire carpenters, motor mechanics – especially those with marine diesel experience – shipwrights, catering specialists, armourers and a dozen other occupations. Burns Philp was eventually contracted to supply and provision the Small Ships which operated out of Australian ports and to also supply fuel at those ports where there were no on-site army supplies. Its contribution would eventually include both water supply and the provision of some specialised staff.

As the organisation grew and the pressure on it increased, Major Gordon Evans was moved from personnel to take charge of the harbourside operations located down the hill, almost at the base of the Sydney Harbour Bridge. There, the Small Ships operation based on 10 Walsh Bay also continued at the same furious pace. In Evans' office on the wharf, all the hiring and the signing on and off of staff took place while outside, in the section known as the victualling wharf, the newly acquired vessels were painted and fitted out, provisioned and armed with two .30 or .50 calibre machine guns, several of which proved to be of World War I vintage. Further down York Street, a clothing store was established, administered by a young man named Cliff Callen, where the new recruits would receive their Small Ships working outfits.

As soon as it became obvious that the size of the section, and the scope and reach of its operations, would exceed the early estimates, a decision was made to decentralise its operations. Bases would be established where needed closer to the war zone in the north, and those bases would be given the responsibility for local decisions as long as they were made in conjunction with the local army command structure. Sheridan Fahnestock was sent to Cairns in early July to oversee the establishment of a Small Ships base there, while others were despatched to Townsville, Port Moresby and Milne Bay for the same purpose. The civilian, Jack Savage, was also required to move northward with the Small

Ships, to oversee repairs and salvage, and to advise precisely what facilities were needed at the bases to be established.

By mid-July, the planning and preparation for the despatch of the first Small Ships to operational bases in the north had been completed. Although some referred to them as a fleet, the dozen or so ships that sailed from Sydney had different destinations and different objectives. Some were to sail to either Townsville or Cairns to await further orders. Others were to sail, via those ports, to Darwin, where they were to be loaded with rations and ammunition before being sent on to Port Moresby, which was rapidly becoming a major garrison and supply base around its port facilities. A large number of Papuans who had been evacuated to Darwin would also be taken back to Port Moresby where they would resume their roles as carriers for the Australian Army.

Among the boats that made up the fleet was the *Shangri-La*.

•

There may have been several levels of worry and upheaval in and around the various Allied commands in Sydney with responsibilities for naval and amphibious matters, but none of that filtered down to Ralph Andrews. They probably wouldn't have disturbed his equanimity anyway. He had learned shortly after signing on with the Small Ships that he would not be required to sail aboard the *Willyama II*, his former boat, if and when it headed north, and that another vessel would be given to him to command. In the meantime, he was asked to await further orders, which weren't long in coming. In fact, he was told, there was something he could do while he was waiting, and that was to collect another boat recently acquired by the Small Ships.

It gave Ralph something to do and, accompanied by two armed American military policemen, he was driven to a small dock on the harbour at Mosman. There, he took possession of 'a lovely little motor cruiser', the *Shangri-La*, once a millionaire's plaything but more recently part of the Volunteer Coastal Patrol. When Ralph arrived back at Walsh Bay aboard the launch, he was greeted by the American officer in charge there, a Major Leon Lancaster, and George Bradford, the section's commander. The men offered Ralph his next assignment, sailing the *Shangri-La* to Brisbane with a new crew and a passenger, another American officer named Doran who would ultimately be a base commander for the Small Ships somewhere in the north. Bradford also explained that the *Shangri-La* was slated to become the section's command vessel in the north.

After his new command had been fuelled, provisioned and given an engineer and deckhand, Ralph steered her out of Walsh Bay and Sydney Harbour, turning to the north once clear of the heads. It was a slow trip to Brisbane because of ongoing problems with the boat's diesel engines, but they reached the city safely around the middle of July. There, Ralph was asked to take the *Shangri-La* further up the eastern coast to Townsville where he would be given further orders. It was big news rather than fresh orders that greeted the *Shangri-La* when she tied up in Townsville; the Japanese had landed in the north of New Guinea and it was believed they were working their way south towards their target, Port Moresby.

At this point, the *Shangri-La* did not have a working radio, and no one in Townsville seemed to know more than what had been broadcast on the (presumably) censored radio news bulletins, so Ralph probably knew about as much as anyone else in Townsville. He was told to continue north to Cairns, where still further orders would be waiting. As Cairns had once been posited as the Small Ships' most northerly operational base, Ralph speculated on where their journey might now end.

Naturally enough, things weren't exactly clear-cut when the *Shangri-La* arrived at Cairns. It seemed the Japanese were continuing their push across the Owen Stanley Ranges towards Port Moresby. The port town itself was subject to regular air raids and was now the focus of a massive influx of men and material destined for deployment against the Japanese. Port Moresby, Ralph learned, was also the *Shangri-La*'s next destination. The journey would be delayed somewhat, though, for the boat had to be prepared for the war zone into which she was about to sail, which meant several coats of grey paint, the fitting of some machine guns and some additional work on the engines.

•

While Ralph Andrews and the *Shangri-La* were being prepared for an uncertain future, the first tranche of Small Ships vessels sent north were arriving at a variety of ports on a variety of missions. As more boats were acquired and refitted in Sydney, they too were sent north, where it was becoming increasingly obvious that the Japanese would need to be stopped. Sheridan and Bruce Fahnestock were again among the leading elements of this move north, with Jack Savage not far behind. The stresses and strains were on them all, and the trip north was not always plain sailing. One of the seine trawlers, the *Ulladulla*, was part of that first movement north. Her captain, Tom Prestnol, suffered a major heart attack en route and died at Gladstone after the boat docked there. The *Ulladulla* remained at Gladstone until her pre-war skipper, Jim Alsop, arrived to take his boat north to the war zone.

The first mission for the Small Ships, then, was to carry supplies to Allied bases in the area bounded by Darwin, Port Moresby, Milne Bay, and Townsville and Cairns. In the forward bases, Port Moresby and Milne Bay, the Allies would establish enormous supply dumps of ammunition, rations and other items necessary to firstly stop the Japanese and, once that had been done, undertake offensive operations against them. It was while doing just that, on a supply mission to Milne Bay, that the first Small Ship sailed directly into harm's way.

•

Milne Bay is a sheltered deep-water harbour, around thirty-five kilometres long and fifteen kilometres wide, at the very eastern tip of the island of New Guinea. Early in his appraisal of the war situation, MacArthur recognised the area's strategic importance. Airfields constructed there would protect the eastern approaches to Port Moresby and the Torres Strait, and it provided a large and sustainable base for operations further along the north coast of the island. An added advantage would be that aircraft based there, if adequate facilities could be built, would be able to attack Rabaul and ocean areas to the north and north-east without having to fly over the Owen Stanley Ranges.

Australian and American engineers arrived at Milne Bay in June 1942 to commence the construction of both airfields and port facilities. They would be protected by Australian Army units, while RAAF Kittyhawks would provide aerial protection against the inevitable Japanese air attacks. Both army and air force personnel soon learned that there were some less than ideal aspects to the place. It was low and swampy, and therefore very attractive to the swarms of mosquitoes that arrived in clouds to welcome each new arrival. The area also had a low cloud base for most of the year and the nearby mountains could make flying a dangerous proposition. While the Kittyhawks could provide aerial defence, aerial resupply was problematic, so most of the supplies and reinforcements would need to be brought in by sea. The only vessels immediately available for this at Milne Bay were some mission luggers and an RAAF launch, so suddenly the Small Ships had an important role to play.

Again, Japanese military planners saw the same opportunities at Milne Bay as MacArthur, but their intelligence was nowhere near as comprehensive as his. They believed the Allies had only put a small force ashore at the bay, and so made plans to overrun that force and take the strategic site for themselves. Late in the evening of 25 August, around midnight, three Japanese cruisers began bombarding what had been the village of Ahioma on the north shore of Milne Bay. When the bombardment ended after an hour, Japanese barges and landing craft put 1900 soldiers and marines, and two light tanks ashore. The Australians held up the Japanese advance that night, and in the morning the Japanese positions were attacked by RAAF Kittyhawks who just had time to gain operational height before sweeping down to attack.

In the midst of all this, a Small Ship steamed happily into Milne Bay.

•

The *Minston Brae*, a relatively new South Coast trawler, had been designated the number S-14, and, as the number suggests, was one of the first boats acquired for the Small Ships Section. George Ling, her pre-war captain, had retained command of the fishing boat and had been given a three-man crew as well-travelled as he was. Ling was a Scotsman, a fisherman from the island of St Kilda, who had followed his profession all the way to the South Coast of New South Wales. Two of his crew were Yorkshiremen. Norm Oddy was a former marine engineer with Vickers-Armstrong who had found himself working at a munitions factory in Australia before joining the Small Ships in July 1942 as a ship's engineer. The other was the cook, Arthur Slight, described as 'tubby and balding'; he had served with the British Army in World War I and afterwards in India. He had gone to sea in this war and had already been sunk twice, once off Norway and once off Dunkirk. The boat's New Zealand-born deckhand, Norm Byrne, had also served in World War I, winning the Military Medal on the Western Front, and, more recently, had been a Singapore Docks policeman.

The *Minston Brae* was part of the original fleet that had left Sydney in July, but she was among the last to leave and had sailed slowly north to Townsville. There, they were told to wait until further orders were issued, which they were around the middle of August. Called to the Small Ships office there, George Ling was informed that the *Minston Brae* would be required to take a load of supplies across the Coral Sea directly to Milne Bay, a part of the world that he had never visited.

It would not make any difference in the end, because none of the other crew had ever been there either. All four agreed that this would not be a deterrent, and with the two Norms and Arthur Slight in full agreement, the *Minston Brae* sailed away. Using dead reckoning, and some fairly old charts, they made it safely to Samarai Island, just off the tip of Milne Bay. From there, it was a relatively easy run up the bay, although the sight of Kittyhawks strafing the jungle on the north shore and the sound of both light and medium weapons firing almost continuously told them that something was wrong. George Ling made the decision to shelter among the mangroves in a tidal creek during the day, before unloading their cargo after dusk.

Ling was forced to relinquish command of his boat when a bout of fever felled him later that day. Norm Oddy took over and sailed the *Minston Brae* to the Gili Gili wharf after dark. There, he supervised the unloading of the stores they had carried and was given an update on the fighting, learning for the first time of the Japanese bombardment and landing. Oddy then made the decision to make a run back out of the bay in the dark. Just as they were about to depart, an RAAF launch pulled up alongside and, using some fairly fruity language, described the arrival of some Japanese warships in the bay.

Feeling that their boat would be a sitting target if it remained where it was, Oddy was still determined to flee the bay and the RAAF launch opted to go with them. By hugging the southern shoreline, Oddy hoped that they would be lost against the backdrop of palm trees and mangroves that dotted the southern side. After several minutes of anxiously peering into the dark to their north, Oddy and Norm Byrne, manning their single machine gun, spotted the outline of the Japanese forces. Oddy believed they comprised a cruiser and several destroyers, apparently engaged in landing additional troops. To the men aboard the *Minston Brae*, the cruiser looked more like a giant battleship. Around the same time as they were peering at the Japanese ships, a Japanese lookout spotted the two small boats creeping along.

Suddenly, they were bathed in the beam of a powerful searchlight, followed by another and then all hell broke loose. If they had wanted to, the men could have watched the muzzle flash of the big ship's guns, but they were concentrating too hard on survival for that. Norm Oddy coaxed the *Minston Brae*'s engine to its top speed of nine knots, and attempted to zigzag without either running aground or running into one of the Japanese vessels. They had no idea how many shells were fired at them, but later agreed that more than thirty had exploded near the vessel without causing any real damage.

The RAAF launch was not so lucky. Caught in a cone of searchlights, the launch disintegrated when a direct hit from a large gun struck home. The *Minston Brae* didn't slow because those aboard knew that no one could have survived the explosion.

They made it to the mouth of the bay and the darkness beyond. Without slowing down at all, Oddy steered the boat out into China Strait and across to an anchorage at Samarai Island. When he, Byrne, Ling and Slight had recovered enough from what they had just been through, they made their way ashore to deliver a formal report to the naval officer in charge at the base on the island. Then they waited.

•

Some distance to the south-east of Samarai Island, Ralph Andrews was experiencing a different kind of war. It was already well into August when the *Shangri-La* was ready to continue its journey from Cairns to Port Moresby. The weather was exceedingly fine when Andrews set out and it continued that way as he sailed into and across the Coral Sea. This was just as well, for as they entered the waters that comprised the expanse of the Coral Sea, Ralph saw something that he would never forget; something that chilled his heart on what was an otherwise clear and hot day. For several kilometres, the *Shangri-La* sailed past dozens of lifeboats, liferafts and Carley floats. Some of them had seabirds sitting on their bulwarks and, from a distance, those birds seemed to be human heads or, if they were flapping or stretching their wings, hands waving to attract attention. The only sound was the *Shangri-La*'s engine and exhaust, and as they sailed on, Ralph realised that every boat and raft and float was empty. He learned later that they had sailed through the aftermath of the Battle of the Coral Sea. They slowed down and hoisted aboard one of the Carley floats, just in case.

•

The Battle of Milne Bay was short and sharp, and was to have important long-term consequences, not the least for the Small Ships. What the crew of the *Minston Brae* had experienced as they sailed into the bay was a harbinger of what was to come. The aerial dominance of the Kittyhawks and the unexpectedly strong resistance by the Australian ground forces pinned the Japanese down on that first day. The Japanese naval forces returned the night after the initial landing to drop off additional troops and pound the Allied positions, but with limited effect. They returned again the next night, too, and landed more reinforcements but by then their troops already on the ground were coming under increasing pressure from both land and air forces.

The climax of the battle occurred on the night of 30/31 August when the Japanese made a determined effort to capture one of the Allies' airfields. The attack was repulsed with heavy Japanese casualties, which prompted a decision by the Japanese to evacuate the forces that remained. The withdrawal was made at night in early September and by 7 September there were no living Japanese present at Milne Bay. The Japanese lost just under half of the 2800 troops they landed. Milne Bay was not a major battle. Its outcome was determined by a series of Japanese miscalculations and Australian feats of arms. And when it was over, the strategic situation in the South West Pacific Area was just a little bit different.

•

The defeat of the Japanese attempt to push the Australians out of Milne Bay gave the Australians there, and the Americans who would soon follow, access to one of the finest deep-water ports in the eastern half of New Guinea. It was not unfettered access; Milne Bay would suffer many attacks from Japanese aircraft in the coming months, and it would always be vulnerable to attack from the sea, but there would not be another ground assault on the area. To many of those who served there, the value of Milne Bay was a lineball decision. Those who had to live through the incessant wet heat, tropical storms and malaria-carrying mosquitoes found it difficult to appreciate that they were serving in the key which could unlock the outer Japanese perimeter and expose what was within to Allied advances.

For that was what they had achieved. Within a few weeks, Milne Bay became the major hub for the build-up that presaged an imminent offensive move against the Japanese forces in New Guinea. Several port areas were developed in the bay, the three main developments being at Gili Gili, at the head of the bay; subsidiary facilities at Ahioma, where the Japanese landed; and at Waga Waga which, like Ahioma, was on the northern shore of the bay. Fourteen docks and a dedicated fuel jetty were built, mostly in water that was at least ten metres deep. Within a few months, these would be joined by a floating dock and large floating cranes to unload the 10,000-ton Liberty ships and freighters that would sail directly there from both Australia and the United States. Their cargoes, once unloaded, would be moved by army trucks to warehouses and open-air dumps established and then camouflaged well inland from the vulnerable port areas.

•

Back in Australia, Clarrie Dawes was continuing his practical education. Among the many things that he learned about being a sailor from Bill Webster was that patience was a virtue that could easily be undervalued. It was a lesson, and a virtue, that Clarrie needed just then because it took several weeks to refit and make the *Leprena* ready for war service, weeks during which other Small Ships arrived and then departed again for destinations in 'the north'. But, soon enough, the *Leprena* was finished, refitted and repainted and with a new captain and crew. As part of that crew, Clarrie did his share of loading and watch-keeping; probably more than his share when he thought about it as very few of his new shipmates had ever been to sea before.

The *Leprena* sailed north with a full cargo, to Townsville, where the cargo was unloaded and all the formal paperwork for the crew was completed. They were then taken to a warehouse ashore where all, Bill Webster included, were given full sets of US Army fatigues and accoutrements. Townsville was also where the *Leprena* was fitted with three .30 calibre machine guns by American armourers. When they were fitted and tested, Webster asked Clarrie to learn how to maintain and fire the weapons; one of the armourers spent three hours on consecutive days teaching Clarrie those skills.

When ship and crew were both ready, they took aboard a full load of military equipment in boxes and began to speculate on where they might be taking them. Most thought that Port Moresby was the obvious destination but one of the new crewmen said he'd been told they would be sailing to a place called Fall River. There was more, he added. Fall River was close to Milne Bay, where there had recently been heavy fighting, and he also knew that the area was full of Japanese soldiers. That crewman and two others shortly afterwards went ashore and were not seen again. Because of this, the *Leprena*'s departure was delayed once more, this time by several days, as they waited for new crewmen to be found and forwarded to the ship.

When she eventually sailed, the *Leprena* travelled under secret orders and it wasn't until they were well out to sea that Bill Webster called the crew together to explain both where they were going and why. Webster said that, yes, they were sailing to Fall River, but that Fall River was actually a codename for Milne Bay. They were going there with a cargo that included a large amount of medical supplies and hospital equipment, much needed now that the Japanese invasion force had been defeated. Two days later, the *Leprena* sailed into Milne Bay at sunset and was soon given an official welcome to the war.

Around 8 p.m., an hour after they had anchored off Gili Gili, a flight of Japanese bombers flew overhead and proceeded to bomb Allied positions inland from the head of the bay. No bombs fell anywhere near the *Leprena*, but there was a scare aboard when she was struck by a nose-cone and several pieces of shrapnel from anti-aircraft shells. The ship's cargo was unloaded without interruption the next day and then, instead of returning to Australia for more, the *Leprena* was put to work towing rafts of logs from a river mouth near the entrance to Milne Bay. The logs were from trees felled upriver and the *Leprena* then towed them to where new wharves were being constructed.

It might have been tedious, but it gave Clarrie a front seat to the massive build-up of resources that was taking place at Milne Bay. There was also the occasional highlight when a native police patrol brought in a Japanese straggler. When this happened, Clarrie was always surprised by the ordinariness of those Japanese. They were neither all-conquering supermen nor primitive savages, although they had been portrayed as both in the past. They were just young men suffering the ravages of war in an inhospitable place.

•

The Fahnestock brothers had accompanied the first Small Ships fleet to Port Moresby. Bruce remained there to establish a base for transhipment and boat maintenance while Sheridan sailed down to Milne Bay once it had been secured. He was impressed by what he saw there and recommended that Milne Bay, rather than Port Moresby, become the Small Ships' primary base in eastern New Guinea. His recommendation was approved and Jack Savage was summoned from Port Moresby to Milne Bay, where he designed and oversaw the construction of a basic slipway and maintenance facilities. Those boats already in Port Moresby now began a shuttle service between the two ports; Milne Bay now became Base A for the Small Ships Section.

•

The repulse of the Japanese at Milne Bay had not only defeated their plans to control the eastern approaches to Port Moresby and the Torres Strait, it had secured MacArthur's southern flank should he choose to take the battle to the Japanese on the north coast, which was precisely what he had been planning to do. The timing for MacArthur's first offensive was the key decision to be made and that timing depended on several other factors. The Japanese advance along the Kokoda Track had stalled in the foothills overlooking Port Moresby. The supply line to the leading Japanese troops was too long and too fragile, and those troops began to experience shortages of everything they needed at a time when they themselves were coming under increasing Allied pressure. The Australian troops who had blunted the

Japanese advance – mostly young and untried militia units – were being replaced by experienced veterans fresh from fighting in the Middle East, and the Japanese began to fall back rather than face annihilation.

The Australian advance along the Kokoda Track began in earnest in September and, after heavy fighting in appalling conditions, progress was made over the old battlefields and towards the little village which gave the track its name. As the hungry and sometimes dispirited Japanese troops retreated, it appeared as though they might be working to a timetable of sorts and that, in fact, they might just retreat all the way back towards the reinforced strongholds based around their original landing place at Buna. Those strongholds would have to be taken, and to support the massive effort that would be required to take them, vast amounts of supplies, rations and ammunition would have to be stockpiled closer to the scene of potential battle than Milne Bay. The Small Ships would be the key to that supply line as only they could manoeuvre and navigate in the coastal waters between Milne Bay and Buna. Their importance grew in direct proportion to the distances the Japanese retreated.

The realisation that the war in New Guinea would be a logistical war caused a number of changes to the way the Allies' frontline and rear echelon units were to be supplied both during and between battles. The role of transportation, both sea and air, rose to a new prominence in this most difficult of battlefield terrains and to cope with those difficulties a new organisational component was introduced. Known as the Combined Operations Services Command (COSC), it was firstly established on paper in September 1942 and became part of the formal New Guinea Force Headquarters in early October. As well as carrying out the normal service of supply functions usually assigned to either or both of the Transportation Corps and Quartermaster Corps, COSC was given direct responsibility for, 'supply, transportation, construction and sanitation'. On 14 October, COSC Headquarters made it plain in a directive: 'Small Ships Section: Organisation, control and movement of all small craft will be under COSC . . .' In early October, the US Army's Brigadier General Dwight Johns was appointed Commanding Officer of COSC, with an Australian, Brigadier Victor Seccombe, as his deputy.

•

Throughout all these changes and challenges, Ralph Andrews had simply been biding his time in Port Moresby. He and the crew of the *Shangri-La* had been kept busy. As the Small Ships command vessel, the *Shangri-La* was at the call of the senior Small Ships officers in Port Moresby – the Fahnestocks and Jack Savage – and they all undertook regular trips to look for suitable anchorages, moorings and the like. That was not obviously war work, though, and the closest the *Shangri-La* crew felt they came to that was when the Japanese bombers came over. Then they could put on their tin hats and watch the dogfights and explosions on the ground and in the sky, and feel that they were part of the action.

At around the same time as he learned that he, the *Shangri-La* and all the other Small Ships in the New Guinea theatre were now part of the COSC, Ralph was ordered to prepare the boat for an important reconnaissance mission carrying an even more important observer, Brigadier General Dwight Johns himself. The very next day, probably around 10 October, Johns and his aides arrived and the *Shangri-La* set off to show the general the estuary of the Fly River, located some distance to the west of Port Moresby.

Before the mission, Ralph had searched for the appropriate shipping charts for the journey. None was available, he was told, but that would not be a problem as they would be able to clearly see the many channels that made up the delta.

They may have been able to see the channels but they certainly couldn't see the many reefs they would have to navigate to get to them. Sure enough, the *Shangri-La* ran onto one of those reefs – although, fortunately, at a low enough speed to ensure that the launch did not sustain any significant damage. Ralph guessed – correctly as it turned out – that his boat would simply float off the reef at high tide, but that would not be until much later that night. Several boring hours later, those aboard the *Shangri-La* heard the sounds of an aircraft circling overhead somewhere nearby.

General Johns, convinced that it was an Allied aircraft sent out to search for him, instructed Ralph to send a signal to the aircraft saying, 'Johns here.' Ralph, equally convinced it was one of the Japanese floatplanes that had been attacking Allied shipping in the area, refused to do so. When the inevitable argument started, Ralph simply pointed out that, as the boat's captain, his was the final decision. It would have been a frosty few hours after that as the *Shangri-La* firstly lifted off the reef then slowly made its way through the dark back to Port Moresby.

Nothing more was said of the incident, at least not in words. Shortly afterwards, Ralph received a new set of orders from COSC Headquarters. It informed him that he was now captain of the *Two Freddies*, another South Coast seine trawler, which was fortuitously tied up nearby. He was to sail the *Two Freddies* to Milne Bay to collect supplies to take onwards to a point yet to be determined. Ralph put on a smile and counted his blessings. There may not have been a lot of them but he was at least drawing closer and closer to the real war.

4.

THE SMELL OF LAND,
THE BARK OF A DOG

The two generals, one Australian and one American, with their aides and advisers and planning staff, had looked at the maps, had read and digested the action reports and intelligence studies, and had produced a plan they thought would quickly reduce the first major Japanese stronghold in New Guinea. The Australian general was Thomas Albert Blamey, recently recalled from the Middle East to take command of the land forces that would defend Australia by stopping the Japanese in New Guinea. Blamey believed the troops he now had under his command, militia and regular soldiers alike, would continue to push the Japanese South Seas Force back all the way from Kokoda to its original landing point on the beaches at Buna. With the Kokoda Track then clear, Blamey would be able to push more men and supplies across it. Those men and supplies would enable him to bring pressure to bear on the Japanese enclave from the north-west, around the small village of Gona.

The American general, Douglas MacArthur, had put together a plan that would push his Americans across the mountains in the wake of the Australians, but his troops were inexperienced in jungle warfare and jungle conditions – in fact, in any kind of warfare – so that plan was changed significantly. MacArthur now said that his commanders would bring an entire division, the 32nd Division, up to the Japanese enclave in two columns. One of those columns would push up the coast from the south, clearing out any opposition they found, until they were in a position to assault the Japanese positions. Another column would also proceed from the south of Buna but would turn inland until they were opposite the centre of the Japanese positions, at which point they too would turn towards the coast and launch their assault.

The pressure exerted by these three major assaults, two American and one Australian, would force the Japanese back to the sea. If they weren't evacuated before this happened, they would be left with just two alternatives: surrender or die. Either way, that part of the coast would be cleared and the Allies could push on to the other strongholds the Japanese had established at key points all along the northern coast of New Guinea.

Unspoken, but implicit in all MacArthur's planning, was the need he felt to achieve some kind of clear victory over a significant Japanese force. While it was important to defeat the Japanese wherever and whenever possible, for MacArthur an equally powerful imperative was to show the chiefs of staff back home what he and his forces could achieve with the limited resources they had. The clear message in this was that, with better and larger resources, and with real assistance from the navy, MacArthur would achieve even greater success. The Buna–Gona complex was the best target within striking range of his land-based forces and he badly wanted a victory there. It should be sooner rather than later, too, as he believed that the longer he waited to strike, the better prepared that stronghold would be. Intelligence suggested that the Japanese at Buna had been, and would continue to be, reinforced by sea using overnight submarine and destroyer runs from Rabaul.

One of the keys to taking the Japanese positions quickly would be a reliable and defensible supply line because MacArthur's soldiers would be fighting a long way from mainland Australia, from which most of their supplies and reinforcements would originate. The waters to the north of New Guinea were still disputed territory and were also a long way from the main supply depots. Milne Bay was rapidly being developed into the type of storage base needed to support ongoing operations at that end of the island but it, too, was really just a halfway point to where the main fighting would be taking place.

In the end, the supply problem was potentially solved by another American general, Major General George Kenney. Kenney was the commander of all American air forces in the theatre, units recently brought together as the US 5th Air Force. Kenney reassured MacArthur that his air force could and would undertake two tasks. The first was to establish and maintain aerial superiority over New Guinea while the second was to support the army's land offensives by flying in both men and supplies to airfields in the rear of the American positions. While continuing to provide that logistical support, other air units would strike at Japanese airfields at Lae and Salamaua, Japanese shipping operating in the coastal waters north of New Guinea and the airfields the Japanese used around Rabaul. Not only would this support Allied operations in New Guinea, Kenney argued, it would also support the US Marines in the fighting that had just erupted at Guadalcanal in the Solomon Islands.

Not all on MacArthur's staff supported Kenney's assessment of the 5th Air Force's capabilities or his vision of future warfare where aircraft ruled the battlefield, some describing both as 'audacious and uncertain', but Kenney had MacArthur's ear and that was all he needed to carry the day.

•

US Army Brigadier General Hanford MacNider had been detached from training duties in Brisbane and sent to Port Moresby on 12 September to report on the embryonic Headquarters' plans for an assault on Buna. Three days later, the first members of the 32nd Division's 126th Regiment, Company E, had flown out of the Amberley air base near Ipswich in Queensland. Their departure was so hurried that the evening before they left their uniforms were sprayed with a mottled green dye at a local dry cleaner's shop for better camouflage in the jungles to which they were heading. When their aircraft took off, some of the men's uniforms were still wet, although they apparently dried off during the flight. Part of their brief, and part of MacNider's as well, was to see whether there was an overland track that avoided the highest of the Owen Stanley Ranges, from somewhere to the east of Port Moresby and across to the rear of the Japanese positions.

A lot of American soldiers suffered a lot of hardship to learn what expatriate planters and explorers could have told them. Yes, there were trails that criss-crossed the area in several directions but no, those trails were not suitable for anything but small teams of men carrying their own provisions. The overland route the Americans sought was never found because it never existed. It was time to consider Kenney's plan and anything else that could support it.

•

If MacArthur needed an additional spur to action, the increasingly successful actions fought by the marines at Guadalcanal certainly provided him with one. He urged Major General Edwin Forrest Harding, the genial commander of the 32nd Division, to start the offensive against Buna sooner rather than later, and began pestering all his subordinates on the subject from early October onwards. As Japanese troops continued to fall back into the Buna–Gona stronghold from Kokoda, MacArthur knew that most would be tired and dispirited but, even so, they were now additional defenders who would have to be winkled out.

The remainder of Forrest Harding's 32nd division arrived in New Guinea by October after a massive and successful airlift into Port Moresby. Harding in turn pushed Hanford MacNider, to whom he had assigned the task of subduing Buna through a movement against it from the south, to proceed with the planning and execution of the battle plan for the assault. Both men knew that logistics would be critical in the forthcoming battle and they, too, applied pressure to those responsible. George Kenney was confident in the capacity of his air force to firstly fly in and then both supply and reinforce Harding's soldiers. Behind him, if it were ever needed, was the long and strong supply chain they all envisioned. Somewhere near the bottom of that chain were a lot of small links that might only ever be a backup to Kenney's aircraft. They were the Small Ships: the trawlers and the schooners – fishing boats that had sailed all the way from Sydney.

·

Those fishing boats, and their command structure, were not idle while the generals were planning their war. The Small Ships operation at Base A, Milne Bay, quickly fell into place. Bruce Fahnestock, still based in Port Moresby, was a regular visitor to Milne Bay and everything he had learned in the past few months was put into practice at their advanced operational base. Local carriers were quickly found and hired, with their payment being made in trade tobacco; Bruce knew that 'Emu' brand twist tobacco was the most highly valued type, and so made sure that his men always had a regular supply. The Gili Gili wharf complex, now complete, was the area used most often by the Small Ships, and they would normally load and unload there. On occasion, and in the deeper water, they would simply pull up alongside one of the larger freighters or Liberty ships and have the cargo lowered down to them. This was the preferred method if that cargo was required at one of the newer bases that were being identified and developed further up the coast, as it avoided double handling.

Clarrie Dawes and the *Leprena* were also at Base A for most of September and October. After they had finished towing logs from the river mouth for the new wharves, they were asked to tow rafts of logs to a small offshore island where there was a mission which had a saw mill. There, the logs were cut into planks which the *Leprena* carried back for use as decking on the various wharves and docks.

One of the more unusual tasks the *Leprena* was involved in was the relocation of a Papuan village. One of the airstrips had to be extended to handle aircraft larger than the Kittyhawks, and a small village stood in the way of the proposed extension. After negotiations with the villagers, negotiations accompanied by suitable payments, the villagers agreed to relocate to that same offshore island for the duration of the war. All their belongings were packed neatly into the *Leprena*'s holds while the Papuans travelled on the deck of the boat to their new home.

The only thing missing at Base A was accommodation and messing facilities for the Small Ships' sailors. This problem was overcome quite simply. The *Mactan* was sailed into Milne Bay and moored near a small landing jetty well away from the main port facilities. There it became a floating barracks and mess hall used by sailors waiting for their next assignment or when en route to or from a posting. It also became very popular when the head chef from Sydney's Carlton Hotel became the vessel's chief cook. The *Mactan* also boasted two barbers and, for a while at least, the only ice-cream machine in New Guinea.

•

Allied intelligence, both secret intelligence from codebreaking operations and from aerial and ground reconnaissance, had long showed that Japanese forces were concentrated in a few key locations along the north coast, the most important of them being the Buna–Gona area, and further along the coast at Lae, Salamaua, Finschhafen and much further along at the old Dutch colonial port of Hollandia. This concentration would allow the Allies almost free rein in the coastal areas between Milne Bay and Buna, but it was free rein with a number of qualifications.

One of those qualifications was that the coastline between those two points was well within range of the Japanese aircraft operating out of both Rabaul and Lae, and those aircraft still had control of the skies over most of that area and for most of the daylight hours. For Allied aircraft, it was a different story. The area was now coming into the wet season, meaning that the Owen Stanley Ranges were wreathed in heavy cloud until around noon each day, making flights over the mountains a very dangerous affair. As well, the Allied aircraft that could fly over the range had a relatively short operational capacity, in terms of time, as they needed to fly back over the mountains before dusk. Air support for shipping and for offensive operations would need to fit into a window covering the early and middle hours of the afternoon.

When navigating the north coast of the island, the Small Ships used what was called the inner passage between Milne Bay and the large promontory of Cape Nelson. The outer passage, passing to the north of Goodenough Island, had the advantage of being in deep water for most of the way but the significant disadvantages of being within easy range of Japanese aircraft from Rabaul, being at the extreme range of Allied aircraft flying out of Port Moresby, and also subject to raids by Japanese surface craft and submarines.

That Inner Passage had been hazardous to all but native canoes and rowboats ever since its discovery by European sailors. Criss-crossed by coral reefs, its depth could vary from one metre to a hundred metres in less than a ship's length. The Small Ships were, quite literally, the only ships available to the Allies capable of sailing in and through such waters with a reasonable chance of being able to complete the voyage without being torn apart on one of the thousands of reefs that infested the seas there.

What complicated matters even more was the almost complete absence of maps. Just two years earlier, the playboy sailors aboard the *Director II* had learned, to their cost, that the Australian government had seized copies and frozen the sales of Admiralty charts of Australian waters for fear of them falling into enemy hands. The same had been done to the charts covering the waters to the north of the Australian Mandated Territory of Papua New Guinea – not that there were many modern charts anyway.

The Small Ships Section was able to obtain one outdated Admiralty map of the New Guinea coastline to the west of Milne

Bay, and it was dutifully traced and copied, then distributed, with toilet paper being the medium used on more than one occasion. The map itself was a classic, with notations including, 'HMS Dart (1885) reported reefs lie three to five miles easterly,' and spidery little drawings which indicated the presence of breakers in the general position indicated.

The Small Ships Section would eventually acquire aerial maps, which were also copied and annotated, with captains and crews being given updates after each voyage. They also drew up their own maps, and these were probably the most useful of all, especially when their experience and the local knowledge they gradually picked up were added to them. Almost literally, the early navigation along the coast was by using the smell of land by day and the bark of a village dog at night. Thus the Small Ships crept slowly along the coast towards their first major objective, the small station and copra port of Wanigela.

•

Earlier in the year, in March 1942, Australian civil authorities had organised for an area of land to be cleared for an airstrip near Wanigela Mission on Collingwood Bay, some 100 kilometres south-east of Buna. Wanigela was to become the initial landing point for the lead elements in the MacArthur–Kenney plan. During the first week of October, Papuan labourers cleared the airstrip of recent growth and then engineer and anti-aircraft troops flown in from Milne Bay upgraded and secured the airstrip and mission buildings. They were followed by several 5th Air Force C-47 aircraft (also known as Dakotas) that brought in the best part of an Australian infantry battalion. No Japanese opposition materialised, either on the ground or in the air, so the Australians secured the immediate area around Wanigela and then sent out scouting parties to look for any Japanese troops and to check that the tracks leading north to Buna were passable. The build-up was now on in earnest.

•

COSC swung into action. The lack of charts for the operational areas leading up to the Buna–Gona stronghold posed a major potential threat to the Americans' supply line and, through COSC, they gained the assistance of the Australians in addressing this priority need. HMAS *Paluma* was a motor launch, built in Townsville in 1941 and firstly requisitioned, and then bought, by the RAN later that year. Her mission was to put individual and small teams of coastwatchers into key locations overlooking Japanese bases in New Britain and, later, New Guinea. The coastwatchers also served as an early warning system for notification of approaching Japanese air raids. The *Paluma*'s shallow draught made her ideal for entering the many small tidal creeks spread across both islands. That draught also made her ideal for marine surveying and hydrography, the marking of significant features and depths at sea.

It was in this latter role that she was engaged by the US Army in late September. She did not completely relinquish her role with the RAN, though, and she would usually carry at least one commando to assist the crew in case she was suddenly called upon to rescue a coastwatcher. For the remainder of 1942, that commando was a young corporal named Lionel Veale.

COSC had also come up with a plan for the seaborne supply line to the troops who would be engaged in the forthcoming assault on Buna. The larger vessels operated by the Small Ships, those of between 100 and 150 tons, would be loaded so as to draw no more than twelve feet (3.5 metres) of water and would carry supplies to Wanigela in the first instance and later, when channels had been identified and sailing instructions drawn up, to Cape Nelson and to suitable ports beyond. In the meantime, and while the *Paluma* was undertaking her surveying work, supplies would be carried forward to one of the ration and ammunition dumps to be set up along the approaches to Buna. To make the whole operation flow more easily, COSC would retain direct control of the larger ships bringing supplies to Milne Bay. The 32nd Division's Quartermaster, Lieutenant Colonel Laurence McKenny, would be in charge of the Small Ships operations from that point.

Using the gathered knowledge of the Small Ships' captains who had sailed the area, and the skills of the surveyor and hydrographer aboard, the *Paluma* commenced its charting work in early October, and remained undisturbed by Japanese aircraft. It found and charted one of the main dangers to shipping in the area, a large coral reef some twenty kilometres to the southeast of Cape Nelson. The reef was spotted by Lionel Veale and was promptly named Veale's Reef in his honour. They not only spotted and charted the reef; they moored a buoy to it, and that buoy had a provision for a lamp to be attached to it to aid navigation at night. Within just a few days, the *Paluma* had charted a clear channel for larger ships to use between Milne Bay and Wanigela and then Wanigela and Cape Nelson. The sea road to Buna was now partially open and the Small Ships could now push it open even further.

•

During the period before the work of the *Paluma* was completed, the Small Ships had navigated the seas off the north coast by guess and by God. At Wanigela, for instance, to enter the inlet on which the mission sat, the best advice was to line up two rock outcrops above the settlement, and then simply sail in a straight line. It was a methodology they continued when sailing beyond Cape Nelson while the *Paluma* continued her work in that area. They found several promising anchorages as well. Just south of the tip of Cape Nelson was the small settlement of Tufi, site of another small government station, and soon to be developed into a significant American base.

To the north of Cape Nelson, two good anchorages were found just a few kilometres apart. One was Porlock Harbour, already home to a coastwatcher; it was a fjord-like inlet, some three kilometres long and 500 metres wide with steep, wooded sides between fifty and 200 metres high. The area was surrounded by hills. There was another nasty reef – Jones' Reef – just outside the entrance and, before buoys were dropped to mark a safe passage, sailors used a notch in the hills as a beacon; if it was kept due west of the vessel entering the harbour, the reef would be avoided. Oro Bay, further along the coast, was much larger and appeared to be suitable for development into a major base close to the Japanese lines at Buna. The passage there was also less risky than others as the final approach was through thirty kilometres of relatively deep water.

The Oro Bay base was established with the assistance of the local Papuans, who were paid with the twist tobacco they preferred. An additional benefit was that the Papuans knew the waters around their villages from a lifetime of fishing in them and many of them took on roles as pilots, sitting at the front of Small Ships and warning the captain of reefs and shoaling water.

The nature of the area through which the Small Ships sailed made night trips problematic before the areas were charted, a problem that was further complicated by the fact that only a few of the Small Ships' captains were familiar with celestial navigation. They would sail at night, if necessary, but always preferred the daylight.

The COSC plan specified certain things and implied others. The specific components were dates, places, timings and the like. The implied aspects were that the people and materials of war would be in the right place at the right time, and that, as a result, everything else would proceed according to the plan and its timetable. There would be supply dumps at predetermined locations along the coastal trail that led from Wanigela to the proposed jumping-off points in front of Buna. The various infantry assault units would march along that trail to those jumping-off points and, when battle was joined, they would smash through the Japanese perimeter defences. Once that initial breakthrough had been achieved, fresh troops would leapfrog over the original combatants, fresh because they had either marched from Wanigela with rest and supply camps along the way, or they would have been flown into Dobodura by George Kenney's transport planes and made the short march to Buna. Those fresh troops would crush any remaining Japanese fortifications and mop up the stragglers. That was the plan.

•

On 14 October, Australian troops set out from Wanigela, travelling in small groups and travelling lightly, to blaze a trail for the Americans to follow from Wanigela to Buna. They moved directly north to cut across the base of the Cape Nelson peninsula, cutting the distance a boat would have to travel by half. It was the opening of the rainy season, and the Australian patrols struggled. They found the main river to the north of the peninsula, the Musa River, in flood and experienced great difficulties in trying to cross it. Eventually, they struggled through to Pongani, another small village that had been identified as a possible base and supply point that was still some forty kilometres short of Buna.

Behind the Australians, the 128th Regiment of the 32nd Division was airlifted into Wanigela in a permanent shuttle run using Kenney's C-47 transport planes between the port and Port Moresby. The airlift began on 14 October and was completed within four days; so far, so good. The division's commander, Forrest Harding, had assigned the initial coastal strike to Hanford MacNider, who flew in with the regiment to oversee the on-ground preparations for the offensive. Accompanying him was the Quartermaster, Laurence McKenny, charged with overseeing the supply line that would be vital to success. McKenny would be able to call on Kenney's transport aircraft and a small group of Small Ships which had been pushed forward to Milne Bay, where they were now engaged in their own shuttle run, taking supplies forward from Milne Bay to Wanigela. At this point, the aircraft available clearly outnumbered the boats.

There were eight boats then available to McKenny at Wanigela. The largest was the *Alacrity*, a two-masted schooner from Port Welshpool in Victoria, capable of carrying in excess of 100 tons and under the command of an experienced sailor named Anderson. Ralph Andrews' new boat, the *Two Freddies*, was there as was his own former boat, the *Willyama II*. They were joined by the *Kelton*, with an all-Filipino crew commanded by Ireneo Ames; the seine trawler *Bonwin*; and the former luxury cruiser the *Minnamurra*. The last two boats available were also seine trawlers: the *King John*, with Bill Priest and Bert Evans from Greenwell Point aboard; and the most distinctive of all, the *Timoshenko*. Of recent construction, the *Timoshenko* was named after the Soviet general then fighting the Germans in

Russia and, appropriately if somewhat incongruously, featured a red hammer and sickle painted on her oversized black funnel. She was under the command of pre-war sailor and adventurer, Neil Sandery.

While the soldiers marched to their jump-off positions, the Small Ships would be moving supplies to the bases that were being established at Porlock Harbour, Oro Bay, Pongani and beyond. Lighter stores and reinforcements would be flown into Wanigela to be carried forward by Papuan carriers or by the soldiers themselves. It was a system that was to be continued after battle was joined and it was a system that would be enhanced when the airfield at Dobodura was completed.

It was also a system with some inherent weaknesses, and McKenny was well aware of some of them. There were no wharves, or port facilities of any kind, in the stretch of coastline between Wanigela and Pongani. Transfer would have to be carried out either at sea or through the use of lighters that would carry the supplies to and from the dumps established at the beach. There were few, if any, craft suitable for this lighterage, but native canoes – the large outriggers – would be able to do the job until something better became available. The natives who manned those canoes, and who carried the supplies backwards and forwards, would have to be recruited and paid. This proved to be relatively easy: the Papuans had no great commitment to the war itself but were willing workers when paid reasonably and treated with respect.

Almost immediately, additional problems became apparent. George Kenney had promised an aerial supply line to support the offensive operations, a promise that was made with no real appreciation of the difficulties involved. To begin with, there was only one terminus for that supply line, the small airstrip at

Wanigela. The weather made flying to, landing on and taking off from Wanigela a sometimes fraught experience, and those three factors worked to decrease the number of men and amounts of material that could be carried. It was sometimes zero because they found that Wanigela could not be used for hours after heavy rain. The other zero was the Japanese fighter aircraft, the Zero (or Zeke), which had established local aerial superiority in the area of operations. And then the reality of what was being attempted kicked in.

A C-47 could carry about two and a half tons of payload. While that may amount to twenty or so fully armed men, in terms of ammunition, rations and the necessary hardware to support a full military offensive, it was not very much at all. Even the smallest of the Small Ships trawlers could carry thirty tons of payload, while the larger trawlers and schooners could carry up to 100 tons. It quickly became obvious who would be the key component of the supply line. A second airfield was under construction at Dobodura, just to the rear of the Japanese outer perimeter and near the village of Popondetta, but it would not be operational until sometime towards the end of November and it, too, would be subject to the same constraints as the airfield at Wanigela.

Airdrops of supplies to the troops were considered, but there were a number of problems with that as well. One was a shortage of aircraft. The C-47s were fully occupied ferrying the troops of the 32nd Division across to Wanigela and if they were to be diverted to airdrops, they would be unable to continue the build-up of troops. The second was that no one had tested the viability of airdrops to troops operating in a jungle environment. In places, visibility on the ground was limited to just a few metres and the drop zones would be very close to a number of large, and almost impassable, swamps and rivers that were now in flood. Until more airstrips and more aircraft could be made available – and there was no guarantee as to when that might be – the reality on the ground along the northern coastline was that all the elements necessary to support a major offensive – men and materials – would be brought forward by land and sea. George Kenney's air forces would play, initially at least, a subsidiary role. With land transportation difficult during the wet season, the boats of the Small Ships Section would become the most critical link in the supply chain supporting the forthcoming offensive at Buna. It might have been by default, but it was a role for which those boats and their crews were certainly, and in that area uniquely, qualified.

5.

FRIENDLY FIRE

The Allied build-up at Milne Bay gathered pace throughout September and into October, mirroring the movement of 32nd Division troops into Wanigela and the work on the new airfield at Dobodura. The waters between Milne Bay and Wanigela were now charted and clearly marked, a process that continued in the waters north of Cape Nelson, allowing significant stockpiles to be built up at both Porlock Harbour and Oro Bay and enabling, as well, the search for suitable bases and command sites ever closer to the Japanese defences at Buna.

On the other side of those defences, the Japanese soldiers – from top to bottom – had a grim determination to hold on at any cost. The retreat from Kokoda, which was still continuing, was not construed as a defeat, as it had commenced as more a reconnaissance in force than a determined push to capture Port Moresby. The retreat was conducted with military precision, and had been undertaken as a series of delaying actions designed to frustrate the pursuing Australians while avoiding any set piece battles.

The retreat had also bought time for the engineers and labourers to build the Buna–Sanananda–Gona enclave into something close to impregnable to normal infantry attacks. There was no talk of defeatism within that enclave. Most nights, fast destroyers from Rabaul or Imperial Japanese Navy submarines would bring supplies and reinforcements to the defenders while the air above the defences was contested by the Zeros patrolling from Lae and Rabaul. They would not surrender and they would not retreat. Theirs' might be one of the furthest outposts of empire, but it was an outpost that Japanese soldiers, sailors and airmen would fight and die to defend. In doing so, they would demonstrate to the Allies just how high a price they would have to pay for success.

●

Laurence McKenny was about to learn that lesson and several others in a short time. Rations and ammunition for the troops being airlifted across the Owen Stanley Range to Wanigela were loaded aboard two Small Ships, Bill Priest's *King John* and Neil Sandery's *Timoshenko*, both trawlers having returned to Port Moresby for that purpose. The supplies were carried aboard on 11 October in an operation overseen by McKenny himself. In addition to their own crews, Priest and Sandery were told they would also carry some troops from the 32nd Division's Quartermaster Company, two or three to each trawler, with an additional two men from the division's Headquarters Company. Those men would be responsible for overseeing the supply dumps to be established at selected points along the north coast. McKenny himself would also accompany them, travelling aboard the *King John*.

The loading of the two boats occupied most of 11 October and it wasn't until early next morning that the boats were able to cast off for Milne Bay on the first leg of their trip. It took them two days and, once there, they tied up at the Gili Gili wharf to take on board more supplies for the soldiers now landing regularly at Wanigela. They also took on another passenger, Lieutenant Bruce Fahnestock, who had been visiting Milne Bay to oversee the growing Small Ships operation there and who, like McKenny, wanted to take the opportunity to see the waters along the north coast and gain a feel for the operational environment in which his Small Ships would be working.

The *King John* and the *Timoshenko* sailed from Milne Bay on the afternoon of 15 October, travelling slowly through the night and arriving off Wanigela just after noon the next day. After the anchors were dropped, Laurence McKenny was rowed ashore in a dinghy. On dry land again, he received the first of what would be several shocks.

•

McKenny had believed that his two Small Ships would unload their supplies and passengers at Wanigela and then simply turn around and sail back to Milne Bay for more. That belief did not survive the opening minutes of his meeting with Hanford MacNider, who had come down to the beach to greet him. MacNider didn't beat around the bush. He was in charge of what had now been termed the 'Coastal Task Force', one part of the enveloping movement about to descend on Buna. He told McKenny that he had sent two battalions of the 128th Regiment to follow the Australians along the tracks across the base of the Cape Nelson peninsula to Pongani, but that reports had already come back indicating that those troops were struggling to make any headway through the jungle. There were rivers in flood and seemingly endless swamps which threatened to swallow men whole, so he now doubted whether those men would be able to make it through to Pongani.

MacNider noted, though not in any detail that he was prepared to share with McKenny, that MacArthur – and through him Harding – wanted action sooner rather than later. Instead of delaying to stockpile both men and supplies, MacArthur believed it would be best to attack the Japanese positions before they could be reinforced further. MacNider knew, and had also noted, the potential problems in relying on a shipborne supply line in waters such as these but he had no other choice at this point, as the air supply situation was becoming problematic.

All this was the preamble to what was the nub of the matter and, without any further discussion, MacNider directed McKenny to have the two Small Ships remain at Wanigela. They were to take aboard a company of infantrymen and carry them to Pongani where they would be landed to secure a position there and then await the arrival of the troops who were marching overland. Because of the general dislocation around them as men and supplies were being moved and then moved again, McKenny asked for, and was given, permission to delay the two boats' departure until the next morning. McKenny knew that Bill Priest and Neil Sandery would both appreciate the extra time. They would literally be sailing through uncharted waters and the skippers would want to make the best preparations possible.

•

At 8 a.m. the next morning, 17 October, a squad of American infantrymen from the 128th Regiment of the 32nd Division lined up at the edge of one of the new airstrips recently constructed on the outskirts of Port Moresby. One of the men standing away from the main body of soldiers looked a little out of place; he was older than most, wore an unadorned uniform and carried no weapons beyond some pens and a notebook, as they were the tools of his trade. His given name was Byron Darnton, although everyone knew him as 'Barney' Darnton, and he was probably the most famous person at the airstrip that morning. Barney Darnton was a reporter, now working as a war correspondent for one of the world's most famous newspapers, the *New York Times*.

That fact alone had already made him one of MacArthur's favourite reporters. Reporters, and what they wrote, were always of vital interest to the general. And recently, the general – or more accurately, his staff – had been painting a glowing picture of what was to come, and had brought the press in for briefings on several occasions. Those briefings were always positive and upbeat, taking as their starting point the American 'can-do' attitude, building upon that and MacArthur's iron will to create an American-led force that would be irresistible when it came to grips with the Japanese and that, folks, would be happening very soon. A few war correspondents – perhaps just a select few – would be given the chance to witness history being made.

Barney Darnton was an obvious candidate for one of those positions, and not just because of which newspaper he represented. He was one of those reporters whose articles always seemed to reflect, or be an extension of, his own sunny disposition. He had earlier met Forrest Harding and would describe him as 'a genial man with a soft side who composed poetry and stashed Kipling verse inside his Army manual'. Harding appeared to reciprocate some of Darnton's admiration, as he would describe the reporter as 'one damn good correspondent and a swell guy'. When Barney asked him for permission to accompany the lead battalion going into combat, Forrest Harding approved the request without hesitation.

This assignment was almost a labour of love for Darnton. To begin with, he had stated right from the beginning of his assignment to the South West Pacific theatre that he wanted to report the story of the war as it unfolded from the ordinary soldier's point of view, rather than from the perspective of those daily briefings delivered by staff officers at a headquarters a long way back from the frontlines. He also believed in writing the little stories that illustrated the bigger story that was the war itself, and that those little stories could be found anywhere and everywhere in a war zone. Darnton should know, too, as he had served in the US Army with some distinction on the Western Front during World War I. What's more, he had served in the 32nd Division, known since those times as the Red Arrow Division from its shoulder patch, made up of boys and young men from the Mid-West. He was about to fly across the mountains to write about the Red Arrows going into battle, about boys and young men from the American heartland facing the challenge of combat, much as he had done twenty-five years ago.

Just a couple of days previously, Darnton had sent home a long report from his vantage point in Port Moresby. His pride in the US Army and its young soldiers was obvious in the report's concluding sentence: 'From a high hill near the aerodrome,' he wrote, 'a man can see his countrymen building with blood, sweat, toil and firm resolution that their sons shall have peace because they will know how to preserve peace.'

Barney Darnton and the squad of young soldiers he was accompanying boarded their assigned C-47 and, within minutes, were flying high over the Owen Stanley Ranges. Less than an hour later, their aircraft made a bumpy landing at the new airstrip at Wanigela, where they disembarked and formed up again. Other soldiers led them along a jungle path in the footsteps of yet more squads just flown in and, as they approached the coconut palms fringing the beach, they spotted the sea and, riding at anchor not too far out, two squat little ships, both flying the Stars and Stripes at their stern. Barney already had his notebook out and was framing the words he would write.

Those notes would be expanded into sentences when he was aboard, and would detail how he was not overly impressed by either vessel: 'The *King John* (was) a 70 foot wooden trawler plucked from its berth in Sydney in July . . . [she had] a balky reverse gear, her engine wheezed, and her sun-scorched decks reeked of fish and copra. She rode low in the water, looking about to sink at any moment, and her most conspicuous feature was the hoist bar angled off the mast for hauling nets.' Nor was he impressed by the *King John*'s companion: 'The Timoshenko looked, if anything, even stranger. Someone had painted a large red hammer and sickle on her funnel, apparently in jest.' Overall, he felt the little boats resembled two pirate ships.

With practised resignation, the soldiers who had flown in with Barney Darnton lined up in squads along the beach and were eventually put on board dinghies and rowed out to one or other of the two ships. Fifty-six infantrymen were put aboard the *King John*, Barney Darnton among them, and another forty-six went aboard the *Timoshenko*. Darnton was introduced to both Bill Priest and Bruce Fahnestock – he had already met Laurence McKenny – before he sat down to record his impressions of what had already taken place that day. Back on the beach, Hanford MacNider growled to one of the aides that hovered nearby, 'The move's so secret we can't even tell the Air Corps.'

•

By the time the last troops had been helped aboard, both ships were quite crowded and sat low in the water. Aboard the *King John*, fifty-six enlisted men, several officers and supplies competed for any flat surface available. Fuel drums had been lashed to the sideboards, and crates of ammunition were stacked on top of each other inside the space bounded by the drums. The choice places, in the few open spaces along the sides and underneath the dinghy now suspended upside down in its davits at the stern, were all occupied by the time Barney Darnton made it aboard, but space was made for him alongside the wheelhouse.

Not long afterwards, and shortly after midday, both ships weighed anchor and headed out into the deeper water before turning to the north-west and proceeding at a slow and careful speed. The *King John* was in the lead, a couple of hundred metres ahead of the *Timoshenko*, and in her bows a young Papuan squatted, staring intently at the water whenever they entered a shallower zone, looking out for reefs and coral outcrops. Whenever he spotted one, he would wave his hand to the right or left. In the wheelhouse, Bill Priest would steer the *King John* in the direction indicated.

At dusk, the Papuan guide switched to a lead-line, calling out the depths to Bruce Fahnestock who was standing next to the wheelhouse. Bruce would pass the directions to Bill Priest inside, and even take control of the steering when Priest wanted to take a star reading to confirm they were still heading in the planned direction. Below deck, Laurence McKenny and several officers pored over aerial photography of the Pongani area while their men, above, tried to find a comfortable position in which to grab some sleep.

The night was clear enough for the *Timoshenko* to close up a little bit to the *King John* and follow her course without mishap. In this way, the two Small Ships rounded Cape Nelson and sailed into the uncharted waters beyond. Priest's steering and the work of the Papuan guide complemented each other, and at 3 a.m. on the morning of 18 October both ships anchored at a spot they calculated to be around 500 metres off the beach in front of Pongani village. Without enough light to see what they would be doing if they started to unload, crews and passengers on both vessels settled down to await the arrival of daylight.

•

When it started to grow light, probably around 6.30 a.m., the troops on both boats consumed their rations. Afterwards, hand grenades were distributed and the soldiers made ready for landing. The engines on both boats were started and the *King John* and *Timoshenko* crept closer to the beach, lookouts in the bows of each. They were lucky; it was a beautiful morning, and the sea was calm and flat and seemed almost crystal clear. There was just enough breeze to occasionally ruffle the American flags at the stern of each ship.

Engineer Bert Evans was on the deck of the *King John* enjoying the scenery. Native houses on stilts were clearly visible among the trees, but as yet there were no signs of people around them. At the rear of both boats, preparations were being made to lower the dinghies to start ferrying the troops to shore when suddenly the sound of aircraft engines broke the silence. From the south-east, a twin-engine, twin-tailed bomber appeared, flying at a height Evans guessed to be around 2000 metres. It flew around the ships twice and then disappeared to the south-east again as mysteriously as it had arrived.

Bert Evans did not recognise the aircraft type and had been unable to see any markings on it. He was not the only one, and a brief discussion broke out among the troops as to what the aircraft was and what its appearance that morning meant. Propped up with his back against the wheelhouse, Barney Darnton took out his notebook and wrote, 'Plane across course. Jap or ours?' He put the notebook away and joined the others watching as the *King John*'s dinghy was slowly winched down to the water below.

As Darnton and the soldiers watched this process, the mysterious aircraft returned, again from the south-east, but this time it was coming in low and fast and with its bomb doors open. Men sprang into action on both ships. Bill Priest and Neil Sandery both called for top speed as their engineers dived down towards their engine rooms. Bruce Fahnestock ran to one of the machine guns on the *King John*, the one at the bow, and swung it around to face the incoming aircraft. Towards the rear, Barney Darnton stood up and leaned against the side of the wheelhouse as he again took out notebook and pen and prepared to jot down the story of what was happening.

And that was about all the time anyone had before the bomber was upon them. The aircraft engine noise was ear-splitting; it was approaching and then it was near, and then overhead, and then it was gone. It had dropped a bomb, though, a bomb that fell some distance away from both boats but that sent up an enormous plume of water before it crashed back into the sea. Barney Darnton crouched over and wrote in his notebook, 'bombed by 2 eng. Plane – 500 yd. miss.' Then, like all the soldiers aboard, he looked around for his helmet. While they donned theirs, he removed the liner from his and placed that on his head; he had always hated wearing helmets.

By now, both boats were zigzagging to present as difficult a target as possible. They also headed in different directions, with the *King John* angling in towards the beach and the *Timoshenko* heading out for the deeper water. Having completed its first bombing run, the aircraft climbed and flew around in a half circle before flattening out into a second bombing run. It was lower this time, and it opened fire with its machine guns as it lined up the *King John*. Barney Darnton, standing alongside the wheelhouse door, watched the aircraft carefully, calling out its every movement to Bill Priest, now concentrating completely on steering his ship.

As soon as the aircraft was within range, Bruce Fahnestock opened fire with his machine gun, and was soon joined by the rifles of most of the soldiers aboard. It seemed a futile gesture, but at least it felt like they were fighting back.

By now, the *King John* was in shoaling water and Bill Priest was certain he felt the bottom scrape a couple of times, although his boat was still moving. In the blink of an eye, Darnton called out that a bomb had been dropped, the aircraft roared overhead and there was a thunderclap of an explosion as a second bomb exploded, still some distance away but noticeably closer this time. Its plume rose at least thirty metres into the air.

Without any warning, Bert Evans suddenly appeared on deck, carrying an axe. He said nothing but rushed to the stern where the dinghy was swinging halfway down the davits. With two swings of the axe, Evans sliced through the ropes holding the dinghy in place and it dropped down into the water. It would make the boat a little bit lighter and perhaps give it a tiny bit more speed. Still without a word, he turned to go back below as the aircraft, which had again circled and flattened out, swung into its third bombing run.

It again targeted the *King John* and again opened fire with its machine guns, this time striking the boat several times but without causing any real damage. Those on board also thought that the plane may have been hit by return fire, but they did not have time to ponder this as – again – it was suddenly upon them. Bert Evans, near the wheelhouse now, watched as it dropped another bomb, and thought that this was going to be a lot closer. It was.

The bomb exploded twenty metres or so from the *King John*'s port side with an enormous noise and rush of air. Shrapnel whistled through that air, past soldiers and supplies, thudding into the ship's woodwork in several places. Evans, looking towards the front of the boat, saw that Bruce Fahnestock had been hit. As he slumped forward over his machine gun, a sudden crimson splash appeared on the back of his army shirt. Alongside the wheelhouse, Barney Darnton jotted down, 'Fahn. Shot – .50 cal.'

The *King John* had clearly slowed by then as Bill Priest tried to navigate through all the coral heads, zigzagging and attempting to avoid the bombs while calling out instructions to all those within earshot.

The aircraft had made another tight turn and was again coming in low and fast at the *King John* for the fourth time. As it flashed overhead, it dropped an anti-personnel bomb which exploded close to the ship's stern on the starboard side. One of its pellets struck Barney Darnton on the left side of his neck, below and behind his ear. He staggered with the impact and then fell headlong through the door and onto the floor of the wheelhouse.

Two metres away, Bert Evans saw Darnton fall through the door but he didn't see much more because he, too, had been struck by bomb splinters. Alongside him, one of the infantrymen, a private named Earl Beecher, had also been hit in the head and was badly wounded.

Then, suddenly, it was over and the aircraft, after a final strafing run along the nearby beach, was now disappearing into the distance just ten minutes after it was first spotted. It left behind a scene of confusion.

•

The *Timoshenko* had escaped unharmed but aboard the *King John* there was a scramble to see how many men had been wounded and how much damage the boat had sustained. The ship's anchor was dropped and the senior officers aboard took charge of what was a scene of some carnage. Bert Evans had staggered forward a few paces after being hit and had then collapsed to the deck, which was where Bill Priest found him. Either a bullet or a pellet from the bomb had passed completely through the upper thigh of one leg and then lodged in the upper thigh of the other. When he saw how much blood Bert Evans was losing, Priest quickly grabbed a sheet from his cabin and tore it up into strips to bind his friend's wounds.

While none of the bombs had scored a direct hit, the near-misses had caused a fair amount of damage to the *King John* and Bill Priest knew she would need a comprehensive over-haul and a number of mechanical and structural repairs to bring her back to top working order. There were also eighteen wounded men aboard, and their wounds ranged from the severe to the superficial. Barney Darnton and Bruce Fahnestock were both unconscious, but Earl Beecher's facial wounds, while horrific to look at, would probably not prove fatal if urgent medical attention could be given. Laurence McKenny had been struck in the right hand by a piece of shrapnel that passed right through, almost severing his ring finger in the process. His was typical of most of the wounds that had been suffered, puncture wounds caused by shrapnel or pellets.

When the aircraft had disappeared, a number of Papuan villagers had appeared and paddled outrigger canoes, which had apparently been sitting under the trees at the edge of the beach, out to the *King John*, now just a couple of hundred metres offshore. McKenny directed that the most severely wounded be taken to the beach first and selected the men best placed to assist in that process. Barney Darnton remained unconscious, still bleeding profusely from the neck wound. An infantryman named Robert Owens wrapped him in a GI blanket and, with another soldier assisting, gently passed him over the side and onto the platform of an outrigger canoe.

Bruce Fahnestock was also unconscious and it seemed that the splinter which had struck him had lodged in his spine, high up. He, too, was wrapped in a blanket and gently carried to the side and lowered down to lie alongside Barney Darnton. Finally, Bert Evans, conscious but in considerable pain, was also passed down to the outrigger. It was just a five-minute paddle to the beach, but some time during those five minutes, Barney Darnton died. Other Papuans appeared from the trees as the canoe grounded on the sand and carried the three men up the beach and into the trees, where they were lowered carefully to the ground.

Bert Evans cradled Bruce Fahnestock and was holding his head, resting it on his stomach, when Bruce Fahnestock also died. By then a second canoe had landed with some of the more lightly wounded, including Laurence McKenny. At his direction, the bodies of the two dead Americans were laid out at the edge of the beach a short distance away and covered with blankets. Two elders from the Pongani village, just twenty metres away, took up a position nearby to watch over the bodies. Others from the village came down onto the beach to help with the wounded and to assist those who were still shocked by what they had just lived through. The dinghies and canoes were turned around and went back out to bring soldiers in from the *King John* and now from the *Timoshenko* as well.

•

Later that day, at a bustling new airfield specially built just outside the town of Charters Towers in Queensland, a B-25 Mitchell bomber touched down in a cloud of dust. The aircraft was named the *Baby Blitz*, a name chosen by its pilot and captain, David Conley of the 13th Squadron of the 3rd Bombardment Group, part of George Kenney's 5th Air Force. The 13th Squadron had given themselves the name the Grim Reapers, and at the debrief with the squadron's Intelligence Officer afterwards, Conley and his crew said that they had lived up to that name earlier in the day. On what was just another reconnaissance flight near the Japanese positions at Buna, they had spotted two small boats packed with troops making for Buna. They had been told that there were no Allied ships operating in those waters, so Conley had chosen to attack them. One ship may have escaped unscathed, he reported, but they were pretty certain that they had hit, and possibly destroyed the second, larger vessel. All in all, they decided, it had been an exciting interlude in an otherwise boring mission.

•

With all the soldiers disembarked, the beach at Pongani was, for a brief time, a hive of activity. The wounded had all been brought ashore in two batches between 8.45 and 9.05 a.m. When that process was completed, the boats' dinghies and the natives' outriggers were put to work bringing all the ammunition and supplies the boats had carried to shore. Though inconvenienced by the wound to his hand, Laurence McKenny supervised the unloading of those stores and approved the establishment of dump sites in the jungle some distance back from the beach. When that task was completed, he ordered that rations be distributed and that the troops sit down in the shade. He encouraged the soldiers to relax after their ordeal earlier in the morning.

Some of the troops were simply too upset to eat. Not only was this the first taste of real combat for almost all of them, but some on the *King John* thought that they had seen large white stars on the wings and fuselage of the aircraft, which was confirmed by others who had been aboard the *Timoshenko* and who had a much clearer view. For some, the fact that they had been attacked by an American aircraft simply added to the shock they were already suffering.

Although the *King John* had been badly shot up and shaken by the attack, almost as soon as she and the *Timoshenko* had been unloaded and patched up, they headed off again. The bodies of Bruce Fahnestock and Barney Darnton were wrapped in blankets and carried back out to the *King John*, which returned them, with the most serious wounded of the infantrymen, back to Wanigela, where they were carried on stretchers to the field hospital that had been established there. Bert Evans, along with one or two others, was subsequently flown back to the Base Hospital in Port Moresby. Evans would eventually be flown all the way back to another Base Hospital in Townsville for specialised treatment.

From Wanigela, the bodies of Bruce Fahnestock and Barney Darnton were flown to an American hospital newly established in an old Catholic mission outside Port Moresby. Two days later, at 9 a.m., both men were buried with full military honours at the Bomana Military Cemetery at Port Moresby. The funerals were attended by a number of high-ranking Allied officers, including a representative of General MacArthur. The funeral had been put back by one day to allow Sheridan Fahnestock, who had been at a Small Ships base in Australia, to attend. Bruce Fahnestock's coffin was carried by serving US soldiers, while a group of war correspondents – American, Australian and British – were the pallbearers for Barney Darnton. Volleys were fired over both men's graves, which were side by side in the cemetery.

Afterwards, back at the house that Darnton had shared with several other war correspondents, the final part of the process was completed. Most of the available correspondents gathered in the house's main room to auction Barney Darnton's last possessions. A number of personal items were set aside for his widow and everything else was sold to the highest bidder, with all the monies also being sent to his widow. Everyone present bought at least one item, even though it might have been something for which they had little or no use. One of those present was an Australian correspondent named Geoffrey Reading, who had been hit hard by Darnton's death as he was starting to model his reporting on the older man's. Reading had no need for any of Darnton's belongings but bought his ration book anyway. He would keep it as a souvenir and as a reminder of someone he rated as the best war correspondent he had ever met.

•

A number of enquiries were made into the circumstances surrounding the attack. Some of those associated with the Small Ships feared that Bruce Fahnestock, who had a reputation for responding impulsively, may have provoked the attack by firing at the aircraft when it came too close to them. This was discounted immediately by eyewitnesses who were there with him on the *King John*. In the end, it all boiled down to a simple lapse in communications. The Allied air forces likely to be operational in the area at the time had been told that all surface craft seen to the west of a certain point, probably Cape Nelson, were to be considered enemy vessels. No one at COSC had been informed of the Small Ships mission to Pongani, perhaps because it was a decision taken by Hanford MacNider on the spur of the moment.

The funerals signalled the end of what was, officially, the first combat-support mission undertaken by the Small Ships on the northern coast of New Guinea. In the end it was successful, as all troops and supplies were safely landed on the beach in front of the small Papuan village. There were casualties, to be sure, but this was wartime and Pongani was only forty kilometres from the Japanese positions at Buna. It was sad as well as successful, and it was also a taste of what was to come.

6.

THE RED ARROW LINE

Work, especially mindless and repetitive work, is often a kind of balm for mental trauma. The simple act of doing something physical, time and time again, with an outcome that can be seen and measured, takes the mind away from whatever has confronted it and allows a person to focus so completely on the task at hand that the images that were so traumatic can, for a time, be banished. So it was with the survivors of the *King John* and *Timoshenko* mission.

When the dead and wounded had been returned to the Small Ships and those ships had sailed off, Laurence McKenny ignored his own wounds and supervised the work of his quartermaster troops while also directing the infantryman to set up guard posts and to patrol just outside the perimeter. There was a genuine fear that Japanese troops may also be close at hand, either in camp or patrolling to the south from Buna. Those fears were assuaged late in the day when an Australian officer was brought in to see McKenny. The Australian was one of those who had overlanded from Wanigela and who was now leading patrols observing and probing the Japanese positions. There were no

Japanese forces in the Pongani area, he said, and he doubted whether there were any on this side of Buna. He also said that there was another Papuan village five kilometres further up the coast, a village called Mendaropu with native houses on stilts sitting over the water's edge, with palm trees providing a canopy above them. More importantly, adjacent to the village was an abandoned church mission known as Embogo. There were a number of usable structures at the abandoned mission.

The next morning, McKenny left a guard detachment to look after the supplies at Pongani and led the remainder of the men along the beaches and up the native trails to Mendaropu, where he found that what the Australian officer had told him was accurate. He believed it to be a better site than Pongani and sent a signal back to Wanigela to that effect. Out at sea and out of sight, the Small Ships loaded with supplies on their way to Pongani, or about to depart, had their sailing orders changed to now deliver their cargoes to Mendaropu, which was now the terminus of the shuttle run to support the build-up for the forthcoming assault. Anchoring off Mendaropu, they would wait initially for the native outrigger canoes to row out to them to start the process of unloading.

Buna was now less than forty kilometres away.

•

The outer passage from Milne Bay to Wanigela and beyond remained too risky to take and COSC was fortunate that New Guinea Force, the headquarters for all operations, recognised the potential importance of the seaborne supply line. The *Paluma*'s work beyond Cape Nelson was now supported by two other RAN launches, the *Polaris* and the *Stella*, and by the sloop HMAS *Warrego*. Between them they had charted a channel, up to five kilometres wide in parts, from Cape Nelson to Pongani and marked that passage with night-vision marker buoys.

The work of those survey vessels, and the observations and notes of the Small Ships' captains, informed the official Sailing Instructions issued by the Allied Geographical Section on 21 October 1942. Those instructions noted that 'the charts of the area are incomplete and inaccurate in places. Difficulty will be found in trying to reconcile them with some of the directions given off the main route.' They noted that in some places, coral patches meant that sailing could only be undertaken in daylight hours, and then only when the sun was in a 'favourable' position. They were stark, and in places almost foreboding, but those Sailing Instructions underpinned all the forthcoming seaborne supply operations; operations that might determine the outcome of the first major clash between MacArthur's new command and an entrenched and fanatical enemy.

By the end of October, the Small Ships' operations in eastern and north-eastern New Guinea were fully established. They were still at the heart of the effort to build up supply dumps at strategic locations to support the Americans' offensive at Buna. They were so busy that they came to be called the Red Arrow Line by Forrest Harding, who realised better than most just how vital those boats were and would remain to his men in the coming weeks.

The supply line, and its processes, soon became standardised. Large freighters, soon to include both the Liberty and Victory ships that were starting to roll off production lines in the United States, would deliver thousands of tons of cargo to one of the four main wharf areas in Milne Bay. Those earmarked for Harding's 32nd Division would be put aboard one of the larger vessels in the Small Ships fleet and sent onwards to Wanigela. There, the materials would either be stockpiled or transferred to one of the smaller vessels for onward movement to Pongani, Mendaropu or beyond. By early November, there was a beyond, thanks to the work of the *Paluma* and other survey ships.

The supply line and process also changed according to circumstances. Wanigela lessened in importance, and was closed as a major base around the end of October, its role now taken over by Porlock Harbour and Oro Bay, two deep-water ports on the other side of Cape Nelson. A cleared and safe passage from Cape Nelson to those ports was declared open on 4 November and could not have come at a better time. On 2 November, MacArthur had selected 15 November as the opening day of the Buna offensive. The next day, he further declared that ten days' worth of supplies be built up before either of Harding's two task forces – one inland and one coastal – advanced any further. The coastal task force, under Hanford MacNider, would rely almost entirely on the Small Ships' shuttle to supply its troops. Secure bases and a secure supply route would therefore determine success or failure.

•

Clarrie Dawes and the *Leprena* would come to know the waters beyond Cape Nelson very well. At just over 100 tons, she was ideal for carrying supplies to both Porlock Harbour and Oro Bay, although her draught made sailing beyond those two bases problematic except in daylight hours. The anchorages at both brought a mixed bag of benefits and drawbacks. Porlock Harbour always reminded Clarrie of an extinct volcano that had collapsed on one side and let the water in. It was not a total collapse, though, as there was an impediment at the entrance, the jagged rock outcrop called Jones' Reef, which so restricted the entrance that ships the size of the *Leprena* and above could only enter in daylight.

Once through that entrance, Porlock Harbour proved to be an ideal, if limited, deep-water port. It was not as large as Oro Bay and sometimes generated a feeling of claustrophobia, and there were several arms off the main body of water. In most of these, the steep sides and overhanging vegetation made them unsuitable for anything but hiding, but at least two ended in small beaches with some relatively flat land extending further inland. The larger of these was considered suitable as a dump site, and a small loading ramp and roller ladders were brought in. The boats were able to anchor alongside the ramp, such was the water depth, and either load or unload cargo using the roller ladders.

When not engaged in moving cargo, the boats would select a suitable anchorage under the overhanging trees – Clarrie Dawes called them willows – knowing they were completely invisible from the air. There was an added attraction at Porlock Harbour for Clarrie. He would take a local guide, if one was available, and a ship's dinghy and row into some of the smaller inlets where there would inevitably be pigeons roosting. He would shoot several and take them back to the *Leprena* where, cooked, they made a welcome addition to the tinned food which comprised the bulk of their diet.

•

Oro Bay had been inspected by the 32nd Division's Chief Engineer, Colonel John Carew, in early November and his report supported what several Small Ships captains had already claimed: Oro Bay could be developed into a very good deep-water port. There was ample water depth and space for the largest freighters operating on the run from Milne Bay and Wanigela, while the hinterland was suitable for both munitions dumps and accommodation because there was none of the coastal swamps that made so many other anchorages problematic. There were no real port facilities there, in the early days at least, but the ingenuity of the engineers soon produced pontoon bridges across rowboats and dinghies, and floating wharves.

The waters beyond Oro Bay and up to Buna remained difficult. The area was criss-crossed with shallow reefs and narrow deep-water leads that soon petered out. It was also an area of high visibility. Japanese troops were dug in at Cape Endaiadere, on a promontory just below Buna, and had a panoramic view back towards Oro Bay. Daylight movement was likely to be observed and, if there were Japanese aircraft or naval units in the area, they could be called in.

Another small promontory to the south of Cape Endaiadere, Cape Sudest, was also a problem because there were reefs close by that were covered by just one metre of water at low tide. Sailing too close risked being fired upon by the Japanese on Cape Endaiadere but sailing too wide risked running aground on the reefs. The situation improved considerably when the Papuans from a village at Cape Sudest were paid to hang out a lantern each night to act as a beacon.

On the positive side, in early November, the Australian and American troops on the ground below Buna reported that Japanese aircraft were becoming less frequent visitors, and the Allies assumed that the aircraft operating out of Rabaul were increasingly being drawn into the fighting taking place at Guadalcanal. Despite this, the lightly protected Small Ships preferred to minimise their risks by operating at night, early in the morning or late in the afternoon.

However, even those night voyages were sometimes interrupted by the Japanese. Their air forces in the area included powerful and heavily armed single-engine floatplanes that operated in both daylight and darkness. Due to their distinctive engine noise, they were known as 'Washing Machine Charlie', and they were a very dangerous enemy. In daylight, they developed the tactic of flying at a considerable height and, if they spotted what they thought was an Allied vessel, of cutting their engine and gliding down into an attack dive. They would start their engines again just before dropping a bomb on the unsuspecting target. At night, they modified that tactic somewhat: flying at lower altitudes, they would approach anything they thought might be suspicious and drop a powerful flare on a parachute, illuminating a large area below. Staying in the darkness, they would move into an attack position and suddenly appear out of nowhere, guns blazing and bombs on the way. The only thing that seemed to stop them was bad weather.

Bad weather might have kept the Japanese floatplanes away, but it also presented a range of problems with sailing and then with unloading. Night supply runs and night landings could therefore be quite fraught. Fine weather was obviously better, but also brought about the possibility of a floatplane being in the vicinity, just waiting to pounce.

Unloading was always therefore quite hurried with the supplies, and sometimes troops, pushed into the dinghies and onto the outrigger canoes that came out to meet the Small Ships. Sometimes those aboard would be rowed to shore by natives or by other soldiers detailed for the task, and sometimes they were just pointed in the right direction and left to their own devices. And sometimes, when conditions were bad or when the men aboard thought they could hear an aircraft on a quiet night with a full moon, supplies would simply be pushed overboard and left to make their own way to shore.

•

The pressure was now well and truly on. MacArthur leaned on his generals, who leaned on their colonels and so on down the chain of command. Close to the bottom of that chain were the Small Ships, and an awful lot was being expected of so few. Calls went out all the way back to Sydney for reinforcements as the ships already in the area worked long hours to support the build-up at the bases and depots below Buna. At the start, there had just been the eight of them: the *King John*, *Kelton*, *Bonwin*, *Timoshenko*, *Minnamurra*, *Two Freddies* and *Willyama II*, all trawlers, and the schooner *Alacrity*. And then, not all of these were always available to take supplies up to Mendaropu and Pongani, as they were frequently detached on other missions.

A lot more ships were on the way, though. There were already more seine trawlers loading up at Milne Bay or Wanigela or then pushing their way forward along the newly marked channels, among them the *Margaret Twaits*, the *San Cristoforo* and the *Charles Cam*. The large ketch, Clarrie Dawes' *Leprena*, was about to be joined by similar-sized vessels like the cray boat *Hilda Norling* and the ketch *Melanesia*, the latter already part of Small Ships' folklore because of the somewhat exotic background of her captain, Alan Reynolds, who had been born in India where his father served in the Indian Army, a background matched by her engineer, Ray Parer, pioneer aviator, adventurer and cousin of the already famous war photographer, Damien Parer. Considered curious was the fact that Parer preferred to work naked in the engine room and, occasionally, appeared topside in the same state of undress. If anyone ever asked, and plenty did, Parer would explain his appearance in a way that suggested nakedness was the most logical way of doing things that could be imagined. It was always cooler with no clothes on, he would say, and he didn't want to risk getting his clothes dirty and thereby creating more work for himself.

Two other vessels, from different navies and different wars, also joined the Small Ships on New Guinea's north coast. One was the old four-stack US Navy destroyer, the USS *Dale*, now the *Masaya*, once again decked out in battleship grey and with a dummy gun made from a coconut trunk proudly displayed on her foredeck. The second had no number and no name. It was a Japanese landing barge that had been left behind when their forces evacuated from Milne Bay in September. It was in good working order and, because it had front-opening doors, would be especially useful in landing men and equipment directly onto the beaches below Buna.

•

The plans had all seemed very sound when presented at staff meetings in air-conditioned offices in Brisbane and Port Moresby. The Allied assault on Buna–Gona would consist of three separate but coordinated attacks. The first would be in the north and north-west of the Japanese enclave and would be undertaken primarily by Australian troops from the 7th Division who would push the few remaining Japanese off the Kokoda Track and debouch out onto the coastal plain. After regrouping there, they would attack the Gona end of the enclave.

Two American columns composed of troops from Forrest Harding's 32nd Division would strike the Buna end of the enclave, in two different places and from different directions. One column would comprise troops airlifted into Dobodura by Kenney's C-47s. Known as Urbana Force, they would attack the Buna complex from the west and south-west. The second column, the coastal task force now known as Warren Force and under the command of Hanford MacNider, would stay close to the coast and attack from the south. The (supposedly) relatively small number of dispirited and emaciated Japanese soldiers would be pushed back to the sea and would then either surrender or be annihilated.

Early probes by Australian and American reconnaissance patrols began to paint a different picture, though. It seemed that the Japanese were well prepared and were waiting patiently for the assault. What was assumed to be a small and dispirited force in makeshift fortifications was a long way from the reality on the ground. All three columns would learn, and pay a high price for the knowledge, that what they would be attacking was actually an extensive complex of defensive strongpoints, all of which were carefully sited, painstakingly concealed and exceedingly well constructed. They did back onto the sea, but that sea was used to bring in reinforcements aboard destroyers, barges and submarines.

The Japanese positions were in an arc stretching almost twenty kilometres from Gona in the north to Buna in the south with the small, well-protected village of Sanananda in the middle. Not only were the positions anchored on the sea; the beaches that fringed the sea for most of the length of the enclave provided a relatively safe passage for Japanese troops at night and messages by day. The terrain also clearly favoured the defenders. On that part of the coast, there were ridges, just a couple of metres high, across much of the coastal littoral. What wasn't ridge was swamp and, at this time of year, the swamp was becoming deeper and more waterlogged with each passing day. The main Japanese positions were all on those ridges, and the only approaches to them were trails above the swamps – all covered by multiple Japanese weapons – or through the swamps themselves. Some of those swamps, however, were so full of water that it was impossible to cross them on foot.

The young men who were going to approach and overcome those defences at the Buna end of the stronghold were the inexperienced soldiers of the 32nd Division, the Red Arrow Division, large numbers of who were farm boys from the Mid-West who had been part-time soldiers until a few months earlier. The climate and terrain could not have been more alien for them. The closest most of them had come to jungle was the brief training they had been given at a camp at Logan, to the south of Brisbane. Here, though, what wasn't water was incredibly thick jungle: solid walls of vegetation that restricted movement to a few trails and also impeded communication. It was impossible to lay telephone cables in such conditions, while the atmospherics were not really suitable for radio communications with mildew and damp playing havoc with radio equipment.

What looked like a green carpet from above was a canopy concealing enemy preparations and enemy movements. It was no wonder that Allied intelligence estimates put the number of Japanese defenders within the perimeter at somewhere between several hundred and several thousand, while any assessment of those Japanese, and of their defensive positions, was little more than a semi-educated guess.

The physical conditions under which the 32nd Division would fight were also far different from anything they had experienced. It was, and would remain, hot and humid. The rainy season was just beginning, and the rivers and swamps were filling with all the extra rain running down from the mountains in the hinterland.

All the river crossings were now problematic and few of the swamps could now be traversed on foot. It was an atmosphere ideal for rot and fungus, and for a host of physical ailments that could debilitate those who remained there. Various skin ailments were among the first to appear, followed by more serious illnesses and diseases, including malaria, dengue fever, scrub typhus and amoebic dysentery. Effective medicines to prevent and treat these were not readily available and the hospitals and clinics to deal with them were still a long way back from where the men were awaiting the signal to advance.

If it were possible to select the worst possible conditions for untried American troops to confront an entrenched and fanatical enemy, the area around Buna would fit the bill, and more. And, to top it all off, those untried troops would be dependent on a very thin supply line for almost everything they would need for the ordeal ahead.

•

On the other side of those defensive positions, the Japanese were experiencing much the same things as the Americans. Both groups of soldiers believed in their cause and in the ultimate success of that cause. The Japanese took heart from the radio reports of ongoing success at Guadalcanal, and rejoiced in the naval victories that they were told had taken place from the Aleutians to Sydney Harbour, without knowing that those victories were no victories at all. They had been in New Guinea longer than the Americans and were now suffering from all the ailments that were just beginning to strike down their enemy. One of them, an Imperial Japanese Navy medical officer, recorded in his diary his concerns about the increasing number of patients he was seeing who were severely weakened by dysentery, confessing that there was very little he could offer them beyond words of encouragement. He expressed, too, concerns about the number of enemy air raids but still remained confident of an eventual Japanese victory.

Another, a young soldier suffering from the effects of malnutrition, took comfort in writing down the words of his unit's marching song, a song written in the first flush of success several months earlier. The song concluded with the verse:

> *A brisk divine breeze blowing*
> *Towards Australia at the limits of the South.*
> *The ultimate place to reach.*
> *The dawn of a new world,*
> *Not quickly but faintly.*

•

The pressure from MacArthur's headquarters did not relent as the presumptive launch date for the Buna offensive, 15 November, drew closer and closer. It was felt everywhere – on land, sea and air – and it began to take a toll. One of the aircraft involved in George Kenney's airlift of troops to the battle zone was a 5th Air Force C-47 named *The Flying Dutchman*, piloted by Lieutenant George Vandervort.

The Flying Dutchman flew out of Port Moresby during the morning of 10 November and headed across the island for the new airstrip recently completed at Dobodura. On this particular flight, the C-47 carried a crew of two, plus a chaplain and nineteen enlisted men from the Red Arrow's 126th Infantry Regiment. They were ultimately bound for Pongani, now one of the main staging points for the Buna operations, scheduled for less than a week away. About half an hour after take-off, the aircraft seemed to be caught in some kind of downdraft, and it clipped the top of some trees before crashing into the jungle. Six of the twenty-two aboard were killed in the crash with several others being critically injured. Six of the survivors would walk out of the jungle several weeks later; the rest died slowly at the crash site.

•

One of George Kenney's oft-repeated claims was that there was no need for artillery support for the Buna campaign. Jungles, he said, would so reduce the effectiveness of any artillery brought in that serving the big guns would simply occupy troops who could be better occupied elsewhere. Besides, he added, if there were any strongpoints that needed to be reduced, his aircraft would assume the role of flying artillery and do the job for the footsloggers below. It was an argument that became less attractive the closer the Americans came to the Japanese positions and, relatively late in the build-up, a call went out for whatever artillery support was available.

It was also an argument that Forrest Harding was not prepared to buy into. Working through New Guinea Force Headquarters, he arranged for two mountain howitzers and their gun crews from the Australian 1st Mountain Battery to be flown to Pongani, and also for elements of the Australian 2/5th Field Regiment to be brought forward from Milne Bay.

That artillery was Australian and the only way it could be delivered was in US Army Small Ships – Australian ships with mainly Australian crews.

At Milne Bay, the 2/5th Field Regiment of the 2nd AIF despatched its F Troop, under the command of a Major Hall, to assist the Americans' coastal task force. They were put aboard the

Masaya, along with their 25-pound field guns, ammunition for those guns, plus another 500 American soldiers. It was one of the first voyages along the newly surveyed route all the way to Oro Bay; the Australians aboard joked afterwards that they seemed to have bumped from one reef to the next, but they made it all the way without undue delays.

At Oro Bay, they were unloaded via one of the new pontoon wharfs and, once ashore, were placed in defensive positions around the now-bustling little port.

Additional 25-pound field guns and crews were also despatched from Milne Bay to Wanigela, where they were broken down and placed aboard one of the Small Ships, the *Kooraka*, which was also loaded up with the guns' crews and American soldiers to be taken forward to Oro Bay. At the last moment, fifty live sheep were also put aboard, leaving no deck space available for anything else.

Just to add to the general misery such crowding engendered, it rained heavily during the night passage around Cape Nelson, causing men and sheep to compete for the little protection available. The next day was dry, but grew increasingly hot; the stench from the sheep and their droppings was soon almost unbearable. For the troops, the ordeal ended when the *Kooraka* anchored offshore at Oro Bay and they were taken ashore to establish defensive positions around the base. It lasted a lot longer for the crew of the *Kooraka*.

•

The problems with the supply line meant that MacArthur's instruction that ten days' worth of supplies be built up before any further movement on Buna occurred put the proposed launch date of 15 November beyond reach, albeit not by much.

The date was pushed back two days with 17 November now becoming D-Day. Warren Force, Hanford MacNider's coastal task force, had the crucial jobs of removing the Japanese from Cape Endaiadere and punching through the southern defences around Buna, creating a ripple effect throughout the entire Japanese position and drawing defenders away from other points. MacNider was a thorough man, and he was not prepared to make mistakes in his role as the first American general to take on the Japanese in territory they considered their own.

MacNider had established his command post at Embogo and, during the night of 15/16 November, he was joined there by a group of American artillerymen under the command of the 32nd Division's Artillery Officer, General Albert Waldron. Waldron had also brought with him two Australian mountain howitzers, all travelling aboard the Japanese motorised landing barge that had been captured at Milne Bay. The barge had already been put to good use, bringing a Marmon artillery tractor from Milne Bay to Porlock Harbour and then returning to collect the mountain howitzers from Wanigela. With MacNider's agreement, Waldron proposed pushing the artillery forward that night, suggesting Cape Sudest, around four kilometres short of Buna, as an ideal place to land them. It was a calculated risk, as the area had not yet been scouted by Allied troops, but aerial reconnaissance had not shown anything and it might save a lot of time later.

Carrying the howitzers, their crews, 200 rounds of ammunition and an American artilleryman, Lieutenant Colonel Melvin McCreary, the barge moved off after dark and, moving cautiously and slowly, was put on the beach at Cape Sudest around midnight. When the men, and the guns and ammunition, had been unloaded, Waldron returned in the empty barge to Oro

Bay where he planned to put two 25-pound pieces and their crews aboard and have them brought forward to support the attack as well.

On the morning of 16 November, MacNider boarded the *Kelton*, which he had temporarily taken over as a mobile base for his continuing moves forward, and travelled aboard it to Cape Sudest. He invited a number of others along, including at least one war correspondent and a newsreel cameraman. They were the lucky ones, as there were several others a bit further back and all were keen to be there for what they had been assured would be MacArthur's first attack on the Japanese. Cape Sudest was their destination because there was a small detachment of American soldiers positioned there. The *Kelton* was also to drop off a consignment of mountain howitzer ammunition there as Cape Sudest was where the two howitzers would be based until they were deployed in support of the attack at Cape Endaiadere.

MacNider was aware that the latest intelligence reports suggested that the Japanese defences at the Buna end of the enclave were manned by relatively few soldiers, and that those soldiers were generally ill and malnourished. He was also aware that there had been few sightings of Japanese aircraft above these waters for several weeks. It may have been this knowledge that led to his ordering Ireneo Ames to sail the *Kelton* past the US troops gathered at Cape Sudest and into the small and shallow bay beyond. When one of the American officers, probably Melvin McCreary, on the shore saw this, he ran down to the water's edge where he removed his shirt and waved it in the air to attract the attention of those aboard the *Kelton*. When not waving his shirt, he would point to the jungle behind to signify that it was where his men were and then point ahead and cross his arms to say there were enemy troops somewhere ahead.

Several of his subordinates questioned MacNider's decision, suggesting that the area had not yet been cleared by Allied troops. One, Colonel Tracey Hale who commanded the 128th Regiment, pointed out to MacNider that he was proposing to land on an unprotected coast, possibly on top of a concealed enemy. The two men had already clashed a number of times and MacNider simply ignored his subordinate. He was confident in his assessment, though, and ordered Ames to anchor a short distance beyond Cape Sudest, two hundred metres out to sea and in front of a small Papuan village which he knew was named Hariko. The outer line of Japanese defences at Buna was now just three kilometres to the north of where the *Kelton* sat.

The small patrol that he put ashore in the *Kelton*'s dinghy soon returned with the news that MacNider had been correct; there was no sign of the Japanese either in or near the little village.

Around noon, MacNider and his staff went ashore and quickly set up a command post in a grove near Hariko village. The ammunition and other stores were also unloaded, after which MacNider directed Ames to take the *Kelton* back to Embogo to collect more troops and supplies as he intended to make Hariko both his headquarters and the jumping-off point for the troops attacking Buna. His little group was soon joined by some of the troops from Cape Sudest who had marched the short distance along the beach when they understood what MacNider was planning to do.

Early in the afternoon, two more Small Ships appeared offshore at Hariko and anchored there. They were the *King John* and the *Two Freddies*, whose skippers, Bill Priest and Ralph Andrews, had learned from the *Kelton* where MacNider had now established his headquarters. They, too, unloaded as quickly as possible before heading back to Embogo. The order went back with them for the Australian 25-pound guns and crews to also be brought up for the opening of the Buna attack. The order also went back for Waldron and his Australian guns and gunners to come forward on their Japanese barge. The fact that the coast below Buna was clear of Japanese troops meant that preparations for the attack could now be hurried up.

Two days earlier, Laurence McKenny's planners had estimated that MacNider's coastal task force would require forty-five tons of rations a week during the forthcoming campaign and a lot of those rations were now at the dumps established around Mendaropu – which was where Forrest Harding had just established his own headquarters – as well as at Oro Bay and Embogo. MacNider was more than happy with what he had found at Hariko and believed it was a suitable site for advanced ammunition and ration dumps. He sent a message down the line calling McKenny to come forward to take control of that side of the preparations.

Around the middle of the afternoon, the troops at Hariko had front row seats to a very heavy US air attack on the Japanese positions at Buna. The bombers swooped down to drop loads of bombs, and their escorting fighters strafed whatever was left after the bombers had done their job. They had been met by quite heavy fire from anti-aircraft batteries, but the infantrymen didn't read anything into that. There was general agreement that whoever was beneath those bombs and those bullets would be dispirited and would have difficulty resisting the American assault that was coming in the next twenty-four hours.

On Cape Endaiadere, the dug-in Japanese troops also had a clear view of the bombing raid. They had, as well, a clear view of Hariko and the waters around the village. They had noted the comings and goings of boats and people, and they reported and waited, hoping they may have a show of their own to watch.

7.

IN HARM'S WAY

That afternoon, Hanford MacNider worked steadily in his temporary forward command post in a tent in a jungle clearing just outside the cluster of huts that made up the little village of Hariko. Planning for the assault on Buna, now less than twenty-four hours away, meant that he needed to be ashore and close to his troops' jump-off points so he could coordinate the thousand and one things he knew would demand his attention when the real fighting started. He was aware, too, that the eyes of the American public and, more particularly, the eyes of Douglas MacArthur would also be focused on what he and his men would achieve in the coming days and MacNider was determined to do everything to prove others' trust in him was not misplaced.

To make certain he was not disturbed in his planning, MacNider had earlier sent out a heavily armed reconnaissance patrol, and that patrol had come under fire from entrenched Japanese positions on Cape Endaiadere, but had also found no other Japanese between Buna and Hariko. When the guns and gunners arrived, MacNider thought he would detail them to blast the Japanese out of their emplacements on Cape Endaiadere, allowing the bulk of his troops to concentrate on the main Japanese positions ahead.

The *Kelton* had returned to Embogo, and could even go back to Oro Bay if that were necessary, to collect more food and ammunition and, hopefully, Quartermaster McKenny to look after that load as well as the hundreds of tons of supplies and ammunition that the Small Ships would be bringing to Hariko in the next few days. MacNider knew that some of those Small Ships were due that afternoon, and even more that evening, but they and their cargoes were a problem for someone else to deal with. Hanford MacNider had a battle to plan.

•

The Small Ships on which MacNider would rely to support his assault on the Japanese positions were under the ultimate command of Laurence McKenny, but the senior US Army officer in any particular area of operations was also able to direct McKenny in their activities. At the next level was the operational commander at the Small Ships base involved in any particular operation. In the case of the Hariko operations, that officer was a US Army captain named Jack Keegan, who was very busy trying to bring together the various elements that would constitute the supply line between the main centres of Porlock Harbour and Oro Bay through to MacNider's headquarters at Hariko. That involved balancing boats and captains and priorities shouted at all of them from several quarters. If anyone in that complex system thought that, perhaps, Hanford MacNider had been a bit peremptory in sailing to Hariko that morning, they didn't mention it – at least within his hearing – and concentrated on doing what they were told they were expected to do.

Early that afternoon, the Hariko shuttle run, the pipeline carrying men and munitions to the front, had been opened by the arrival of two Small Ships bringing the first soldiers and supplies to MacNider's forward command post. The *King John* and *Two Freddies* unloaded their cargoes into the canvas assault boats and outrigger canoes that acted as lighters at Hariko until more substantial craft could be found and brought forward. The trawlers then returned to either Embogo or Oro Bay to load up again while the other Small Ships also took cargoes aboard and slotted straight into the shuttle run. Several more were expected at different times later that afternoon, carrying the needed men and supplies plus the quartermaster MacNider had ordered forward to make sure the supply line continued to function. The whiff of battle was in the air and things needed to keep moving.

•

The first of the Small Ships to bring up men and supplies in the late afternoon was the twin-masted schooner, the *Alacrity*. As well as being the first, she would be the largest and, arguably, the most important. There was very little space aboard her when she departed Embogo at 5 p.m. for the one-hour trip to Hariko. Her holds were packed tight with ammunition, some 100 tons of it, which represented all the reserve ammunition for the 128th Regiment, the unit MacNider had selected to spearhead the advance on Buna. There was, in fact, so much ammunition that the holds could not contain it all, and some of the overload had been placed aboard a steel barge the *Alacrity* was towing with odd boxes here and there on the main deck as well. The size and importance of the ammunition the *Alacrity* carried was such that a young ordnance officer, Lieutenant John Harbert, had been assigned to supervise its transportation and unloading.

As well as the overflow ammunition, the steel barge was carrying boxes of medical equipment and supplies belonging to the US Army's 22nd Portable Hospital, a recently formed unit that was expected to provide the prototype for a new kind of army field hospital, one better suited to the exigencies of jungle warfare than the traditional field hospitals. The hospital's twenty-nine staff members – surgeons, medical and clerical orderlies – were deck passengers aboard the *Alacrity*, as were a number of infantrymen who would be responsible for the security of the hospital once the fighting began.

The medicos were joined on deck by members of a reconnaissance patrol from the 126th Regiment, while forty Papuans had gathered together in a loose group towards the front of the vessel. Those Papuans had been hired as carriers and, once the *Alacrity*'s cargo had been taken ashore by the outriggers and canvas boats at Hariko, they would carry the various boxes inland to where the hospital and supply dumps were to be established. They would then stay ashore and wait for the next Small Ships to arrive. As well as all that equipment and ammunition, the *Alacrity* carried around 180 people from Embogo to Hariko that afternoon.

•

As the *Alacrity* was raising her anchor off Embogo, a hundred metres away another Small Ship, the trawler *Minnamurra*, was dropping hers. It had already been a busy day for both ship and crew, but it would all be over in a couple of hours and they could then relax until the next trip.

Earlier that morning, the *Minnamurra*'s captain, Ted King, had overseen the loading of his little boat at Oro Bay and had been surprised by how much they had been able to squeeze aboard her. The main cargo on this trip comprised boxes of ammunition but there were also crates of rations, radio parts, 81-millimetre mortar tubes, .50 calibre machine guns and a lot of other equipment that was too heavy to be carried through the jungle. The boxes had been carefully carried across the pontoon wharf at Oro Bay by Papuans, and King and his crew had then supervised their loading and storage. To top it off, they had been asked to make a short stop at Pongani which resulted in a squad of twenty-five US infantrymen being ferried aboard before they departed for Embogo.

Like everything else about the operation, though, departure times were very flexible, which was just as well because they had barely got underway when they had to stop again. This stop was brief. Opposite an abandoned mission building and 150 metres off the beach sat two outrigger canoes occupied by Papuan paddlers and two US Army officers, sitting and waiting patiently. They weren't any old officers, either; in one canoe sat General Forrest Harding and one of his aides, in the other, Colonel Herbert Laux, an Army Ground Forces observer sent from MacArthur's headquarters to report on the forthcoming attack. The three men clambered aboard quickly and the *Minnamurra* continued up the coast on the short hop to Embogo for any final instructions before continuing to Hariko.

Almost as soon as the anchor had dropped at Embogo, two dinghies appeared alongside the *Minnamurra*. The first contained two passengers, the local Small Ships controller, US Army captain Jack Keegan, and Geoffrey Reading, the Australian war correspondent for the Sydney newspaper, the *Daily Mirror*. The two men had developed a close friendship in a short time, a friendship based in part on a shared, and wry, sense of humour.

Reading would later describe Keegan as 'a lean young man, much given to laughter. Through thick spectacles he took a long view, and saw the fun in everything.' As they had rowed out to the trawler, Reading had noted a shark fin breaking the surface of the water and slowly circling their dinghy. He pointed it out to Keegan and asked whether it was an omen.

'Only if it's hungry and you're a fish,' came the reply.

As Keegan and Reading climbed aboard the *Minnamurra*, a second dinghy stopped within hailing distance of the boat. This one had a single passenger who both men recognised as Australian Army captain Keith Black, a former journalist who now worked for the Army's Directorate of Public Relations. Black called out to Ted King, asking him how long the *Minnamurra* would be staying at Embogo. From the wheelhouse, King called back that they would be leaving in no more than fifteen minutes.

At that, Black turned his dinghy around and rowed hard for the shoreline. He was back within ten minutes, this time clutching his kitbag, which he threw up onto the deck before he, too, climbed aboard the *Minnamurra*.

While he was gone, Keegan had introduced Reading to Ted King, and the three men were still talking at the wheelhouse when Keith Black climbed aboard. He joined the other three there and told them that Frank Bagnall and Tom Fisher, two Australian cameramen/photographers, were still on the beach at Embogo but were throwing some kit together in the hope that they, too, would be able to get a lift to Hariko. Black didn't seem too concerned about them, though, adding, 'If we go without them, we go without them. They can follow on the next boat.'

And that was what happened. As the *Minnamurra* raised its anchor and moved off slowly, Geoffrey Reading looked across to the beach and saw two figures there looking out to sea. He knew it was Bagnall and Fisher, and he knew as well that they had spotted the next two Small Ships sailing towards Embogo.

●

The first of the two was the Japanese motorised barge that had been captured at Milne Bay and handed over to the Small Ships. The slow-moving barge was low in the water because it was loaded with more than it usually carried. Aboard were two 25-pound artillery pieces, along with their gun crews and a substantial supply of artillery rounds, all under the command of Captain Charles Mueller, a Sydneysider who was now a battery commander in the 2/5th Field Regiment. Also aboard were Albert Waldron, the brigadier general responsible for the 32nd Division's artillery, and Colonel Harold Handy, another observer from MacArthur's headquarters. The barge stopped briefly off Embogo, but because there was no room for more passengers or supplies, and no last-minute instructions for Waldron, it was soon underway again, chugging slowly through the water towards Hariko.

The second of the Small Ships was the *Kelton*, coming from the other direction and returning from Hariko for more supplies and with MacNider's request for Quartermaster Laurence McKenny, who was in Embogo and able to report to Hariko. But there was a hitch: the *Kelton* had been issued contradictory orders, one of which was to stay at Embogo awaiting further orders, and Ireneo Ames was in something of a bind over what to do. The situation quickly righted itself, though, as yet another Small Ship hove into view.

This one was the *Bonwin*, another Sydney trawler with a three man, all-Filipino crew. The *Bonwin* was operating out of Oro Bay where, earlier in the day, she had taken on a full load of ammunition and fuel drums to take forward to Hariko and the new supply dumps being established there. Also aboard was another small group of Papuan carriers. After an exchange of signals between the boats, accompanied by much waving and gesticulating, the *Bonwin* moved in closer to the beach to receive the passengers she had just agreed to take to Hariko. There were three of them and they were rowed out to the *Bonwin* in a dinghy that seemed to be carrying a lot of kit.

First aboard was Laurence McKenny, answering MacNider's summons; once he was aboard, he helped the other two, the Australian newsmen Tom Fisher and Frank Bagnall, and then assisted them to hoist their cameras and recording equipment, plus several boxes of related gear, onto the deck. The Papuan carriers stored the gear somewhere below decks.

Tom Fisher was especially happy to have made it aboard. He had been documenting the American advance along the north coast for the past few weeks and would have been gutted if there had been a significant clash with the Japanese and he had not been there to document it. Frank Bagnall would have been a bit disappointed if he missed the opportunity to get to Hariko, but nothing more than that. As well as being a newsreel cameraman for the Department of Information, he was an accredited war correspondent and knew that all the good stories did not have to originate in the frontlines. Besides, he had hundreds of feet of great newsreel footage in the boxes the carriers had stowed below, and he wanted to start organising its return to Port Moresby and then onwards to Australia.

As he stood there thinking, the *Bonwin* raised its anchor and headed off in the wake of the other Small Ships, heading for Hariko.

•

Geoffrey Reading may well have been the most relaxed person among the 300 or more passengers and crew aboard the four Small Ships now strung out along the route between Embogo and Hariko. There was no battle ahead for him, no deadlines to meet and, after what he had been through recently, this little sea trip was almost like a childhood excursion on a ferry in Sydney Harbour. Reading had spent two weeks covering the Australian advance along the Kokoda Track and then ten days working closely with and observing the American troops. He considered the Americans' approach to coming to grips with the Japanese casual and somewhat unusual. However, he did concede that their apparent nonchalance might be due to their nature rather than a lack of understanding of just what they would be going up against.

For now, though, he was content to relax, take stock of his surroundings and compose the mental photographs that he would use at some future date when reporting on his short voyage aboard the *Minnamurra*. As he glanced around, those pictures came into focus: 'a chocolate-skinned coast boy with a red flower in his hair stood at the bow throwing out the plumbline and calling out the depths. Laux chatted with Harding and Black read his letters.' He noted the *Minnamurra*'s two .50 calibre machine guns on their shoulder-high mountings in front of the wheelhouse looking to him like 'gaunt scarecrows'.

Ahead, he could see that the *Alacrity* had dropped her anchor opposite what he thought must be the village of Hariko somewhere back from the beach in the jungle. Up ahead a few kilometres, and still out of sight, were the Japanese positions at Buna. Astern, the other two Small Ships were still trailing the

Minnamurra. The slow-moving barge had been overtaken by the *Bonwin*, but neither would catch the *Minnamurra* before she, too, anchored off Hariko to unload her passengers and cargo.

Looking ashore, Reading thought the land resembled the tropical paradise described in books and attempted in Hollywood movies. It was probably around 6.30 p.m., he thought, with the sun slowly sinking towards the sea, soft shadows falling across the shoreline and a gentle breeze blowing. It was almost twilight, normally the best part of the day, a time to relax and let your thoughts wander where they will.

•

All the officers and men of the Small Ships Section operating in the waters around New Guinea were aware of their little vessels' vulnerability to enemy attack, whether that attack was mounted from sea or air. They knew the machine guns they carried were as much for show as they were for protection, as they would do little to deter either enemy ships or aircraft. Around Embogo and Hariko, they should be relatively safe though. Hostile aircraft had been spotted further up the coast but none seem to have ventured down as far as Hariko, where villagers said they had not seen one for several weeks. The Japanese troops dug in on Cape Endaiadere would have a panoramic view of the Allies' movements in and around Cape Sudest but, earlier that day, when a large force of American aircraft had pounded Buna, their only opposition was from ground fire and no Japanese aircraft had ventured into the area. The consensus was that the fighting on Guadalcanal had dragged most of the enemy aircraft away to the east.

•

The *Alacrity* had dropped anchor around 500 metres from shore and around 500 metres past the little promontory that was Cape Sudest. With her relatively deep draught, it was probably about as close to the beach as she could safely go. The dropping of the anchor stimulated some activity on the beach as a motorised canvas assault boat was launched and Papuans could be seen pushing outrigger canoes towards the water. There was movement aboard the *Alacrity*, too, as orders and directions were given as to who was to do what, and what was to go where. There was such a hubbub that orders had to be shouted if they were to be heard.

By contrast, the atmosphere aboard the *Minnamurra* was calm and unruffled. There were voices, but they were quietly spoken, in conversations about what was behind, what was ahead and the qualities of the part of the world in which they now found themselves. Geoffrey Reading was having one of those conversations, chatting idly with one of the American soldiers. A few metres away, Forrest Harding was finishing a cup of coffee; he had just been informed by his aide that his evening meal was waiting for him in the aft saloon, and had stood and turned in that direction.

Reading stopped mid-sentence and Harding stopped mid-step when they – and almost everyone else aboard – heard a faint whisper of sound from the sky, a distant droning noise that steadily grew in intensity. At that sound, all aboard the *Minnamurra* stopped talking, as if on command. Heads swivelled around and upwards, looking out to sea towards the north where a number of small dots had appeared high in the sky, flying in formation and heading south.

Reading counted them to himself, and stopped at a total of seventeen. By then, the question of whose side they were on could also be answered; the blunt noses of the now-recognisable aircraft stated emphatically that they were single-engine fighter aircraft. To no one in particular, Reading said, 'They're Japanese. They're Zeros.'

●

A kilometre or more behind the *Minnamurra*, Frank Bagnall on the *Bonwin* was having a similar conversation to Reading's, but he was talking with the American colonel, Laurence McKenny. They were admiring both the scenery and the quiet when they heard the drone of aircraft and spotted the little black dots in the sky. Because neither of them had seen Japanese aircraft for several weeks, both assumed that the aircraft above were either American or Australian. The matter settled, they returned to their conversation.

●

On the Japanese barge, conditions were close and crowded and clear lines of sight were limited. When someone aboard spotted the high-flying aircraft and pointed them out to the others, the only response was someone's call of 'Good old Yanks!'

●

The seventeen aircraft flew overhead towards the south and disappeared from view for perhaps two minutes, lost in the clouds and the high country inland from Hariko. But then they reappeared, most at a much lower height than before and in groups of three. They were now coming in hard and fast and were diving straight towards the little ships spread out across the calm sea.

•

There was a kind of logic to the Zeros' attack, with the largest target – the *Alacrity* – hit first, and the other Small Ships attacked in descending order of size, which also happened to be the sequence of their final approach to Hariko.

Three Zeros attacked the *Alacrity*, each swooping down several times to pour machine gun and cannon fire into the schooner. The attacks created chaos aboard and around the ship. The assault boat that had motored out to help with the unloading turned around immediately and made a run for the beach. Although under fire, its coxswain opened up the engine for maximum speed, making it to shore and putting it up onto the beach before he abandoned it and ran into the cover of the nearby jungle.

Crouching behind ammunition boxes back on the *Alacrity* was Private First Class Bill Vana, one of the infantrymen who had been attached to the Portable Hospital. Vana had never been this scared in his life and, if he survived, he didn't believe he would ever be this scared again. Like many of the other soldiers, Vana's first impulse had been to jump into the water but – again like many of the other soldiers – he couldn't swim, so he sought the first cover he could find on the deck.

Two of the Zeros swept past so low that Vana could see the pilots in their cockpits, and it was that sight which galvanised him into action. He ran to one of the machine guns and, after working out how to operate it, emptied the magazine in the general direction of the attacking aircraft. While he looked about for more ammunition, he saw that another soldier was now firing the other machine gun at the Zeros. Vana was still scared, but not quite as scared as before.

•

Aboard the *Minnamurra*, the captain, Ted King, and the pilot, the Papuan boy with the red flower in his hair, were probably the best prepared when the Zeros began to attack them. King had watched the aircraft fly overhead through his binoculars and when he was positive they were Zeros, he stepped back into the wheelhouse, turned the trawler towards the nearest part of the beach and increased the engine speed, all without saying a word to anyone. The Papuan boy simply slipped over the side and started swimming towards the distant shoreline.

Others took a more military response to the threat from the Zeros. Jack Keegan picked up an ammunition belt and fed it into the port-side machine gun, then ran his hand along the weapon as if reassuring it. A dozen or so soldiers swore and cursed at the Japanese aircraft, but loaded and cocked their rifles and took up firing positions. Four Zeros did a flypast, looking carefully at the *Minnamurra*, then swooped up and back into a dive towards the ship. This time, all their guns were blazing.

Unlike the soldiers, Geoffrey Reading was not prepared to sell his life dearly, nor was he prepared to give it away either. His first movement had been to seek the shelter of the cabin at the stern of the *Minnamurra*; when he looked into it, though, it was small and dark and reminded him very much of a coffin, so he left. He next sought cover among the boxes stacked high amidships, but those boxes all had 'AMMUNITION' stencilled in green on them, so he kept going all the way to the ship's bow. There, he took off his boots, socks and shirt. He was a good swimmer and knew that, if he survived what was coming, he would have no problems swimming to shore.

•

A kilometre behind, the *Bonwin* was caught in the open, with no obvious escape route to safety. The reappearance of the aircraft that had previously flown over them, now in attack formation and diving steeply, prompted the realisation that they had been mistaken and that the aircraft were in fact Japanese. When that realisation hit, Laurence McKenny turned the seamanship over to the Filipino crew and ordered all those around him to go to either the large cabin aft – large being a comparative term – or to the smaller cabin forward; as soon as they were inside, they were to lie flat on the floor. McKenny, Tom Fisher and several others went back to the main cabin, while Frank Bagnall and two of the Papuan carriers went forward to the smaller cabin as the Zeros swept down.

Bagnall threw himself down as soon as he was inside, but made sure he was near the door with a clear view back along the deck. He saw the two machine gunners swivelling the weapons on their mounts, firing short bursts at the fast-moving Zeros. Then he heard and felt, rather than saw, a storm of machine gun and cannon fire raining down upon the *Bonwin*, cracking overhead and smashing into wooden decks and bulkheads.

As he tried to press himself even flatter against the floorboards, Bagnall was aware of bullets passing through the walls of the cabin as a second Zero swept past in the wake of the first. Looking out, he saw one of the machine gunners falling back slowly, bleeding profusely from a bullet wound somewhere in his abdomen. He also saw that the fuel drums at the stern of the vessel had been set alight by incendiary bullets and that the flames were spreading. A third Zero then raked the *Bonwin* from end to end with machine-gun fire, and although Bagnall's cabin was again struck several times, neither he nor the Papuans were hit.

Frank Bagnall had to make an urgent life or death decision. The second, or maybe the third, Zero had done greater damage than he realised. The boat's engine was still running, but either the captain was dead or the steering had been disabled, as the *Bonwin* was now just going around in a fairly tight circle.

There was a brief respite between attacks, and Bagnall used every second it offered. He stood and ran out onto the deck. Flame was advancing towards him, and the heat was growing intense. He paused for just a second or two. He knew his cameras and precious film were somewhere behind and below those flames and he knew that they were now lost forever. It was a momentary pause, a break in step really, and then Bagnall kept running, right up to the railing where he simply dived over, hit the water and swam as hard as he ever had in his life.

At some point, perhaps thirty seconds later, he stopped, trod water and looked back at the *Bonwin*. The fuel drums were all alight now, some exploding, and a burning river of fuel was pouring down into the main cabin. Anyone still aboard the ship was either dead or doomed. Frank Bagnall turned his back and started the long, slow swim towards the distant shore.

Mercifully, the *Bonwin* burned quickly and sank out of sight.

•

Geoffrey Reading had a front-row seat to the death of the *Bonwin*. He saw the three Zeros break away from the larger formation and dive towards the little trawler. The thin lines of tracer bullets were clearly visible against the darkening sky and he could hear clearly the deeper thud of the aircraft's cannon. There had obviously been fuel drums aboard as the *Bonwin*'s stern had exploded in flames. By then, though, those aboard the *Minnamurra* had more pressing concerns. Without the Papuan pilot to guide her, the *Minnamurra* had run up onto a coral reef, still well out from the beach. It hadn't been a violent impact, more just a loud squeal and a lurch as the ship ran up onto the shallow reef; she was now stuck fast, a sitting target for the Zeros.

With the *Bonwin* now a blazing wreck behind them, Geoffrey Reading, Ted King, Forrest Harding and all the others aboard the *Minnamurra* could do little beyond praying for deliverance and waiting for their turn to die.

8.

HARIKO

The scene aboard the *Alacrity* was one of absolute chaos. No
sooner had one aircraft swept by, spraying the boat with its
machine guns, than it was replaced by another, machine gunning
or bombing or sometimes both. It would then be replaced by a
third and a fourth until anyone who was trying to keep count
lost all track of what was happening. The noise alone was deaf-
ening and frightening for the inexperienced soldiers aboard but,
fortunately, after a while it simply became an ongoing shriek
in the background. There were noises in the foreground, too.
Men calling out in mortal agony or mortal fear, calling for their
mothers or their sweethearts, or for just someone, anyone, to
help them.

The Portable Hospital had already suffered a number of
casualties from the early strafing runs – a quick head count
revealed four dead and five wounded – and its commanding
officer, Major Parker Hardin, now ordered the rest of his men
to take to the water. The Papuan carriers had already done
just that, and were now grouped together in the water a short
distance from the *Alacrity*. As Hardin was directing his men

into the water, a bomb exploded in the middle of the group of Papuans, killing most of them instantly.

A number of infantrymen attached to the hospital stayed aboard the *Alacrity*, firing their rifles at passing aircraft in the vain hope of providing some protection for the men in the water.

Young Bill Vana was in the middle of it all. There was so much noise that he feared that he would go deaf and in among the high-pitched whines and screams he heard a deeper *whump*! Looking back, he realised the sound was that of the last little ship – the *Bonwin* – exploding in flames.

Vana felt a kind of panic taking over. The water around the boat seemed to be full of men swimming, or attempting to swim, while others simply flayed their arms and splashed the water around while calling out for help, saying they couldn't swim or simply saying some kind of prayer aloud as they suddenly real-ised their own mortality. For a while this assault on the senses almost overwhelmed him. Vana couldn't swim and had a real fear of drowning; he looked around for a lifeboat or a life vest, but couldn't see either. What he did see, though, was quite a large group of men, perhaps a dozen, milling about towards the stern of the boat and calling for help because none of them could swim.

Bill Vana decided that he was not one of them and that, if he was going to die, it would at least be while he was doing something to try to stay alive.

Nearby, one of the steel-framed canvas assault boats had been lashed to the deck and Vana thought that if he could somehow release and then launch it, he might just survive. However, it proved too heavy for him to move, and even when two other soldiers came to his assistance, they were unable to release, let alone move, the boat. By then, there were a number of dead and wounded lying on the deck nearby, and Bill Vana understood that the end was near for all of them now.

He moved across to join the group of non-swimmers at the stern of the *Alacrity*, in the shrinking space between the flames and the sea. Back behind them, the other three boats were all on fire now, but discussions and arguments still raged over what the best course of action could be. One of the men suggested they throw their packs into the water and use them to help stay afloat until they could be rescued. They should do it soon, too, as the various fires aboard the *Alacrity* were now spreading and soon the whole ship would be alight.

Vana stripped off almost completely, leaving just his socks and his watch on, believing in his state of semi-shock that they were his most important possessions. He threw a pack into the water – and watched as it immediately sank out of sight. He glanced around once more before jumping and saw that a group of soldiers had somehow managed to release the assault boat and get it into the water. Moreover, they were beginning to paddle it away from the *Alacrity*. Without hesitating, he ran across the ship to the railings and jumped as far as he could. As his feet hit the water, he stretched out with one hand and was just able to grasp the side of the assault boat. He hung on for grim death, knowing that if he let go, he would sink below the surface and never come up again. That thought alone gave him a strength he hadn't known he possessed.

•

When the *Alacrity* had anchored off Hariko, Lieutenant John Harbert, the ordnance officer, had been given the task of transferring the ammunition aboard the boat into the barge being towed behind. Harbert and a small team had filled perhaps a quarter of the space available on the barge when the Zeros swept down, forcing them to seek whatever protection they could find on the barge or in the water. When burning material from the *Alacrity* fell into the barge, Harbert grabbed it in his bare hands and threw it overboard before it could set fire to the ammunition boxes.

As well as boxes of ammunition, the barge was carrying general supplies and some of the non-medical equipment – tents, tables, lights and the like – for the establishment of the 22nd Portable Hospital with its operating theatre and support services. Some of the hospital's medical staff, joined by a number of infantrymen, had climbed down or jumped into the barge with Harbert to save as much of the irreplaceable equipment as they could.

They were soon joined by two officers, Colonel John Carew and Lieutenant Herbert Peabody, both staff officers who had remained aboard the *Alacrity*, rescuing wounded men from the flames, helping others into the water and throwing overboard any item they thought might assist the men struggling in the water below. Finished aboard the boat, they now jumped into the barge to assist there.

The *Alacrity* was doomed and Harbert and all the others knew it. Without any real discussion, Harbert, Carew and Peabody quickly climbed back onto the boat for a final sweep. They found two medical chests which they passed back down to those in the barge, and recovered a couple of badly wounded men. They, too, were passed back down into the barge, but with a lot more gentleness. Then, and only then, did the three officers return to the barge, where Harbert untied the rope that had tethered it to the *Alacrity*. Harbert asked several men to join him in the water. With some pushing and some pulling, those men slowly moved the barge through the water until it was shallow enough for them to drag the barge and its precious cargo onto the beach.

For this, and for several other actions that day, Lieutenants John Harbert and Herbert Peabody and Colonel John Carew would all later be awarded the Distinguished Service Cross.

•

The *Minnamurra*, and those aboard her, also fought hard to stay alive. Forrest Harding crouched behind ammunition boxes alongside his infantry privates, rifle in hand, firing at the attacking aircraft as they flashed past, just twenty-five metres above the water and seemingly impervious to all the bullets fired at them. Jack Keegan, manning the port-side machine gun, loosed off bursts of fire whenever a Japanese aircraft presented itself, but his gun jammed and he was struck in the leg by a bullet in quick succession. Just across the deck from where he stood, the starboard machine gunner was also hit, and slumped to the deck with what seemed a much more serious wound. Clearing the jam and ignoring the pain from his wounded leg, Keegan continued to fire at the Zeros until advancing flames forced him to abandon his post.

After the *Minnamurra* had run aground, and at Harding's direction, several soldiers moved along the boat, looking for wounded. Three of the seriously wounded they found were carried to the stern where they were gently lowered into the boat's dinghy, which had been tethered behind. Some lightly wounded and fit soldiers jumped into the water and swam to the dinghy, which they untied. Then, clinging to the sides, they began to push the dinghy towards the shore. When Harding saw that they were clear of the *Minnamurra*, he put down his rifle, took off his outer clothes and dived into the water. When he surfaced, he began to swim slowly after his men.

Elsewhere along the boat's rails, an army chaplain named Schneider had also stayed aboard until the last moment, looking for empty fuel cans which he then threw overboard to act as flotation devices for the non-swimmers, of whom he was one. He followed the last can in and began to push it towards shore.

Down towards the bow of the *Minnamurra*, Geoffrey Reading also understood that the little boat would not last much longer. He watched as another Zero dived down and flattened out just above the palm trees that framed the beach. As it lined up on the *Minnamurra*, Reading calmly climbed up onto the boat's railings and looked briefly at the water. Spotting what appeared to be a pothole in the almost solid coral below, he dived and propelled himself through the water, down as far as he thought he could go. When he briefly touched coral he stopped moving and let his body rise slowly to the surface.

After the quiet of the depths, everything on the surface suddenly seemed very loud. He could hear cries and shouts and two deep concussions as bombs exploded somewhere on the other side of the *Minnamurra*. It felt like two solid punches to his solar plexus.

Reading turned on his back and floated as he struggled out of his long pants, and then trod water as he looked around. He guessed that there was now no one alive on the *Minnamurra*, and wondered why the Zeros continued to attack a boat that was obviously abandoned and on fire. He also spotted the boat's dinghy and thought that it had probably been holed as it was sitting very low in the water.

As he watched, two Zeros in succession came in low and fast and Reading believed they were actually aiming at him, so he again dived as deep as he could; when he surfaced, the aircraft had disappeared. He then realised that the dinghy had been their target, as the men who had been hanging onto the sides of it had also swum away before the attack and were just now returning to it. From the shouts and calls for help, it seemed that one of the wounded who had been placed in the dinghy and one of the non-swimmers who had been hanging on to its sides had both been hit in the attack.

With a sense of shock, Reading realised as well that it was now growing dark quite rapidly. The two-masted schooner that had been ahead of them, the *Alacrity*, now resembled an enormous bonfire and, by swivelling around in the water, he could see that the little Japanese barge was also on fire.

As Reading turned towards the shore, two Zeros swept over the jungle fringing the beach, spraying it with cannon and machine-gun fire. Then they swept up into a steep climb to join the others already much higher up in the sky. With the sun glinting on their wings and fuselages, they rejoined the formation, which soon disappeared to the north-east.

•

Frank Bagnall swam as hard as he had ever swum in his life to get away from the *Bonwin* and the horrors he knew it held. Like Reading, he stopped in the water and looked around to both get his bearings and to see what was happening elsewhere.

About 200 metres away, sitting low in the water because it was obviously holed and equally obviously empty, sat the *Bonwin*'s dinghy and Bagnall decided to swim across to it. The rope that had tethered it to the Bonwin was still trailing in the water, and he assumed that it had either burned or been shot through. The dinghy had indeed been holed by bullets or shrapnel but was otherwise in good condition and seemed unlikely to sink. Bagnall pulled himself up and over the side and made himself comfortable inside.

The oars and rowlocks were still where they had been carefully stowed, so he put them in place, gripped the oars and began to row towards a group of survivors whose heads he could see bobbing up and down in the water some distance away. As soon as the dinghy moved forward, water began to spill in through some of the holes in its upper sides, so he stopped again. He plugged the two largest holes he could find with his socks and a smaller hole with his handkerchief. It worked; the water coming in was reduced to a trickle, so he took up the oars again and continued rowing.

As Frank Bagnall rowed, he noted in the middle distance that the *Alacrity* and the *Minnamurra* were both burning brightly but were also still being attacked by passing aircraft. When he thought about just how bright the flames and tracer bullets were, Bagnall, too, realised that it was starting to grow dark.

The men in the water he came across included both of the machine gunners from the *Bonwin*, each suffering from wounds they had sustained in the opening minutes of the attack. One had suffered a leg wound – something Bagnall had not seen occur – and was inconvenienced but was still able to operate almost normally, but the second man had a bad stomach wound which would require treatment as soon as possible if he was to survive. Nearby were two of the *Bonwin*'s Papuan carriers; between them they were able to lift the badly wounded soldier into the dinghy. The increased weight when they were all aboard meant that water sloshed into the boat from a number of holes that Bagnall had been unable to plug, threatening to sink the dinghy if something wasn't done to stop the flow.

Bagnall found that by changing positions in the dinghy, bailing constantly with their hands and having one person in the water at all times, they were able to make reasonable progress.

He guessed it was around 7 p.m. when they finally started for the shoreline, which he estimated was around two kilometres distant. Those who could took it in turns to row and swim, but it still seemed to take a very long time to get close to the beach. Finally, the swimmer said that the water was now shallow enough to stand up in. All but the badly wounded soldier jumped out into the water and pushed the dinghy through the shallows and up onto the sand. They found a suitable place at the back of the beach to lay the wounded man down, and all lay down near him.

Frank Bagnall knew that they would be found sooner or later but for now all he wanted to do was sleep.

•

With the *Alacrity* burning like a Roman candle behind him, Bill Vana was determined that he would not let go of the assault boat no matter what happened. He guessed there were about ten men already crammed into the boat and three or four others like himself hanging onto the sides with grim determination and wishing they were inside. When a space did present itself as the passengers crowded closer together, Bill quickly climbed aboard and grabbed a paddle that someone had dropped. Someone else plucked an oar out of the water and they began to paddle towards the shore just a few hundred metres away.

As they did so, a Zero suddenly dived towards them and opened fire. All aboard quickly jumped over the side and into the water. Vana almost drowned when two other non-swimmers grabbed him and started to drag him under. Fortunately, they let him go when he began kicking them as hard as he could underwater. As he did so, he spotted his best friend, Herb Grew, in the water nearby. Grew was another non-swimmer and he had left his uniform on when he had jumped into the water. Vana called out to Grew, but his friend's eyes were focused on something in the distance and he gave no sign of recognition. As Bill Vana watched, his best friend quietly slipped beneath the water. Vana watched and watched the spot where his friend had disappeared but he didn't come to the surface again.

Bill Vana was now one of many bobbing and floating in the water, all seemingly crying out for help. He knew that if he went under he would certainly drown, so he put all his energy into finding ways to stay afloat. He soon grew tired from these efforts and was beginning to feel dispirited as well; it seemed that no matter what he did, the shoreline was further away than it was when he first dived in. But, as he looked at that shoreline, he and several others could see the shape of a small boat at the back of the beach. The men began calling out at the tops of the voices for someone to get into the boat and row out to rescue them.

•

After the crescendo of noise had died away, the silence around Geoffrey Reading took on an eerie, almost menacing quality. He listened hard, but could hear little beyond the sound of his own laboured breathing.

The *Minnamurra* was a wreck; the wheelhouse had been largely shot away and the amidships region had been gouged and splintered. Bobbing incongruously alongside the wreck were two of the Zeros' belly tanks, empty and shining in the reflected light. Reading swam slowly towards the beach, staggering through waist-high water for the last thirty metres before collapsing on the sand. Looking across what was now a calm sea, he was able to pinpoint all four of the Small Ships because three were burning furiously and the fourth, the *Bonwin*, had left survivors, smoke and debris to mark where she had once been. The three ships still burning looked, he thought, like large beacons warning of the hell to come.

•

Nearby, frantic efforts were being made to save as many of the survivors from the stricken *Minnamurra* as possible. The vessel's dinghy was well clear of the wreck, and both Harding and Laux swam across to it. There was enough room for both of them aboard but neither stayed in the dinghy for long. Firstly, Harding spotted a young soldier floundering in the water nearby. He climbed over the side and swam across to the young man, calming him down before helping him across and into the dinghy. Harding then chose to remain in the water.

Colonel Laux also returned to the water, making more space in the dinghy for wounded and shocked soldiers. What made this even more noteworthy was that Laux was a non-swimmer himself. It made no difference to him; using anything that floated, he paddled around, finding wounded men and other non-swimmers before somehow shepherding them back to the *Minnamurra*'s dinghy. By the time he and Harding finished assisting those in trouble, the dinghy was very crowded and sitting very low in the water. Five further survivors were in the water clinging to the stern, while others were holding onto the sides. As it grew dark, those in the water began to push the dinghy towards the shoreline, a little over a kilometre away.

•

The Japanese barge was the smallest of the four Small Ships and the furthest back in the little line they had made, but that didn't save it from the fury of the attack. While some aboard took advantage of whatever cover they could find, it was really no cover at all in a confined and exposed space. Others fought back. American infantrymen and Australian artillerymen used their rifles, and the barge's two machine guns were brought into action. One man, the Australian gunner Allen King, rested a Bren gun against the side of the barge and fired long bursts at the aircraft, pausing to change magazines before resuming his firing. However, this considerable firepower did little, if anything, to delay the inevitable.

In one of its passes, machine-gun fire from a Zero tore into some fuel drums, causing a fire which quickly spread. As it took hold, someone – either Captain Mueller or maybe even Albert Waldron himself – called out the order to abandon ship. In the scramble that followed, men dropped anything they thought might impede them in the water and climbed over the barge's sides to either jump or simply fall into the water. The last to leave was Allen King, throwing the now-useless Bren gun aside and following the others into the water.

Sixteen of those who made it into the water were carrying wounds they had sustained in the attack. In the barge behind them they left the bodies of one American and three Australian gunners, John Weatherston, Louis Bearden and John McDonald. Two other Australians, Roy Young and Stewart Shaw, both died shortly after entering the water. The survivors' ordeal was not over yet, though. Since the barge was the last in the line, the survivors were faced with the greatest distance to swim to shore or, if they chose to stay where they were, the longest wait for possible rescue.

Waiting was not a realistic option in the rapidly failing light. Organised by Waldron, the headquarters observer Harold Handy and the senior Australian Charles Mueller, the survivors came together and looked firstly for anything that would assist them in the water. The barge had no lifeboats and no dinghy trailing behind, so anything that floated was collected and brought to where the largest group of survivors had gathered.

One of those survivors was an Australian gunner named Paul O'Neill, who had suffered a nasty head wound. Despite this, he swam away from the main group, looking around until he found his best friend, who had also been wounded. O'Neill supported, cajoled and encouraged his mate until they both made it to shore several hours later. Both would later be able to share in the joke that O'Neill's only motivation in saving his friend was to make sure he recovered some money he was owed.

Another Australian who survived unscathed was a man named Tommy Hale. Perhaps the strongest swimmer among the survivors, Hale recovered an empty, wooden Bren gun case, which he used as a flotation device. Realising there were survivors in much greater need than him, he then used it to support three wounded soldiers, and pulled them towards the shoreline by hooking one of his feet through the case's carrying loop. He also attached his group to four American wounded who had found an empty fuel drum and were supporting themselves with that.

•

The struggles of the soldiers, sailors and carriers had been witnessed by dozens of pairs of eyes ashore. Among those observers was Don Caswell, an American United Press war correspondent who had landed at Hariko earlier in the day with Hanford MacNider's headquarters troops. After looking around, settling in and making some preliminary notes about the build-up to the Buna assault, he found a spot in the shade overlooking the waters off Hariko late in the afternoon. From that vantage point among the coconut trees, he watched the Japanese attack on the Small Ships.

Caswell had counted twenty-three Japanese aircraft, but couldn't be certain of either the number or type because it quickly developed into what he believed was the most intense and concentrated aerial attack on a small number of ships yet seen in the war. At one point, eight aircraft had flown directly above where he crouched as they lined up to attack the ships offshore. He still shuddered later when he thought of what might have occurred if just one of them had spotted MacNider's camp among the trees.

His best view was of the *Alacrity* and the *Minnamurra*, and he had seen both boats destroyed before his eyes. He knew there were another two vessels further out because he had seen the Japanese aircraft diving down on them, too, and had also seen the bright flames lighting up the darkening sky. As soon as the last of the aircraft had departed the area, he relaxed and started gathering his thoughts about what he had just witnessed. He was jotting down the notes that would form his first newswire report when the first rescuers ran down the beach and the first survivors staggered ashore.

•

The beach in front of Hariko, which had been so quiet during the attack, now sprang into life. A number of boats, including dinghies, canvas assault boats and native outriggers, were dragged from beneath the trees and down to the water's edge, where they were pushed into the water by a number of soldiers, some Australian, some American. They were rowed and paddled out into the gathering gloom and could soon be seen dragging men from the water. The calls of those wanting to be rescued could be heard faintly above the sound of waves breaking on the beach and, as the light faded, the flames from the *Alacrity* and the *Minnamurra* provided enough light to see the boats, if not the bobbing heads of the survivors.

One of those bobbing heads belonged to Bill Vana, who believed that the collective prayers of those around him had been answered when he saw two men come out of the trees and manhandle a dinghy across the beach and into the water. By now, he was almost completely spent and, although he called out to the men after they launched the boat, he wasn't certain whether they had heard him; besides, his entire focus was now on simply staying alive from minute to minute. Then, without any warning, he felt strong hands under his arms and the next thing he was being hoisted into the dinghy by two men who spoke to him with broad, flat Australian accents, asking him if he was all right.

Within just a few minutes, he was more than all right and so asked the Australians if he could help them. For the next quarter of an hour, the three men rowed around in a relatively small area of open water. At the end of that time, they had twenty-five people in the boat and another five hanging onto the sides; they simply couldn't accommodate any more people and so turned around and rowed back to shore. When all their passengers were safely on the beach, the two Australians turned the boat around and rowed back out into what was now semi-darkness to look for more survivors.

Bill Vana's was just one of many rescues and attempted rescues that evening. Further along the beach, four Australians had carried an assault boat from the trees and down the beach to the water before rowing out to what was left of the *Alacrity*.

They spotted four American soldiers huddled at the ship's rails near the bow watching the fire creep ever closer to them. The Australians called out to the Americans to jump and they would pick them up. Between their boat and the *Alacrity*, the water was on fire as an oil slick burned. The Americans would have to either try to jump over it or dive right through the flames and swim underwater until they were past it. The Americans were not prepared to do either; all four died on the ship.

Earlier that day, the Australian 1st Mountain Battery had moved their howitzers from Cape Sudest to a new position some 500 metres north of Hariko in the jungle. A number of the gunners were also beachside when the boats were attacked and they, too, sprang into action as soon as the aircraft had cleared the area. Led by a bombardier named Les Snape, a group of them grabbed two canvas boats and joined in the search and rescue operation. There were simply too many men clamouring to be rescued, but the gunners did what they could and, when their boats were full, they also returned to the beach before setting out again. Snape himself dived in several times to rescue soldiers but his scariest moment came when he was back in his boat. He was pulling an American soldier aboard no more than 300 metres offshore when the man was suddenly pulled from his grasp, disappearing underwater. It was a shark. Although others were believed to have been taken by sharks, this was the only loss that could be confirmed.

Long before the boats stopped looking for live bodies in the water, the survivors themselves had started to struggle ashore. Those from the *Alacrity* were the first to arrive. The survivors who pushed the *Alacrity*'s barge were among those early arrivals and, once they had run the barge up onto the beach, they helped the wounded up into the palm trees fringing the beach and made them comfortable before returning to unload the supplies they had been able to salvage.

Major Parker Hardin then moved further inland with some of his Portable Hospital medical staff, seeking somewhere suitable to establish an aid post and, when he found a site, sending some of his men back to the beach to find whatever had been saved of their medical supplies and equipment.

While Hardin's men were setting up their medical facility, Bill Vana and the more than twenty of his fellow survivors who had been aboard or alongside the Australians' dinghy also came ashore – most of them, like Vana, either naked or wearing nothing but underclothes. A number were also carrying wounds they had sustained either in the attack or from coral they had bumped into while in the water. They were followed soon after by those who had made it onto the *Minnamurra*'s dinghy and then by the survivors from the *Minnamurra* who had managed to swim ashore unaided.

The two generals, Forrest Harding and Albert Waldron, had both managed to swim ashore from their respective boats, and they soon attracted an entourage, some seeking directions, others seeking information but most seeking nothing more than reassurance. The fact that their commanding general was issuing orders while wearing nothing but his underpants did not seem incongruous to anyone who was there.

Others from Waldron's Japanese barge, Tommy Hale and Paul O'Neill among them, managed to keep pretty well together and, after four hours in the water, made it to the beach between Hariko and Cape Sudest. Hearing voices in the jungle, a small group set off to investigate and found the voices came from an American outpost. They had survived.

Back towards Hariko, another survivor made it to shore wearing only his underpants. Geoffrey Reading was tired from his long swim to shore from the *Minnamurra* but he was also heavy-hearted from what he had seen and from what he hadn't seen but guessed had happened on board the *Bonwin*. Reading made his way out of the water and up the beach to the trees that fringed it and sat down there, staring out at the burning remains of the little fleet.

Some American soldiers suddenly appeared from the undergrowth behind where he was sitting, one of them asking what had happened. Reading felt an unreasoning anger at what he thought was the insensitivity of the question, and was about to snap back a sarcastic answer. He realised, though, that the Americans themselves had been scared out of their wits by what they had seen, and that the question had been asked out of naivety and nervousness as much as out of curiosity.

He mumbled an answer and, as he did, one of the other Americans gave him a cigarette while two others produced items of clothing, a pair of pants and a jumper, both of which he put on before excusing himself and walking back down to the water's edge where he simply stared out at the burning boats. At some stage during the night, the Australian Army Public Relations man, Keith Black, suddenly appeared on the beach in front of Reading, limping from a leg wound and repeating aloud, 'The bastards, the bastards.' Reading spoke to him, commiserated with him over the friends and colleagues they may have lost that day, but then had to walk away.

He found a packet of cigarettes one of the Americans had given him and walked back to the spot where he had been sitting when he first made it to shore. There, he sat down again and smoked cigarette after cigarette, looking out at the sea and at the ships, still burning brightly, and let his mind go blank.

•

Long before the last survivor had staggered ashore at Hariko, the Japanese aircraft and airmen responsible for the attack had landed at Rabaul and compiled their after-action reports. The attack had been carried out by a mixed force of Val dive-bombers and Zero fighters despatched earlier in the afternoon on a search and destroy mission against the Allied forces building up around the Buna–Sanananda–Gona stronghold. The nine Vals and six of the Zeros came from one unit, the 582nd Kokutai of the Imperial Japanese Navy. The other six Zeros, which had flown as top cover during the attack, were from another naval unit, the 252nd Kokutai.

Both units' commanders agreed that it had been a copybook attack and ordered that it be used as a practical example in all future unit training.

•

At Hariko, the generals and the colonels, and their respective staff officers, were up late trying to understand the scale of the losses they had suffered that day and what those losses might mean for the immediate future. It was clear that the day had been a disaster on several levels. A lot of good men had been lost, not the least of whom was Laurence McKenny. His skills as the division's quartermaster would be sorely missed, as would his knowledge about the capacity of the various supply dumps he had set up and how the Small Ships would operate to bring supplies from those dumps forward to MacNider's fighting men.

The *Alacrity* was probably the major loss because of all the ammunition she was carrying, ammunition that continued to explode and shoot up into the heavens throughout the night. The early calculations were that McKenny and around twenty American soldiers had been killed, plus up to ten Australians and around thirty of the Papuan carriers that were on board all the boats except the Japanese barge. A number of the correspondents and cameramen were also missing. The loss of the barge and its contents was also a setback as the two 25-pound artillery pieces it carried were vital to the initial assault on the Japanese positions. All the ammunition for those pieces had also gone down with the barge. Most of the rations being brought forward for MacNider's men were also gone. The only supplies that had been saved were the boxes of ammunition in the *Alacrity*'s barge and two boxes of medical equipment, all of which would also have been lost if not for the efforts of John Harbert and his men.

As the raw numbers were being totalled up in MacNider's headquarters hut, nearby another kind of calculation was also being undertaken, this one a calculation of how many of the wounded could be saved: who would live and who would die.

On flat land between coconut palms, the 22nd Portable Hospital had set up a makeshift surgery, protected from rain by canvas and lit by army torches and the flickering light of the burning ships offshore. The wounded walked or were carried in, and all received the most sympathetic care and the best treatment that compassionate medical staff and two boxes of surgical instruments and medicines could provide. The staff worked throughout the night dealing with the more than 100 wounded who had made it to shore. Among the survivors of the 22nd, Parker Hardin was clearly the senior officer. He had an officer's bearing and was also the only one there dressed in regulation army shorts.

•

Well away from the beach at Hariko, two other activities were taking place out of sight of the senior officers. One was in the American lines inland where, within an hour of the attack ending, every soldier had dug himself some kind of shelter using anything that was at hand. With small trenching shovels, knives, bayonets, mess kits, helmets and even bare hands, the men dug holes as deep as they could, aware now of just how deadly aerial attacks could be.

Further away, some kilometres to the north, in the heart of the Japanese positions, a group of Japanese soldiers and engineers met at the beach to prepare the landing area and inland tracks that would be used by the 1000 fresh reinforcements from Rabaul who were being brought down by fast destroyers some time after dark.

•

Daylight at Hariko on 17 November revealed that the hulks of the *Alacrity* and the *Minnamurra*, although burned down to the waterline, were still smouldering; there was no sign of either the *Bonwin* or the Japanese barge, which might never have existed for all that was left of them. The *Alacrity*'s barge had been pulled well up the beach to the protection of overhanging palm trees, which was just as well as daylight also brought back a flight of Zeros, either attracted by the smoke or the memory of the previous day's easy pickings. They searched for new targets but there was nothing at sea and nothing to see on the land. They made a couple of strafing runs over the jungle fringing the beach, firing almost for the fun of it. Some of the huts now sheltering the wounded were hit, but there were no further casualties. The Zeros then disappeared towards the south, hoping for better hunting there.

•

Frank Bagnall walked into the bustle of activity in and around Hariko at midday. After he'd made it ashore with the wounded men in the dinghy in the early hours of the morning, he had promptly found a quiet place where he had gone to sleep. When the sun was well up, he decided to complete his journey to Hariko on foot. He walked around the bustling little village, looking for familiar faces but, apart from a few he recognised from earlier contacts, there was no one he knew really well. He had been hoping against hope that Tom Fisher would somehow appear, but realised that it was a foolish hope as no one could have survived the inferno that the *Bonwin* became.

All his films and equipment had gone with the *Bonwin* and there was nothing to keep him at Hariko so he decided to walk back to Embogo along the beach. He did not travel alone. A number of the Australian gunners who survived the sinking of the Japanese barge had also decided to head back. They were able to borrow some American clothing, while a few had some rations they were willing to share as well as some personal items. They put these into sandbags they had found, dropping everything in, tying the neck and then slinging the sandbag over their shoulders. Bagnall figured the little group would be back at Embogo around the time the evening meal would be served.

•

At the end of that day, 17 November, a gentle rain fell on and around Hariko well into the night. The rain finally brought an end to what remained of the fires that had slowly consumed the *Alacrity* and the *Minnamurra*; by the morning, nothing would remain.

With the rain that night came another Small Ship, the *Kelton*, which arrived without any fanfare, signalling her presence to those on shore with a signal lamp and recognition signs. It was close to midnight, and when her signals were answered correctly from the shore, the *Kelton* came in as close as Ireneo Ames dared bring her. A number of assault boats and outrigger canoes were paddled out through the gentle rain, returning with boxes of ammunition and crates of rations. When all had been brought ashore, those same assault boats and canoes began making trips back out to the *Kelton*, taking a more precious cargo, human beings wounded on other Small Ships just over twenty-four hours earlier. The *Kelton* would carry them back to Embogo where another Portable Hospital, the 14th, was setting up its own medical centre.

The *Kelton* was small even for a Small Ship, with limited deck space, so it could carry only a dozen wounded on that trip. It wouldn't do to crowd the wounded too close together. Two other passengers boarded as well, Forrest Harding and Herbert Laux, both returning to their respective headquarters to report on what they had seen and learned from their excursions to Hariko. Harding was also trying to understand what the attack meant for the well-crafted plans of MacArthur and his staff.

9.

INTO THE MAELSTROM

By any measure, the loss of the four Small Ships off Hariko during the late afternoon and evening of 16 November was a disaster. It would be some time before the final accounting of the losses would be made, but by dawn on 17 November the extent of the disaster was staring both Forrest Harding and Hanford MacNider in the face.

The coastal task force, Warren Force, had suffered more than 150 casualties: at least twenty-four American servicemen were dead, five Australian gunners and twenty-eight Papuan carriers were confirmed dead or missing, with double those numbers wounded. One Australian war correspondent and the Filipino crew of the *Bonwin* were also missing, and no one was in any doubt that they would never be found. All of MacNider's reserve ammunition, which would have been sufficient to support the first week of MacNider's assault on Buna, had been lost. Most of the heavy weapons needed to support that assault, the 25-pound field guns and the 81-millimetre mortars, had been lost along with the guns' ammunition and several of the gunners.

McKenny, the quartermaster who was overseeing the deployment of rations, supplies and ammunition to the forward and rear dumps, was also missing, believed killed, while the task force's only self-sustaining medical unit was basically out of action until its lost equipment and missing staff could be replaced.

As worrying as those losses were, the fact that a vital part of Harding's supply line had been destroyed carried even more import.

The loss of the schooner, two trawlers and the motorised barge placed even greater pressure on the remaining Small Ships available for the Oro Bay – Hariko shuttle run. The *Kelton*, *Two Freddies* and *Willyama II* would have to sail the route almost continuously, stopping at the various dumps and bringing up as many troops as they could manage in the hours, or even days, before the ships that had been sunk could be replaced. If they couldn't, and if there was a delay in replacing the lost ships, the offensive simply could not go ahead.

There were other Small Ships en route to Milne Bay or en route from there to Oro Bay and Porlock Harbour, but no one was certain when they would join Harding's movement forward. And both Harding and Hanford MacNider needed everything *now!*

•

Early on the morning of 17 November, just down the coast from Hariko at Embogo, Ralph Andrews supervised the loading of additional ammunition and other supplies to accompany the 110 American infantrymen he already had on board on one of those remaining Small Ships, the *Two Freddies*. Just as Andrews was easing away from his mooring with his overloaded boat, he spotted three Zero fighters and three Val dive-bombers and, with a sinking feeling in his heart, realised that there was precious little he could do to prevent what he knew was about to happen. Even so, he would give it everything he had. Calling out a warning to both his crew and the soldiers aboard, Andrews opened up the *Two Freddies'* throttle as wide as it would go.

Deprived of a target at Hariko minutes earlier, the Japanese aircraft moved into an attack formation as soon as they spotted the little trawler. Ralph Andrews knew a lot about boats, and he knew that it would not be possible for him to either outrun or outmanoeuvre the attackers; his boat was simply too slow and cumbersome for either, so there was no point in making a run for the open sea. The only chance of saving the boat, its passengers and crew, and all the supplies they were carrying, lay in making a beeline for the shore and beaching the boat. And so, as the machine gunners and several of the soldiers who carried weapons blazed away at the aircraft, which were moving into the attack runs, Andrews drove as hard for the beach as the *Two Freddies* could take him.

With a series of loud groans and bumps, the trawler came to a gradual halt short of the beach, but it stopped in water shallow enough for all aboard to be able to splash ashore and then run across the beach to the cover of the trees. The *Two Freddies* was stuck hard, but of the 100-plus soldiers and crew aboard her, only five were injured by enemy fire and only one of those seriously.

•

The six Japanese aircraft ceased their attacks on the grounded *Two Freddies* when they spotted another small ship chugging along further out to sea. It was the *Kelton*, en route from Mendaropu to Hariko. The ship's log noted that six Japanese aircraft were sighted at 0800 hours and that the *Kelton* was under intermittent attack for the next thirty minutes. A combination of good seamanship, poor marksmanship and sheer good luck meant that the *Kelton* would survive those thirty minutes with no casualties and, apart from some cannon shell holes in her stern, no significant damage.

•

Fifteen kilometres south of Embogo was the equally tiny village of Mendaropu, the site of both Forrest Harding's headquarters and a large cache of munitions and supplies. That morning, it was also home to the trawler *Willyama II*, whose skipper, Jack Simcock, was also just heading out to sea with a full load of supplies and a squad of infantrymen, all bound for Hariko. When Simcock spotted a flight of Japanese aircraft moving into attack positions, he did exactly the same as Ralph Andrews had done over half an hour earlier. Pushing for as much speed as the trawler could possibly make, Simcock spun the wheel and headed directly towards the Mendaropu beach.

The result was almost a carbon copy of the *Two Freddies* at Embogo. The *Willyama II*, grounded in the sand short of the beach, and all aboard were able to scramble through the shallows and across the beach to shelter. There was one difference from the earlier attack, though. Possibly frustrated by the morning's relative lack of success, the Zeros each made strafing runs over the stranded *Willyama II* before rejoining the bombers and flying away to the north-east.

An examination of the *Two Freddies* later in the day showed that, while there was some structural damage to the hull and quite a lot of battle damage to the superstructure, the former was not fatal and the latter was mainly superficial. The boat was repairable, and she was floated and fishtailed into deeper water on the high tide. Ralph Andrews nursed the *Two Freddies* back to Jack Savage's slipway and repair facilities at Milne Bay. The *Willyama II* had sustained considerably more damage and, while she was still seaworthy, her engine was damaged, her rudder was questionable and she needed a complete overhaul. Jack Simcock took her back to the Small Ships dockyard at Milne Bay, too, but it was at the end of a towrope.

By midday on 17 November, Forrest Harding had just one Small Ship on the Hariko run, the *Kelton*, to support the opening of the offensive against Buna scheduled to begin early the next day.

•

Back at COSC Headquarters in Port Moresby, Dwight Johns and his staff also recognised the scale of the disaster that had befallen the Small Ships' north coast supply operations, and took immediate action. During the following day, 17 November, a flurry of orders and directions were fired off. Three of the Small Ships then at Milne Bay – Clarrie Dawes' *Leprena*, the *Torres* and the *Moreton* – were ordered to depart for Pongani at 11 p.m. that night to replace the lost vessels. Any troops the vessels were carrying were to be offloaded at Pongani; they could march to Hariko. From that point forward, the Small Ships would carry supplies to replace those lost the previous day. The orders also contained the admonition that, 'Small Ships must, repeat must, operate forward of Porlock at night only.'

It was clear that it would be several days at least before the maritime supply line could be brought back into full operation, and a number of short-term measures were put in place to bridge that period. Laurence McKenny's replacement, Major Ralph Birkness, was in Port Moresby and immediately approached George Kenney's Air Force headquarters for urgent and immediate assistance to get supplies north. That assistance was offered but it came with restrictions. The airstrip at Dobodura was almost ready, but was not yet suitable for air operations, while the airstrip at Wanigela was too far away and was, in fact, in the process of being abandoned as an operational base. Supplies for the Buna campaign would therefore have to be airdropped, with all the losses that entailed. Kenney's transport aircraft would also require fighter escorts, meaning those aircraft would not be available to protect the Small Ships; night operations were therefore the only realistic option.

•

When Forrest Harding learned of the attacks and the beaching of both the *Two Freddies* and the *Willyama II*, he was reported as saying, 'That finishes the Red Arrow freighters.' He knew that it didn't – there were dozens more in a pipeline stretching back to Sydney – but he knew as well that his fragile supply line had just been stretched to breaking point.

Much of what had been lost on 16/17 November could be replaced in a relatively short time, but the losses also meant that MacNider's task force would be expected to go into battle with virtually no heavy weapons, limited reserves of ammunition and only enough rations for a day or two. Harding asked for the attack to be postponed, and it was, but only until 19 November. The other two thrusts of the three-pronged attack were at their starting lines: the Australians at Gona, and the second American task force, Urbana Force, inland from Buna; they could not be held in readiness for much longer given the conditions under which they were all operating.

MacArthur approved the postponement but his patience with Forrest Harding, like the supply line, was starting to wear thin.

•

Irrespective of anything else, the Buna offensive would open at
dawn on 19 November 1942, and the full might of the US Army in
the South West Pacific Area was put into action to make it happen.

All the Small Ships in the New Guinea theatre, and those
already on the way, were urged forward to Milne Bay and from
there to Oro Bay and beyond. There was also an increased
effort to use George Kenney's air forces to fill the temporary gap
created by the loss of so many Small Ships. An assumption was
made that the new airfield at Dobodura would overcome most
of the supply problems when it opened on 21 November, but
that assumption was built on others, like the weather remaining
clear for flying, no aircraft losses through enemy action and the
ability of the aircraft to operate at full capacity for long periods.
None of these assumptions were based on the realities of the
New Guinea theatre of operations.

A lot of hope was attached to the idea that the troops could
be supplied through airdrops, but when these were ramped up
it soon became obvious that Kenney's claims were well off-track,
both figuratively and literally. The problems sometimes began
even before take-off, with weather conditions delaying, and at
other times preventing, the transport aircraft from even getting
off the ground. On 19 November, for instance, heavy rain at
Port Moresby stopped all flights on the day the Buna offensive
commenced. If the planes did get into the air, they faced the
immediate dangers inherent in flying over the Owen Stanley
Ranges and, on flights to and from the north coast airfields and
drop zones, the ever-present danger of Zeros.

The early supply and resupply drops revealed even more
problems. The supplies were either dropped inaccurately or the

parachutes carried them into inaccessible terrain so often that it sometimes took ground troops a full day to recover just 20 per cent of what had been dropped. Despite the best intentions, and the best packing, fragile ordnance like 81-millimetre mortar rounds were always damaged when they landed. Any foodstuffs with damaged packaging would be spoiled by the end of the day.

•

If there weren't enough problems, when the offensive began on 19 November, it stalled just beyond the jump-off points. The terrain and the weather, plus the inexperience of the American troops involved, had probably made it inevitable. All over the Buna–Sanananda–Gona front, the only approaches to the Japanese positions were along the paths that already existed in the area. Those paths were on the highest land, highest being a relative term as the swamps all around them were now full of water from the seasonal rains. Thus it was that the Australian and American attacks became 'canalised': forced into very narrow fronts along the only possible attack routes.

After four months of waiting, the Japanese were very familiar with the area, knew the attack routes the Allies would be forced to follow, and had built their defences accordingly. All the approaches were covered by interlocking fire from well-prepared and mutually supporting positions. Those strongholds were dug as deep as the water table would allow, heavily reinforced at the front and sides and with overhead protection from thick tree trunks and steel drums filled with sand. Well camouflaged in the first place, the fast-growing jungle now made them almost impossible to see. They were the kind of defences that were impervious to anything but a direct hit from a large aerial bomb or a number of hits from field artillery.

On MacNider's front, that heavy artillery was now rusting in the waters off Hariko.

As well, the troops involved were as green as their newly dyed fatigues. The 32nd Division had had no meaningful jungle training before being flown to the jungles that would be their battlefield. With the loss of the Small Ships at Hariko, the main body of infantrymen who would carry the attack was landed at Pongani and then expected to march to their jump-off positions before Buna. A journalist who joined one group on that march has left a telling description of the troops on who so much depended:

The American boys in their mottled green uniforms eventually got going on the long trail up the coast. Then for the first time they realised what jungle warfare really could mean without actual combat. They staggered along with sixty pounds each on their backs under a broiling New Guinea sun that was frequently obscured by sudden torrential downpours. But the rain brought little relief to the sweltering soldiers because after a rain, the jungles in the lowlands were turned into dank, steaming morasses that dragged them down to their hips in their sticky, slimy embrace. Sharp, stiff undergrowth shredded their clothing and tore legs, arms and faces.

On top of all this were the myriad insect pests of the jungle – swarms of malarial mosquitoes which could bite through thick drill trousers, land crabs of all kinds, voracious large brown ants and persistent sandflies and leeches.

The boys were caked with slimy mud that covered them from head to foot. But they could always wash or swim in any of the numerous little streams they had to wade through, and there

*they had nothing to worry about except the crocodiles, which
even the natives feared more than sharks.*

When, in response to a stream of questions from headquarters
asking why the American troops were not advancing, Forrest
Harding outlined the realities described above, adding that
there was now a chronic shortage of basic supplies, MacArthur
read the messages, replied in sometimes harsh and intemperate
language, and began the process that would inevitably lead to
the replacement of Harding with someone more attuned to his
commanding general.

●

For the remainder of November, the 32nd Division made practically no progress in its attempt to overwhelm the Japanese
defences; the advance on Buna was no advance at all.

In those eleven days, the Americans confronting the Japanese
were also confronting many of the other harsh realities of jungle
warfare at the end of a fragile supply line. For one thing, they were
slowly starving. By the end of the first few days of fighting, their
rations had been reduced to a single can of bully beef and a bar of
hard chocolate a day. Some had even taken to seeking out edible
bush tucker in the jungle. Their boots and clothing, and much
of their accoutrements, were rotting in the damp heat and many
– far too many – had nothing to sleep under at night.

Not only were they tired and demoralised; increasing numbers
were suffering from tropical diseases and vitamin deficiency-
related ailments. There was little or no medicine available to
treat the sick, just as there was little or no gun oil to prevent
their weapons from rusting and seizing up. There was not a lot
of ammunition for those weapons anyway.

•

Although the airstrip at Dobodura was operational from 21 November, the weather and other circumstances limited its use. Parachute drops were proving to be largely ineffective; by the end of November, just under sixty tons of freight had been brought in by air for the American troops in front of Buna. The *Alacrity* had been carrying almost twice that amount when she was sunk and even the smallest trawlers in the Small Ships fleet could carry up to thirty tons on each trip. If Buna was to be taken, the Small Ships' supply line had to be restored.

•

The Small Ships' chain of command, from the irascible Dwight Johns down, prepared itself for a maximum effort to support the struggling troops. Increasing numbers and types of small ships were pushing towards both Milne Bay and then Oro Bay from Port Moresby, Townsville and Sydney. Among the competing and sometimes conflicting priorities, the failure to make any inroads against the Japanese positions on the opening day of the offensive meant that the delivery of artillery and ammunition was at the top of the list.

For the opening of the offensive, the only artillery pieces available to support Hanford MacNider's Warren Force were the two Australian mountain howitzers that Albert Waldron had pushed forward on the Japanese barge to Cape Sudest the evening before the disaster off Hariko. They were probably better suited to the accompanying attack on the Japanese positions at Cape Endaiadere, where the terrain suited their capabilities, but they were also used to support the attacks on Buna.

Additional artillery was on the way. On 21 November, two more 25-pound pieces were delivered to Oro Bay aboard the *Karsik*, one of the Dutch freighters that had been transferred to the Allies when the Netherlands East Indies were overrun by Japanese forces. There, they were dismantled and, using a boat 'borrowed' from the *Leprena*, taken across to the *Kelton* where they were loaded aboard along with ammunition and as many boxes of rations as could be squeezed aboard. The *Kelton* departed Oro Bay at 11 p.m., stopped at Embogo to collect Albert Waldron and then, rather than offloading at Hariko, took the cargo to another point, the creek mouth at Boreo, around one kilometre north of Hariko. They arrived there shortly after 1 a.m. and landing the guns proved difficult as the sea was quite choppy. The only craft available were canvas assault boats but, with a good deal of pushing and shoving, and accompanying language, the field guns, ammunition and stores were all brought ashore. The material dropped off was quickly replaced by as many American wounded as the *Kelton* could carry, plus Forrest Harding, who was returning to his headquarters at Mendaropu.

It was shortly into that return journey that the *Kelton*'s luck finally ran out. She was barely underway when her rudder fouled one of the stays (cables) attached to the masts of the sunken schooner *Alacrity*. Unable to steer, her passengers were transferred to another boat and she was towed, firstly to Harvey Bay en route to Oro Bay and ultimately to the Small Ships repair facilities at Milne Bay.

The guns and gunners the *Kelton* dropped off fared a little better. As the guns were being reassembled the next morning, the activity was spotted by a flight of Zeros on a search and destroy mission. The area where the gunners were working and the surrounding jungle were strafed several times, resulting in a number of casualties; fortunately, none of them proved fatal. The works resumed and by 11 a.m. that morning the guns and gunners were in action supporting the ground troops.

•

As soon as the Small Ships from the south and west arrived at Milne Bay, they were checked, loaded and sent forward to join the shuttle run then operating between Porlock Harbour, Oro Bay and Hariko/Boreo Creek. The pressure to keep the supply line functioning, and the haste with which boats were loaded and turned around, inevitably led to problems that might not otherwise have occurred. On 21 November, the *Charles Cam*, another Sydney-based seine trawler, ran aground on an unmarked reef and – a sitting target – was shot up badly by Japanese aircraft. The *Charles Cam* was so badly damaged by the grounding and the attack that she was left where she lay. When there was practically nothing of her left, the hulk was used as a navigation beacon by the other Small Ships. When there were no remains to be seen, the reef was given a name, the *Charles Cam* reef.

Just a few days later, the *Helen Dawn*, a wooden fishing trawler originally from Ulladulla, also arrived to take part in the shuttle run, under the command of a former fisherman, John Plumb. She was destined to also have a short career on that run. On US Thanksgiving Day, 26 November, while carrying a full load of ammunition, she ran aground on a sandbank just five kilometres short of Hariko. She was also carrying Forrest Harding, who by now must have been regarded as a harbinger of ill-fortune.

Harding completed the remainder of his journey in the boat's dinghy, while the *Helen Dawn* was left where she was until she could be towed off at high tide. This was not to be. Spotted by patrolling Japanese aircraft early the next morning, she was bombed and strafed, and reduced to a smouldering wreck. John Plumb rowed out to her to salvage what he could late in the day and returned with the boat's logbooks and his own sextant, now with shattered glass and a neat bullet hole all the way through.

•

If the reefs and the Japanese did not provide enough problems, gross incompetence and hidebound military procedures were occasionally added to the mix. On 27 November, the Australian 2/5th Field Regiment received an urgent order from New Guinea Force Headquarters to send two more 25-pound artillery pieces and gun crews from Wanigela to Oro Bay for transhipment to Hariko to assist the Americans in their stalled assault. They were to be carried forward by the *Kurimarau*.

At 500 tons, the former Lever and Lever freighter with her crew of Solomon Islanders would be one of the largest vessels to attempt that passage but her captain, Bert Cummings, was a North Queensland fisherman used to sailing in tropical waters. Cummings had taken command of the *Kurimarau* in Cairns, where she had been converted for service as a Small Ship. From Cairns, she had sailed across to Milne Bay and had been operating between there and her new base at Porlock Harbour.

After a pleasantly uneventful trip from Wanigela, the *Kurimarau* arrived at Oro Bay shortly after midnight, with Cummings steering carefully between what appeared to be several sunken vessels. After anchoring a short distance offshore, Cummings could get no response to his lamp signals, so he and an artillery officer named Nix rowed ashore in the *Kurimarau*'s dinghy. They searched along a blacked-out beach and eventually found some sort of guard post and woke up the Americans inside.

Those Americans directed them to the harbour master who told them, with some exasperation, that he had requested food for the troops at Buna rather than guns and ammunition. After having his say, he contacted the US Army's Dock Operation Unit, newly arrived and responsible for the loading and unloading of all ships at Oro Bay. (At this point, there were no permanent wharfing facilities at Oro Bay and all cargoes had to be offloaded using barges lighters and a temporary pontoon wharf.) However, the Dock Operations Unit would only work at night if that work was illuminated by powerful lights.

Cummings was well aware of the night-time operations of the Japanese floatplanes – Washing Machine Charlie – and had no intention of making his ship a spotlit target for them. After a sometimes acrimonious exchange, Cummings and Nix returned to the *Kurimarau*, where the anchor was lifted, the engines were started and ship and cargo sailed off, this time only as far as Porlock Harbour.

Just to add to his general disgust, Bert Cummings had another shock from that aborted attempt to bring the guns forward. When he had been easing the *Kurimarau* towards her anchorage at Oro Bay, he almost hit a large log floating in the water. Soon afterwards he was informed, reliably he thought, that the Japanese had been caught using such logs as observation posts after hollowing them out and fitting them with small and silent engines. He decided that the next log he saw near one of the Small Ships bases would be rammed at high speed.

•

Just a few hours after the *Kurimarau* sailed out of Oro Bay, the *Timoshenko* sailed in. The previous day her skipper, Neil Sandery, had been advised that Harvey Bay, the next inlet to Oro Bay, was a good place to hide from Japanese aircraft during the day, but with the pressure building to get supplies forward to Hariko, he thought Oro Bay was a risk worth taking as it would save time in the turnaround between shuttle runs.

Around noon, a single Japanese aircraft swooped down and made just one strafing run along the bay before disappearing as quickly as it had arrived. The *Timoshenko* was damaged, but the damage was mainly superficial. Her cook, who had been standing on the deck, was hit and killed instantly though.

That night, fully loaded with supplies, the *Timoshenko* resumed her place in the shuttle run to Hariko.

•

In those eleven days of November, there was no single experience shared by the Small Ships and the sailors who crewed them. The pressure to push the supplies and equipment forward prevented any real system or pattern of movement; it was very much do what you could when you could and then wait for the next consignment. To Clarrie Dawes, just sixteen years of age and still the youngest of those sailors, every day remained an adventure.

When the weather cleared in the days following the opening of the offensive, Kenney's aircraft returned to the war front with a vengeance. Early one morning towards the end of November, the *Leprena* was hiding in one of the many little arms of Oro Bay when Clarrie and the others aboard heard the deep throb of many aircraft engines coming from the direction of Port Moresby. A number of them went ashore and found vantage points looking along the coast towards Buna; they were just in time to see a flight of B-25 Mitchell bombers coming in low and fast.

The aircraft were met by a storm of anti-aircraft fire. However, as Clarrie and the others quickly realised, the anti-aircraft shells were incorrectly fused, exploding too high and allowing the B-25s to pattern bomb inland from the beach without any real impediment. As the first flight of bombers departed, a second arrived and, through a growing haze of blue and black smoke, continued to pound the Japanese positions before flying off.

It was impressive to see but caused little real damage to the defences below.

From the opening of the offensive, the *Leprena* had been directly involved, making the short run from Oro Bay to Hariko every second or third night. Loading supplies during the day, they would sail after dark to a spot off Hariko beach where they would be met by a collection of barges, assault boats and outrigger canoes. Troops and carriers from those craft would assist in unloading the *Leprena*'s main hold and deck cargo, passing the boxes and crates down to those waiting on the water below. The various craft would then take those supplies into the beach where they would be collected and carried to the dumps well back from the beach. The small craft would also make their way back to the *Leprena*, this time with their own cargo of sick and wounded soldiers. In those early days, most were walking wounded, but space could always be found aboard for any stretcher cases.

The *Leprena*'s skipper, Bill Webster, would estimate the latest time they could leave Hariko and deliver the wounded to Pongani and still find shelter before the sun was up and the Zeros were out hunting. After just a few of those nights and a few of those sights, Clarrie began to experience nightmares. Some were about what he had already seen but most were about what he was afraid he might see.

•

The last few days of November 1942 and the first few days of December were bleak days for the Americans bogged down in front of the Japanese defences at Buna. Most were sick, all were hungry and none could see a possible solution to overcoming the defences. Artillery would help, certainly, as would tanks and a more accurate and sustained aerial attack, but none of those things seemed likely in the short term. There was a general feeling of resignation rather than defeatism, a belief that they would probably prevail in the long run while in the short term they would just continue to waste away because of disease or they would be frittered away in fruitless attacks against an enemy so well dug in that the Americans could not even see the men who were killing them.

The Small Ships' sailors charged with supplying and supporting those men were also feeling the pinch. For two days, the only boat on the Oro Bay to Hariko shuttle run was the *Kelton*, and they were just fortunate that, when she fell into difficulties, the other Small Ships despatched from Milne Bay and beyond were already bringing supplies forward.

If the sailors had an ongoing fear, it was of the Japanese aircraft that had proved to be so deadly. Their first response to this threat had been to switch all their operations on the north coast to night operations, but a lack of boats and a lack of time meant that the troops they were supposed to support would fail unless a more reliable and larger sea supply operation was put into place, and soon. In December, all their energies would go into making that wish a reality, but they would pay a heavy price for doing so.

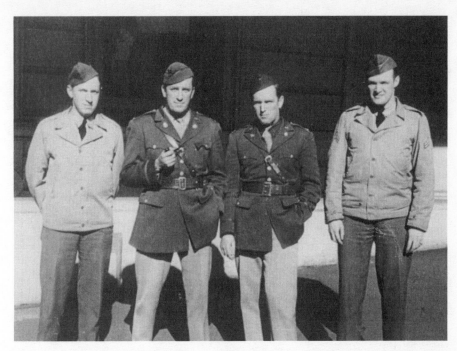

Four of 'The Originals': Heath Steele, Bruce Fahnestock, Sheridan Fahnestock and Frank Sheridan. *Photo courtesy of Gladstone Maritime Museum*

Seine trawlers at Walsh Bay undergoing conversion for war service. Note the deck-mounted machine gun. *Photo courtesy of Gladstone Maritime Museum*

Bill Priest's *King John* departs Walsh Bay for New Guinea. *Photo courtesy of Gladstone Maritime Museum*

American troops at Wanigela preparing to board the *King John* and *Timoshenko*, in the background with the *Alacrity*, for carriage to Pongani.

Photo courtesy of Australian War Memorial/AWM 127513

Frank Bagnall, Australian Army news cameraman, with two Papuan carriers.

Unloading 25-pound field guns from the captured Japanese barge at Oro Bay on 11 November 1942. *Photo courtesy of Wikimedia Commons/Tom Fisher*

The *Tassie III* (S 188) hiding in a Papuan river to avoid Japanese aircraft during daylight hours. *Photo courtesy of Wikimedia Commons/Arthur James Carfax-Foster*

Geoffrey Reading (*left*) and Frank Bagnall in borrowed clothes after the disaster at Hariko.

The *Kurimarau* (S 105) tied up at a wharf, probably in Far North Queensland. Note the bridge had been cemented and steel-plated for protection from strafing by Japanese planes. *Photo courtesy of Gladstone Maritime Museum*

Jim Carfax-Foster, with holstered pistol, with his crew and carriers aboard the *Miena* (S 115), with jury-rigged machine gun mounting.

The *Mactan* (S 188) docked, probably in Far North Queensland. *Photo courtesy of United States Signal Corps*

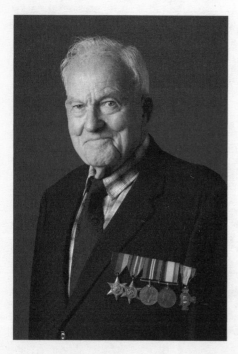

Melville Clarence 'Clarrie' Dawes on Anzac Day, 2016: there at the beginning, there at the end.

Photo courtesy of Sharpshooting Photography/ Tom McNab

10.

THE RETURN OF THE RED ARROW LINE

Douglas MacArthur was not a man to accept failure unless that failure could somehow be turned around to become a necessary part of a larger success. It was something he had some knowledge of.

Just a few days after the opening of the Buna offensive, he was becoming increasingly concerned about the 32nd Division's lack of progress against the Japanese positions at Buna, especially as he had been led to believe that those positions were lightly held by a small number of sick and demoralised Japanese troops. As important as the lack of progress at Buna was the fact that he, Douglas MacArthur, had announced to the world that this, his first victory against the Japanese, would be a short, sharp affair.

And so MacArthur despatched a team comprising his senior aides to Buna to report on Forrest Harding's sputtering offensive while MacArthur took over Government House in Port Moresby, holding briefings for selected newsmen and hosting functions for senior army officers from both the Australian and US armies. While MacArthur's men were conducting their investigations, Forrest Harding was writing to Ned Herring, the Australian lieutenant general then commanding Allied land forces in New Guinea. He, too, was trying to detail the issues that were impacting on the success of his offensive, and he noted in some detail the problems caused by the interruptions to his seaborne supply line.

'During the Buna campaign,' he wrote to Herring, 'all was going well until the 16/17 November when six Small Ships were lost together with their cargoes. The Small Ship situation has since gone from bad to worse; another Small Ship went on a reef yesterday, another got stuck on a reef and was bombed, another three vessels have been bombed and sunk and today there is only one vessel available.'

The reports that MacArthur received from his aides, if they touched on supply line problems, touched on them very lightly. Instead, they suggested that the American troops' failures at Buna were due to a lack of leadership from the top, from battalion and regimental commanders and all the way up to Harding himself. MacArthur was told stories of soldiers with beards, wearing rotting clothes and carrying dirty weapons. Many of those soldiers neglected to salute the visiting staff officers and some even seemed to resent their presence.

That was enough for MacArthur. He summoned one of his senior generals, Robert Eichelberger, a corps commander who was then in Brisbane overseeing the training of the second American division that had been sent to Australia. MacArthur's instructions to him were short and to the point, and could be summarised as, 'Take Buna, Bob, or don't come back alive.'

Eichelberger went forward to Buna to gauge the situation for himself. On 2 December, he told Forrest Harding that he was being recalled to Australia and then replaced Harding with Albert Waldron, the 32nd Division's artillery chief. Several of

Harding's subordinate commanders were also replaced. When all that was done, Eichelberger sat down and prepared to finish the Buna campaign as quickly as possible.

•

When Laurence McKenny was killed at Hariko, Harding had at first feared that he would be impossible to replace. Major Ralph Birkness soon proved to be a more than adequate replacement. He addressed the immediate need for an increase in airdrops, knowing there would be some difficulties with them, and pushed hard to have a second airstrip at Popondetta completed ahead of schedule. He also pushed hard to have every available and suitable Small Ship relocated to the forward bases at Milne Bay and Oro Bay, and for the facilities at both to be upgraded.

•

In contrast to some of the claims put forward about what was achievable at Buna and beyond, Dwight Johns and the COSC planners, including the Small Ships executive, appear to have based their operational planning on a mixture of past experience and careful, objective assessments. It was a combination that would stand them in good stead at Buna and in the battles that would be fought later. Through COSC, the RAN sent two of its own small ships, HMAS *Petrula* and HMAS *Matafele*, to Porlock Harbour on 16/17 November where they were to act as a floating reserve should the US Army Small Ships operation collapse. When Oro Bay became the main Allied base on that stretch of coastline, both vessels relocated there. A COSC liaison party also arrived at Porlock Harbour on 27 November; it, too, would later relocate to Oro Bay.

Porlock Harbour and Oro Bay were also designated Advanced Supply Depots. In the US Army's scheme of nomenclature, this meant that each depot was required to hold ten days' worth of rations, ammunition, POL (petrol, oil, lubricant) and sundries for 10,000 troops. The COSC and Small Ships planners took it from there to undertake their own calculations. To maintain the reserves at that level during the forthcoming campaign would require daily deliveries of sixty tons of each consumable at each site, a total of around 200 tons each and every day to both Oro Bay and Porlock Harbour. Given that the trawlers being used – and lost at an alarming rate – could carry up to thirty tons each, and given that those trawlers were the only vessels capable of carrying supplies forward to Hariko, it was suddenly very obvious that many more, and larger, vessels would be needed.

The COSC also set up its own administration on the ground on the north coast. In mid-November, they appointed a beach master at Porlock Harbour, a 53-year-old member of the Royal Navy Volunteer Reserve, Commander John Sinclair. Like several others involved in Small Ships operations, Sinclair had escaped from Singapore shortly before it was surrendered to the Japanese. A similar arrangement was put in place at Oro Bay where Jack Gilmore, formerly of the Rabaul Hotel, was appointed salvage master.

COSC also issued orders and directives, as and when they deemed it necessary for the safety and security of their supply operations. On 7 December, for instance, COSC issued a new set of orders, active from that date. Those orders specified that there were to be no ship movements forward of Porlock Harbour before 1830 hours each day unless there was an urgent operational necessity and air cover was provided. There were also to be no movements between Tufi and Porlock Harbour after 1230 hours each day. COSC also kept pressure on the Small Ships command to keep pushing boats and crews forward. From the top down, they were now all under pressure.

•

The stories of the different Small Ships illustrate the issues and problems they all faced in the pressure to support the stalled Buna offensive. When the call went out for all available Small Ships to move forward, to Milne Bay in the first instance, those ships were scattered from Sydney to Port Moresby and a number of places in between. Those that were specifically directed to Oro Bay were, in the main, the smaller trawlers and motorised yachts, boats whose capacity to navigate in the treacherous waters between there and Hariko was already known. They, however, comprised only a small part of the considerable Small Ships fleet, and the call was for other, larger vessels as well. One of those en route was the *Hilda Norling*, the Victorian cray boat acquired earlier that year.

The *Hilda Norling* had been part of a second Small Ships convoy assembled at Walsh Bay in Sydney in mid-October and despatched from there to Port Moresby. Apart from her capacity as a cray boat, the *Hilda Norling* had a crew regarded by some of the others as a cross between notable and distinguished. The *Norling*'s captain was Horace Horder, a member of a well-known Sydney cycling family. Horace had joined the Small Ships in September 1942. Chief Engineer aboard the *Norling* was Horrie Horton, assisted by a second engineer named George Smith, formerly a cleaner at the Mark Foy's store in Sydney. The final crewman was cook George Barry Brooks, or simply 'Georgie', a pre-war champion swimmer.

The *Norling* might have been a good ship but she certainly wasn't a lucky ship. Three days out of Sydney, the convoy ran into a large storm and she was separated from the others. Under the pounding of the waves, her engine pumps began to give trouble and shortly afterwards her gearbox failed. There was also misadventure among her crew. George Brooks found himself in some discomfort after he slipped and broke a toe during the rough weather on 12 October. To add insult to injury, the following day he burned himself on the galley stove.

Worse was to come. Later that same day, the *Norling*'s engine broke down completely and Horder anchored his stricken vessel off Byron Bay. From that anchorage, George Brooks swam ashore, made it to a telephone and contacted the Small Ships' office in Brisbane seeking assistance. Shortly afterwards, the tugboat *Wanda Belle* was sent out and towed the *Norling* to Coolangatta, where both ships anchored and awaited further orders. Still later, a tugboat arrived from Brisbane and towed the *Norling* up to the Brisbane River, where she promptly ran aground. Another boat eventually arrived and towed the *Norling*, successfully this time, to her allocated berth up river.

By then, Horrie Horton was over the whole thing; he liked Horace Horder personally but regarded him as a disaster as a ship's captain. He requested a move and was transferred immediately to the *Melcustoms*, another Small Ship and the vessel that had pulled the *Norling* off the sandbar in the Brisbane River. Horder was also transferred, while George Smith was promoted to chief engineer. The *Norling* was duly repaired and set sail for Port Moresby again, this time under the command of Clifford Peall, a young fisherman from the Queensland port city of Bundaberg.

The problems continued, though, and they came in all shapes and sizes. Two days out of Brisbane, the ship's generator failed, just after the only frying pan they carried was lost over the side. The generator simply seemed to defy repairing while the engine continued to operate at well below peak performance. Just on dark on the evening of 5 November, the *Norling* limped into Townsville for another layover and overhaul. There, another new captain was appointed: Norm Oddy, still fresh from his Milne Bay heroics as chief engineer on the *Minston Brae*.

The *Hilda Norling* departed Townsville on 12 November with a unit of American soldiers and Gubby Glover aboard. The next day the engine seemed to be losing power again. Just to rub some salt into the crew's wounds, George Smith had a bad fall that day in the engine room and broke a bone in his ankle. As the engine seemed to fix itself, Norm Oddy took a side trip to show Glover and the soldiers the wonders of Green Island before sailing into Cairns on 15 November. There, they dropped their passengers off and loaded up with spare parts and supplies, the latter including twenty eighteen-gallon kegs of beer donated by the Castlemaine Brewery for 'the boys in the islands'.

They departed Cairns on 18 November – and returned four hours later with further engine problems. By then, they were sorely needed in New Guinea where a lot had already happened and a lot more was about to begin.

•

This time, the repairs seem to have worked, and the *Hilda Norling* sailed from Cairns across the Coral Sea to Goodenough Island, just off the eastern tip of New Guinea and to the north of Milne Bay. There she dropped off the supplies she had brought from Australia, including the kegs of beer, received by some very grateful and very thirsty diggers. From Goodenough Island, she doubled back to Milne Bay, tying up at the Gili Gili wharf where they dropped off fifty drums of diesel fuel they had been carrying and took on board fifty tons of rations for the soldiers on Goodenough Island. They also took on some additional passengers: Laddie Reday, heading for Oro Bay, a new deckhand named Gilder and a supernumerary, a Filipino named Augustin Guerrero. From Goodenough Island, Norm Oddy steered the *Norling* along the north coast to Porlock Harbour where they loaded around fifty tons of rations for the troops at Buna. It was Friday, 4 December and they were now part of the Hariko shuttle run.

They sailed again later that evening, heading for Oro Bay. Once there, Oddy had trouble finding their berthing marker so he simply continued on to Embogo and found a mooring under cover there. The *Hilda Norling* remained at anchor all day, leaving its mooring at 5.30 p.m. and sailing back to Oro Bay where they arrived just on dusk. Laddie Reday disembarked, the supplies were unloaded successfully and the crew made ready to depart again at midnight. They were scheduled to take another cargo of supplies back to Pongani, which was now bypassed by the larger ships, before returning to their temporary base at Porlock Harbour.

Again, a change of luck intervened.

It began with a sudden tropical storm which delayed their departure from Oro Bay for several hours. When it cleared, they took some wounded soldiers and medical attendants aboard, bailed out the lifeboats that had taken water aboard during the storm and set off just after the sun rose at 7 a.m. Just two hours later, they anchored off Pongani and sent the wounded and the medical orderlies ashore. George Smith accompanied them as his recently broken ankle continued to give him trouble. When he returned to the ship shortly after 11 a.m., they weighed anchor and headed back to Porlock Harbour.

Just two hours into the voyage, the *Hilda Norling* was firstly spotted and then attacked by a flight of fifteen Zeros. Oddy called for speed and took whatever evasive action he could. He counted twelve bombs dropped in that first attack. None of those bombs scored a direct hit, but there were several near-misses and these put both of the ship's machine guns out of action. Cook George Brooks, who was manning one of the guns, was killed instantly by a bomb splinter.

After that initial attack, eleven of the Zeros climbed into the sky to act as top cover for the other four, who now made a series of attacks on the *Hilda Norling*. During one of these, one of the medical orderlies returning with the ship and one of the Papuan carriers jumped into the dinghy tethered behind the *Norling* and cut it adrift in an attempt to escape the attackers. However, the dinghy had been shot full of holes and quickly sank beneath them. The orderly disappeared below the water but the Papuan survived by hanging onto the oars.

During another attack, engineer George Smith was struck by a machine gun bullet. He fell to the deck, unconscious, and died there a few minutes later. Elsewhere, the second engineer, a sailor named Vaughan, donned a lifejacket and jumped overboard, and another two of the Papuan carriers were both hit in the legs as they dived for cover during an attack. Miraculously, and somewhat ironically, the *Hilda Norling*'s engine now ran better than it had during the previous three months.

Now defenceless in the face of the continuing attacks, Oddy turned off the engine and ordered everyone to abandon ship. Those still alive made their way through the water to the beach, the Zeros making one or two further runs spraying the water with bullets and cannon fire. The attacks continued until the last survivor had made it to the protection of the jungle. When he was certain that the aircraft had gone and would not return, Norm Oddy swam back out to his boat, becoming painfully aware as he did so of the shrapnel wounds that he had also suffered.

Oddy climbed aboard the *Norling*, which was just drifting along, and found that both the engine and the steering gear were intact. However, he would be unable to anchor her because the donkey engine that raised and lowered the anchor had been shot away. Hearing a shout, he spotted engineer Vaughan drifting as well, so he steered the boat across to him and, when he was safely aboard, carefully steered the *Norling* into some soft sand not too far off the beach and left her there. They both swam ashore and made their way to the small Papuan village of Sebaga a short distance back from the beach.

The rest of Norm Oddy's day was fully occupied with trying to look after what remained of his ship and crew. With the assistance of the villagers and his Papuan carriers, Oddy returned to the *Norling* to recover the bodies of his dead crewmen. The villagers had made two crosses and dug two graves in a coconut grove near the village and there they buried the two Georges, Smith and Brooks, who were the last members of the *Hilda Norling*'s original crew. They were lonely graves, a very long way from home, and Oddy took photographs of both to send later to the men's next of kin. The wounded were treated and the survivors moved into the village where the villagers had agreed to look after them. One villager volunteered to walk to Porlock Harbour to raise the alarm and two of the fit crewmen agreed to accompany him. Oddy rowed out to the *Hilda Norling* in a borrowed outrigger canoe and gathered as many supplies as it would carry back to the beach.

While his men remained ashore, Norm Oddy lived aboard the *Hilda Norling*, organising food from the ship's stores and the supplies they were carrying for both his crew and the villagers helping them, while also making whatever running repairs he could to his ship. A single Japanese aircraft circled the stranded boat the next day, but flew off without attacking, probably convinced that the *Hilda Norling* was now just another wreck. Three days later, on 8 December, a launch arrived with orders to take all the survivors back to Pongani from where they would be taken to Australia for medical treatment. Norm Oddy's time as a Small Ships sailor was over.

•

At Buna, the change of commanders organised from the rear had made little difference to the troops at the front. Harsh words and an aggressive mindset did not put extra food in the soldiers' stomachs, nor did they substitute for medicines, extra ammunition or heavy weapons. The Japanese defences remained as strong as ever, and even if the defenders were in as poor a shape physically as the attackers, they also had the high ground, the protection of their bunkers and a resignation to their fate that the Allies lacked. For those Japanese defenders, a life given in the service of their emperor was a life blessed; the Allies struggled to understand this, and certainly had no desire to emulate it.

Hanford MacNider was no longer at that front by this time; he had been struck by splinters from a rifle grenade on 26 November and was evacuated back to Australia for treatment. Prodded by Eichelberger, Albert Waldron ordered a major attack on 5 December, an attack supported by several Australian Bren gun carriers brought up on barges towed by Small Ships. The barges had also carried forty tons of food and ammunition, a shipment that was particularly welcome to the men at the front as the coastal task force had that day consumed the last of its rations.

Rushed into Waldron's offensive, the open, lightly armoured Bren gun carriers proved to be almost completely useless for that type of jungle warfare and were easily knocked out by the Japanese defenders. Observing the action from a forward post, Albert Waldron was also wounded be enemy fire and he, too, had to be evacuated to Australia for treatment.

The failure of the 5 December attack proved conclusively that, if Buna was to be taken, much more artillery and armour would be needed. This alone made George Kenney's claim that 'the artillery in this theatre flies' ring hollow to the troops on the ground. The only way to bring in the necessary armour and artillery was by sea, along a sea route that, while increasingly reliable by night, was also increasingly deadly by day.

•

Bert Cummings had sailed the *Kurimarau* back to Porlock Harbour, planning to return with the guns and gunners to Oro Bay later whenever common sense and army orders made that operation possible. Waiting at Porlock Harbour were the harbour master, John Sinclair, and a large steel barge measuring some thirty by thirteen metres that the *Kurimarau* had towed up from Milne Bay on its last run along the coast. With a possible solution in mind, Cummings approached Sinclair, explained what had happened at Oro Bay and asked him whether it would be possible to transfer the guns and gunners from his ship to the barge which he could then simply tow to Oro Bay and leave there.

Given his recent experiences, Cummings told Sinclair, he thought the barge would be easier for the dock unit labourers at Oro Bay to handle. It might even be possible for one of the shallow-draught Small Ships to simply take over the tow at Oro Bay and continue with it all the way to Hariko. Sinclair agreed with Cummings and asked whether he could accompany them to see how the system operated at Oro Bay and beyond.

That day – it was 5 December and Waldron's offensive was already in trouble – was spent manoeuvring the *Kurimarau* and the steel barge together and then transferring guns, ammunition, gunners and other supplies from one to the other. Somehow an army jeep was included in the transfer; it fitted, and no one seemed too concerned about how it had come aboard the barge in the first place. Porlock Harbour had few facilities but many backwaters and inlets for hiding in, and late in the day the *Kurimarau* towed the barge and its cargo of soldiers and guns into one of these, where it was pushed hard up against a belt of mangroves, before the *Kurimarau* itself sought shelter nearby.

They were soon joined by several other craft. Earlier that afternoon, the HMAS *Paluma*, the launch that had charted the main shipping channel from Cape Nelson to Oro Bay, was working in tandem with one of the Small Ships, the *Wato*, towing a large barge packed with ammunition from Oro Bay to Hariko. The little convoy had been attacked by a single Japanese aircraft but both ships and the barge had escaped without sustaining any real damage. However, as there were still several hours of daylight left, the skipper of the *Paluma*, Ivan Champion, decided that it might be best to sit out the evening in Porlock Harbour. Lionel Veale, still serving aboard, thought this a good idea; he was beginning to become a bit 'windy' in the open during daylight hours. Conscious of the possibility of a Japanese air attack, Champion pushed his barge into another mangrove thicket and took cover in a nearby tidal inlet.

There were mountains immediately inland from Porlock Harbour and they normally were shrouded in mist during the morning. At around 7 a.m., just as the men aboard the various boats and barges secreted in the harbour's inlets were getting ready for the day, the mists parted just as a single Japanese aircraft roared out of the clouds, flying over the harbour bombing and machine gunning everything it thought might be an Allied vessel. It was a well-planned attack: the aircraft had gained height over the mist-covered mountains and then glided down from the top of the cloud until just inland from the harbour where the engine was switched back on and the aircraft continued its dive to make just a single bombing and strafing run.

As well as the gunners aboard each ship, anti-aircraft defences were in place at several points around the harbour, but the attack was so sudden that all anyone had to fire at was the rapidly shrinking rear of the aircraft as it flew away after just one bombing run.

Fortunately, the damage it had caused was not great. While most of the ships and barges had fired at it, it seemed that the main target of the attack was the *Kurimarau*, obviously not as well hidden as Bert Cummings had thought she was. Most of the damage was from gunfire and while the structural damage itself was largely superficial, there had been casualties aboard. A bullet had struck third engineer Ted Deverill a glancing blow along the side of his head, one of the Papuan carriers had been hit in the shoulder and one of the American machine gunners had been hit in the buttocks. All the wounded were given first aid before being taken ashore for treatment at the aid post there.

The attack and its aftermath set the *Kurimarau*'s sailing plans back several hours, and it wasn't until early afternoon that the ship, with the barge being towed behind, actually cleared Porlock

Harbour. While there was still a lot of daylight left, the barge reduced the *Kurimarau*'s speed and Cummings knew it would be an especially slow voyage. It would also be a dangerous voyage for, after covering fifteen kilometres, the ship and the barge were spotted by four Japanese dive-bombers. Cummings thought they may have been spotted first by a reconnaissance aircraft as they left Porlock Harbour, or they were perhaps just unlucky to be spotted by a search and destroy flight, but he didn't waste time pondering this as he had a ship and a barge to save.

As the first of the Japanese dive-bombers went into a power dive, the two American machine gunners stationed towards the stern opened fire, while there was general pandemonium among the others still on deck. One of them, a gunner named Shaw Brown, had grabbed his camera when the aircraft were first spotted but, as the scream of the bomber's engine grew to a crescendo, he joined the other artillerymen all looking for cover among the boxes stacked on deck, even though most of them contained ammunition.

Just as Brown reached the bottom of the companionway from the upper deck, there were two tremendous explosions not twenty metres away from the side of the ship and towards the stern. The blasts seemed to lift the ship right out of the water and sent up huge grey spouts composed of smoke and water, some of which then fell back down on the *Kurimarau*.

Looking at his fellow artillerymen, Brown noted a range of reactions which he thought probably mirrored his own: looks of total fright, beads of perspiration running down foreheads and even a few holding their hands over their ears as if that could somehow make it all go away. He noted, too, that at least two of the gunners had been wounded by bomb splinters: one a sergeant named Carson, and the other a gunner named

Keith Coates. Fortunately, their wounds seemed slight. Others aboard were not so fortunate.

Porlock Harbour Beach Master John Sinclair had been below deck, eating his dinner, when the planes were spotted and the machine gunners opened fire. Wanting to see what was happening, he rushed topside and had just reached the deck when the two bombs exploded nearby. He, too, was struck by a bomb splinter and collapsed onto the deck in a growing pool of blood. The ship's chief engineer, Kenny Dhiem, and one of the Solomon Islander crewmen, a Malaitan named Willy, had both been on deck near the stern when the bombs exploded and both had also been hit by bomb splinters. Willy's was the more serious wound and he was now unconscious and stretched out on the deck. Kenny Dhiem was also bleeding profusely from where the piece of hot metal had sliced open his forearm.

Both the stern machine gunners, American soldiers named Edgar Heater and William Parriott, had also been hit. Heater's was the worse injury. Two bullets had struck and penetrated his helmet, but had luckily done no more than gouge deep creases in his scalp. Another bullet had struck him in the leg and he reeled back from his machine gun, seeking shelter and assistance on the lower deck. One of the Australian artillerymen nearby, Bill Semmens from Enfield in Sydney, had been firing a Bren gun at the attacking aircraft. Seeing Heater's distress, he dropped his weapon and assisted the wounded American to cover.

Semmens returned to his Bren gun and found its firing mechanism had been smashed by a Japanese bullet. He ran across to Edgar Heater's machine gun but found that its magazine was empty and he didn't know how to reload it. Semmens then noticed that the other gunner, William Parriott, had also been wounded in the leg. It wasn't a bad wound but Parriott agreed to hand over his machine gun to Semmens while he sought treatment for the wound. He showed Semmens how to fire it before limping away. Semmens stayed there for the remainder of the assault, firing at the aircraft as they swept in to attack; he would later be awarded the Military Medal for his actions that day.

Up on the bridge, Bert Cummings was doing everything in his power to save his ship. It had a minor problem with its steering which had caused it to yaw slightly if a firm hand was not on handle but even that was absent that day. Towing the barge not only reduced the *Kurimarau*'s speed, it also made it difficult to zigzag, so Cummings waited until the attacking aircraft were well into their dives before swinging the wheel hard to either port or starboard. It was crude but effective. Another eight bombs were aimed at the *Kurimarau* before the aircraft flew off and while several were near-misses, none hit the ship itself.

The officers aboard, Australian and American, surveyed the damage as soon as the Japanese aircraft had disappeared. The barge, with its precious artillery, ammunition and rations, appeared to have survived completely unscathed. The same could not be said for the *Kurimarau*. The above decks area towards the stern was a mess. One of the lifeboats there had one of its davits shot away and there were hundreds of perforations in the superstructure, both bomb splinter gashes and bullet holes. A couple of small fires started by incendiary bullets were extinguished before they could take hold. Overall, however, the damage was mainly superficial and could be either patched or plugged and then painted over.

Inside the hull and below the waterline, the story was quite different. The near-misses had damaged both the propeller and the drive shaft, and the ship could now only manage to make half speed. It also appeared that the ship's electrical systems had been damaged.

Among the soldiers and sailors on deck, the disappearance of the planes was quickly followed by calls for both medical assistance and field dressings. A quick survey found that seven men aboard had been wounded. Of those, two were critically injured: John Sinclair and the deckhand Willy. Blood was still streaming down Edgar Heater's face but he appeared likely to survive the wounds.

The men also reacted with the exuberance of those who face death, believe they are about to be killed but survive, and survive in the company of those who also thought themselves doomed. Amid the backslapping and jokes about how brave they really were came an agreement that the captain and the machine gunners may well have been the difference between life and death. Bert Cummings had seemed to be able to almost predict where the next bomb would fall, while the machine gunners stood at their exposed posts as long as they could, only moving when they were wounded.

Several of the aircraft were forced to abort their bombing runs because of the fire directed at them, and there were those who believed at least one of the attacking aircraft had been hit and damaged.

•

The damage to his ship and the injuries to his passengers and crew convinced Bert Cummings that the only realistic option open to him was to turn the *Kurimarau* around and return to Porlock Harbour. He radioed ahead with a brief outline of what had happened and a request for medical assistance. As the *Kurimarau* approached the entrance to the harbour, a launch came out to meet them and the doctor it carried boarded the ship while it was still some distance from its anchorage. That doctor was unable to save Willy, who died on the deck as he was being treated. He did what he could to help the other casualties but said that both Sinclair and Heater needed specialist treatment that wasn't available at Porlock Harbour.

Cummings and the doctor agreed that the course of action most likely to save the badly wounded was for the *Kurimarau* to continue back to Wanigela where Heater and Sinclair could be landed and transferred to an aircraft for the short flight to Port Moresby, and beyond if necessary, for the urgent treatment that Sinclair in particular needed.

At Porlock Harbour the *Kurimarau* let go of the towline that connected her to the barge and Cummings and his crew wished the gunners good luck for whatever was to come their way. At this, several of the gunners expressed their belief that their fate was to be stuck on a barge in Porlock Harbour for the duration of the war. The *Kurimarau* then sailed at 2 a.m. and limped to an anchorage off Wanigela later that afternoon. The wounded were rowed ashore and later transferred to a cargo flight to Port Moresby. While Heater was returned to full health, John Sinclair died quietly in hospital the next day.

The *Kurimarau* continued slowly eastwards and made it to Milne Bay where an examination of the damage she had suffered revealed that it was even more serious than Bert Cummings suspected. In fact, the marine surveyors there doubted whether Jack Savage's shipyard at Gili Gili was capable of undertaking the necessary repairs and the *Kurimarau* was sent on her way, this time down to Brisbane. There, other marine engineers found that the near-misses had not only partially twisted the drive shaft but had actually bent her propeller blades forward. The *Kurimarau*'s war was temporarily over.

Back at Porlock Harbour, the artillery troop's commander, Charles Mueller, had arranged to have the barge towed up to Hariko by two of the Small Ships, Neil Sandery's *Timoshenko* and the newly arrived trawler, the *Pat*. The operation took place that night, 8/9 December, and although the seas off Hariko were unusually large, the barge and all its contents were successfully put ashore and taken to a designated area. Two 25-pound field pieces and a jeep were not going to turn the course of the Buna campaign but they were a step, however small, in the right direction. The guns and gunners finally got to the war they had been chasing for quite a while now and they, and the rations they carried on their barge, put a smile on faces that had not smiled in quite a while.

•

The successful arrival of the *Kurimarau*'s barge at Hariko was just one of a number of occurrences in the days following the opening of Albert Waldron's offensive on 5 December that were to have a significant impact not only on the outcome of that offensive – it was doomed from the start – but on both the course and the outcome of the larger Buna campaign. The smallest and least noted of those occurrences was the departure of HMAS *Paluma* from the waters around Oro Bay on 8 December. The little launch had done her job for the surveyors she carried, and had done it well. Instead of using the Small Ships methodology of lining up lights and rocks and wrecks, the *Paluma*'s work meant that there was now a deep-water channel charted and marked all the way into Oro Bay, allowing the larger freighters to sail directly to that point to offload their cargo.

Semi-regular shuttle runs were also established between Oro Bay, Porlock Harbour and Hariko, with supplies going into Hariko and wounded and ill soldiers being brought out. These runs were almost exclusively undertaken during the hours of darkness for, despite an increasing Allied presence in the air, the Japanese continued to be the major threat to the operations of the Small Ships.

They were all, by themselves, small steps but taken together they had begun to create a critical mass that had previously been missing in the Allied battle preparations.

11.

WAITING FOR THE CAVALRY

There were a number of outcomes that flowed from the failure of Albert Waldron's first offensive of 5 December. Two of these were of immediate import to the Buna campaign and, though not immediately apparent, to the way that MacArthur's plan to march back across the Pacific to the Philippines would be undertaken. The first and most immediate outcome of that failure was the recognition that the tactics the American commanders had been using were badly flawed. Unsupported infantry attacks on an entrenched enemy who dominated all avenues of approach would never succeed at Buna, and a lot of young Americans had died proving this rather obvious truth.

A second outcome was another realisation, this one about the equally obvious fallacy of George Kenney's claims about just what his air force could do. The two claims he had pushed most vigorously throughout the planning stages of the Buna campaign were now shown to be hollow and self-serving. Those air forces could never supply a field force of 10,000-plus soldiers in a campaign fought under the conditions that prevailed at Buna. With the failure of the airdrops, there were simply too few aircraft and too few airfields to provide the level of support that was needed. The claim that aircraft had made artillery irrelevant in jungle warfare was equally hollow. The design and construction of the Japanese defences made their strongpoints all but impervious to anything but a direct hit from an armour-piercing bomb.

Against a background of some distrust between Australian and American commanders over the relative value of each other's troops came another realisation: success at Buna would only come when a greater level of cooperation was achieved. An obvious lesson from the first three weeks of fighting at Buna was that the Japanese lines there would not be broken, nor would their strongholds be reduced, by infantry alone. The lack of success to date could be turned around by two other arms of service, artillery and armour. The big guns, especially the 25-pound field pieces, could reduce the Japanese positions if enough could be brought forward, while an even better solution seemed to be the use of armoured vehicles. The experiment with the Bren gun carriers had been an abject failure, but tanks might succeed where they had failed.

After 5 December, discussions between the Allies were focused very much on these things and, to the surprise of some, the outcomes of those discussions were uniformly positive. The Australians would supply additional troops, the three infantry battalions of the 18th Brigade. They would also supply the armour: the M3 Stuart tanks of the 2/6th Armoured Regiment. They would even supply some of the transportation – three RAN corvettes – to take those troops part of the way to the front. The rest, the final delivery of men and machines to Buna, was up to the Americans and their Small Ships Section.

●

Forrest Harding must have sensed either the implausibility of George Kenney's claims about artillery flying or that tanks might become an important weapon at Buna as, even before his offensive opened, he had asked for armoured vehicles to be sent forward. A tank was available at Milne Bay, possibly a one-off sent forward by the 2/6th Armoured Regiment, and it was decided to send that one forward as a test of the system for delivery of such vehicles to Buna. The 2/6th was equipped with the American M3 Stuart tanks. Designated a 'light tank', the Stuarts had been designed for reconnaissance work in the flat, arid and semi-arid battlefields of the Middle East, where their speed and light weight would make them a valuable forward scout car. The armoured corps had larger, heavier battle tanks, but they were in Australia and there was as yet no transportation system to deliver them to the jungle battlefields of New Guinea.

Within three weeks, a solution appeared. The work of the Small Ships skippers and the accurate surveying and charting undertaken by those aboard HMAS *Paluma* meant that larger ships could now carry tanks as far forward as Oro Bay. The bulk of the 2/6th Armoured Regiment was at that time based in and around Port Moresby, building roads and guarding airfields there, when orders arrived from New Guinea Force Headquarters on 7 December. Those orders were for a troop of four Stuart tanks, two officers and twenty-five other ranks to prepare for immediate embarkation to the frontlines on the north coast of the island.

That afternoon, Captain Norm Whitehead, his men and the four tanks that made up C Troop were taken aboard the *Karsik*, a 3000-ton freighter with a chequered history. Actually a German ship, the *Karsik* had been impounded and then seized by Dutch authorities in the Netherlands East Indies in May 1940. After fleeing to Australia ahead of the invading Japanese, she was chartered by the US Army in mid-1942. Departing late on the evening of 7 December, the *Karsik* picked up a consignment of ammunition and rations at Milne Bay before continuing on to Oro Bay, where she arrived during the night of 9/10 December.

That night, the tanks were unloaded in an operation that would become a template for future operations at Oro Bay and elsewhere. Under the direction of US Army Major Marion Moffatt, the tanks were carefully lowered, one by one, onto the floating pontoon wharf and carefully driven into the jungle. The operation was orchestrated by members of the army's 287th Port Battalion, who had also travelled aboard the *Karsik*. While the tanks spent the next day hidden in the jungle, their crews remained aboard the *Karsik* and spent the day under the cover of a mangrove swamp in nearby Harvey Bay.

After dark the next evening, the *Karsik* departed Harvey Bay, dropping its passengers off at Oro Bay before returning to Port Moresby for another troop of tanks and crews. A few days previously, a number of flat-bottomed steel barges, specially designed and built in Australia, had been delivered to Oro Bay where they, too, had been carried into the jungle and hidden. This night, they were brought out, launched and tied up to the pontoon wharf.

Again, the tanks were driven from their jungle hideouts and, one at a time, driven out onto the pontoon wharf and down a small ramp onto the barges. Two tanks, side by side, fitted nicely, with enough space around them to pack in supplies and munitions. A number of other barges were loaded with boxes of rations, boxes of ammunition, fuel drums and the like, and then towed behind several Small Ships to the beach above Hariko and close to the mouth of the creek at Boreo. There, the towlines were cast off and the barges pushed up towards the beach as far as possible. Ropes attached to the barges were then taken ashore and held by teams of soldiers to keep each barge stationary and square to the beach. Hardwood planks were used as ramps from the front of the barges to the beach, but were almost impossible to keep in position.

The tank drivers found the best way to make certain of reaching the beach was to accelerate hard when they passed onto the planks and then rush up the beach. The tactic meant that the planks had to be replaced after a tank had passed over them, but it also meant that none of the tanks was lost or stranded. The tanks were then driven several hundred metres further into the jungle to a laying-up area to the north of the landing place. Before dawn, the Small Ships towed the barges back to Oro Bay while troops back at Boreo filled in and then raked over the tank tracks. From the air, it would be impossible to tell that anything had been landed there.

While this delivery was being made, the *Karsik* had collected another four tanks and crews and more much-needed ammunition, all of which she again delivered to Oro Bay for onward movement. On the night of 15/16 December, eight more tanks were landed successfully at Boreo and made secure in the jungle, waiting with their crews for some action.

•

Coincidental with the arrival of tanks in the theatre and, more specifically, shallow-draught steel barges designed for use in shallow, tropical waters carrying such loads, was the arrival of another specialised vessel. In late October, COSC had received a shipment of eight small wooden landing craft known as LCVPs – for Landing Craft, Vehicle, Persons – but better known as

Higgins boats after their developer, Andrew Higgins. These were some of the 20,000 that would eventually be produced and they were a boon to those planning amphibious operations. Constructed from marine plywood, they were six metres long and powered by petrol engines, which gave them a top speed of twenty knots. Each boat could carry a squad of fully armed and equipped soldiers, or a vehicle like a truck. The boats were equipped with a mounted machine gun and had a very shallow draught. They were ideal for what MacArthur wanted to see happen on the north coast of New Guinea, but they came without crews. Each boat was designed to carry two crewmen: a coxswain steering the boat from the stern and a deckhand who also manned the machine gun in the bow.

It was decided that the Small Ships would operate the boats and the AIF would supply the crews. Detached from their parent unit, the 2/7th Infantry Battalion's Carrier Platoon was at Milne Bay when the Higgins boats arrived there in late October. Almost immediately, the platoon's thirty-five members volunteered, or were volunteered, to join the Small Ships Section for six months in order to crew the boats. On 28 October, two NCOs and eighteen privates started training on handling the boats under the direction of a US Army Small Ships officer, Marion Moffatt. They all expected to be in action sooner rather than later, a not unrealistic expectation, but found themselves simply sitting around, still undertaking their regular army functions until the Buna campaign was well underway. On 10 December, they were warned to be ready and the following day they departed Milne Bay.

Sheridan Fahnestock was given responsibility for the operational deployment of the Higgins boats and he oversaw their loading with much-needed ammunition for the Buna front. Under

Moffatt, they were despatched in a high-speed convoy travelling from Milne Bay up to and around Cape Nelson before making the run across to Harvey Bay where they anchored, huddled together, for the night. It had been a trouble-free run, exhilarating to the Australians and Americans aboard, and it took them close to the battlefront and coastal areas which would soon become their working environment. It was also completed with no breakdowns and no interference or even observation by the Japanese, an important consideration as this would be the first time such landing craft had been deployed by the Allies in the South West Pacific Area.

Marion Moffatt and his eight boats successfully delivered the ammunition they had carried to the beach master at Oro Bay before returning to lay up under cover during the remainder of the day. Their night would be occupied with what was classified as 'Operation Hammer'. The three infantry battalions the AIF had agreed to supply for the battle at Buna were encamped on Goodenough Island. That night, the Higgins boats were to meet the RAN corvettes assigned to bring the troops into position in the deeper water off Cape Sudest. There, the Australian infantrymen would be transferred to the landing craft, which would then deliver them directly to the beach at Hariko. That operation would be under the command of the assistant beach master at Oro Bay, an RANVR lieutenant named Reg Verdon.

The three corvettes assigned to the job were the HMAS *Broome*, HMAS *Ballarat* and HMAS *Colac*, and they all arrived on time at Milne Bay on 12 December to collect supplies and orders. From there they sailed the short distance to Goodenough Island, where they took on board twenty-six officers and 638 other ranks from the 18th Brigade, comprising the Brigade Headquarters, two-thirds of the 2/9th Battalion and the commanding officer of the 2/10th Battalion, who had flown in from Wanigela the previous evening. When all men and equipment had been loaded aboard, the corvettes set off on a fast run to the rendezvous point, almost directly north of Cape Sudest and some five kilometres out to sea.

The three corvettes and eight Higgins boats made contact at midnight and manoeuvred into position to begin the transfer of men from corvette to landing craft. It was a nervous time for all the stationary vessels. Shortly before they had all come together, an unidentified aircraft had dropped several powerful flares some distance off, and that aircraft was thought to still be somewhere in the area. The last straw came when the captain of the *Ballarat*, the senior naval officer present, received a message suggesting that two Japanese cruisers and four destroyers had been sighted at a distance of 150 kilometres north-east of Cape Sudest steaming southwards at forty kilometres an hour.

The transfer of the troops had already begun, but orders were issued instructing that transfer to cease immediately with around eighty troops aboard two of the Higgins boats. The corvettes immediately sailed for Oro Bay, where they would remain for the coming daylight hours. All the Higgins boats made haste to Hariko where the two loaded boats ran up onto the beach, disembarked the soldiers and rejoined the others. There was even an element of danger in this. An aircraft, possibly the same one that had been operating in the area earlier, dropped parachute flares further out to sea at regular intervals. Japanese machine gunners on Cape Endaiadere also fired towards Hariko. Fortunately, a number of rain squalls swept across the landing site, effectively covering the actual landings. The Higgins boats then returned to Harvey Bay where they, too, lay up for the day.

The plan was not followed as closely again, probably because the transfer at sea left both men and ships horribly exposed. Instead, the corvettes and the Higgins boats all sailed to Oro Bay, where the transfer was supervised by Reg Verdon. It was completed without incident and the corvettes returned to Milne Bay to await further instructions. They would return with the remainder of the troops from the 18th Brigade in the coming days.

The Higgins boats, again led by Verdon, made the run to Hariko and successfully unloaded all the troops in an operation that took up most of the night. Early next morning, soon after sunrise, the little flotilla was making its way back to Oro Bay when it was spotted and attacked by a single aircraft. In an unfortunate repeat of the earlier incident at Hariko, the attacking aircraft was from the Allied air forces, in this case a Boston bomber from the RAAF's 22 Squadron. The Boston made several attacking runs over the Higgins boats, sinking one and forcing a second to be beached. Nine crewmen were wounded in the attack, one of whom later succumbed to his wounds.

When the aircraft had departed, Verdon led the boats straight to Oro Bay where the wounded were taken ashore. The remainder of that day was spent patching the boats and drafting new men onto them to replace the casualties of the morning's clash with the aircraft. The former was quite easy; the wooden boats could easily be plugged with timber cut to size. The latter proved a bit more difficult, but by sundown all the boats were repaired and seaworthy, and all were fully crewed. When the last soldier was on dry land, Operation Hammer officially came to an end.

•

The Stuart tanks and many of the Australian troops landed by Fahnestock's Higgins boats went into action alongside American

troops in a joint attack on the troublesome Japanese positions at
Cape Endaiadere on 18 December. The build-up to the attack
included a number of ploys to keep the Japanese defenders
unaware of what was being planned. To bring the tanks into
position before the assault began, they were taken from their
jungle hiding places and driven along the beach at low tide with
Allied aircraft flying low over the Japanese positions. Those
aircraft drowned out the noise of the tanks moving up into
position while the tracks they left behind were obliterated by
the incoming tide.

The opening of the attack went as planned, and the tanks
added the element of surprise that enabled the attackers to this
time almost literally come to grips with a well-entrenched enemy.
Like all Buna battles, it was a battle of attrition against not just
the Japanese but against tropical disease and the general debil-
itation that came with fighting a determined enemy in a hostile
environment. When the assault started to run out of steam,
Operation Sledge Hammer was activated.

Sledge Hammer was the natural successor to Hammer and
followed the pattern established several nights earlier. On the
night of 19/20 December, the Higgins boats again sailed out to
the rendezvous point off Cape Sudest and there met the RAN
corvettes. The transfer of several hundred more Australian
troops to the landing craft was completed without hindrance,
but this time the troops were to be landed under Japanese eyes,
and weapons, directly on Cape Endaiadere. The troops were all
landed ashore successfully and there were no casualties during
the landing, but the boats came under sustained fire as they
pulled away from the beach.

Most of the boats were holed and there were two casualties among their crews. A gunner named Russell was seriously

wounded and Henry Loye, a twenty-year-old infantry private from Queensland, was killed. Both had been coxswains on their respective craft.

It was the start of what was to be a very busy and dangerous period for all the Small Ships, and the Higgins boats were at the heart of much of the action. They began their own shuttle run from Oro Bay to Hariko, operating without air cover and relying on their speed and manoeuvrability to keep them safe from harm. Each boat would carry a full load of soldiers, supplies or ammunition and would travel as fast as it could between the two points. Mostly they dropped off their cargo and returned to Oro Bay empty and anxious for a quick turnaround, but they were also increasingly asked to take back Japanese prisoners under escort to the rear echelon. Without exception, those prisoners would be suffering badly from starvation as well as the tropical diseases which plagued all combatants and non-combatants at Buna.

The first few shuttle runs were completed without any interference, but then several went awry. On one of the runs, coxswain Harry Hopperton was standing on the beach at Cape Endaiadere, talking to the beach master, when a Japanese shell hit his boat amidships and reduced it to splinters. On another run, Hopperton was acting as deckhand/gunner when their boat was attacked by a Japanese aircraft. In that attack, the boat's coxswain was hit in the head and killed instantly. Hopperton took over but ran the boat onto a coral reef as he attempted to evade the aircraft.

The loss of Hopperton's second boat reduced the number now available for the shuttle run to four. Two more were brought up from Milne Bay a few days later along with the remaining fifteen original soldier volunteers to crew them. However, by the end of December, when the boats were taken off the run for a few days' rest, only two Higgins boats remained in action, the others being lost to a combination of enemy action, coral reefs or because they were cannibalised for spare parts.

•

There were dangers even when there should not have been. On 23 December 1942, Alan Reynolds had loaded his Small Ship, the *Eva*, with stores and ammunition at Oro Bay and then sailed to Cape Sudest where he anchored off the beach at 10 p.m. In the moonlight, Reynolds could see two small vessels sitting out on the water some distance to the north of his anchorage. They were too far away to be recognisable but Reynolds assumed that they, too, were Small Ships either waiting to unload their cargo or perhaps just having a rest. He gave them no further thought as he organised the unloading of the *Eva*, then he and several of his crew sought out a comfortable spot on the beach and lay down to sleep.

Reynold stayed awake and, shortly after the others fell asleep, he saw the two boats he had spotted earlier approaching Cape Sudest at speed, throwing up large bow waves. There were still a number of Papuan carriers aboard the *Eva* and, as the boats sped up towards his ship, Reynolds saw the flashes and heard the hammering as their machine guns opened fire. One boat appeared to be firing at the *Eva* while the other had opened up at the soldiers and carriers still on the beach. His crew were instantly awake and they joined Reynolds in pressing themselves as far down into the sand as they could go. As they did so, machine gun bullets cracked overhead and fizzed into the sand around them.

The *Eva* exploded into flames after the first burst of firing and at the same time Alan Reynolds heard one of his men cry out in pain somewhere nearby. Throwing caution to the wind, he crouched and ran along the beach, found the wounded man and helped him back into the jungle as the two boats moved closer, firing at the beach and the jungle behind in long bursts.

Convinced that the attackers were Japanese, Reynolds led his men back to the American defensive positions where they were all issued rifles to help in repelling the Japanese attack which was now expected at any minute. As he waited, Reynolds looked out at the *Eva*, now burning fiercely with a number of explosions rocking the ship as the ammunition it was carrying exploded from the heat.

There was no attack that night, and the following day Reynolds and his crew were interviewed by US Army Headquarters about the circumstances of the attack. Afterwards they were looked after very well by the Americans. They were given whatever rations they asked for, and were also issued with new clothing to replace that which they had lost on the *Eva*. They were told as well that they would be given places aboard the next ship that came to Cape Sudest. Having just lost their own boat, that was not something they were particularly looking forward to and, after a discussion, Reynolds and his men decided that they would prefer to walk back to Oro Bay. It was hot, and there were occasional showers, but they all made the twenty-five kilometres back to their own mess where they arrived just in time for an evening meal. After little or no sleep the night before and a solid trek that day, Reynolds and his men slept well.

By the next day, Christmas Day 1942, it had been confirmed that the attack on the *Eva* had been carried out by US Navy

Patrol/Torpedo (PT) boats operating out of their new base at Tufi; the unit had arrived in New Guinea less than a week earlier.

Afterwards, there was quite an unusual series of consequences from the loss of the *Eva*, and it almost seems as though there was an attempt to cover up the incident.

The night of the attack on the *Eva*, Shaw Brown and the other gunners who had survived the attack on the *Kurimarau* were sleeping peacefully in their tents near their guns then located between Hariko and Cape Sudest when they were awakened, he thought around 11 p.m., by calls of 'Stand to!' and the sound of machine-gun and cannon fire. Brown wasn't certain but he thought that he could also hear bombs dropping somewhere in the distance. Brown and his troop grabbed weapons and jumped into the slit trenches they had dug around their gun emplacements. There, they watched tracer bullets passing through the treetops above.

At one point, they were ordered to move one of the 25-pound guns down to the beach, an order that was quickly countermanded. At another, American sick and wounded passed back through their gun emplacements convinced that their hospital was under direct attack.

Brown recalled that the moon was bright that night, although it was also occasionally obscured by cloud, creating shadows that morphed into shapes creeping through the trees towards them until the moon came out and there was nothing there anymore. He and the other gunners remained on alert but, apart from some explosions that seemed to be some distance off, there were no further indications that they were under attack.

The next morning, Brown and his troop were told that the action during the night was an attack on an Allied launch loaded with explosives by two Japanese boats using machine gun and cannon fire. The story of the Japanese then landing troops had been started, he learned, by 'some scared Yank'.

Not all that far from where Shaw Brown's gun troop was based, Alan Williams, an Australian medical orderly with the 2/10th Field Ambulance was also awakened by the sounds of machine-gun fire; he would later clearly recall what happened that night, but from a slightly different perspective. He would write that on the evening of 23 December 1942, an attack was made by Japanese E-Boats on a US schooner just off the coast. The E-Boats were engaged by coastal defence guns and there was some heavy firing from and at the Japanese boats. In fact, that firing prompted a rumour that the Japanese were preparing to land troops to the rear of the Allied forces.

As most of the army units that had been camped around the field ambulance had by then moved forward to the Buna front-lines, there was a real concern among the ambulancemen that they could be surrounded and cut off by the Japanese. Hurried preparations were made to move to one of the 25-pound artillery bases, the nearest Allied forces.

Williams recalled that the incident had begun just after dark – it was, in fact, a couple of hours later – and that the first the ambulancemen knew of an attack was when bullets began to hit the unit's tents, at which point they all sought cover behind trees. He said the firing continued for some time and thought that it only ceased when the field guns started shelling the attackers' boats. He also said that further rumours soon swirled around, suggesting that it was in fact American boats that had attacked the schooner and the shoreline because they had mistaken the location of the Japanese positions along that part of the coastline. However, he added, the rumours were wrong and the next day they were all told that it had really been an attack by Japanese forces.

What was even stranger was that the first official US Army account of the Buna campaign, published just three years later, would contain the passage: 'On 23 December, two enemy PT-type boats sank a ship off Hariko and machine gunned the supply base. However, through most of the period, the Allied forces on the east flank were successfully supplied by the sea route.' They were partly wrong but they were also partly right.

•

After talking to Alan Reynolds and several others who had either seen or were aware of the attack on the *Eva*, Ralph Andrews was in no doubt as to who had attacked the boat off Hariko and was determined that such an incident would not occur again. The American PT boats had only been operating in the area for less than a week, coming out of the new base they had established at Tufi. The next time the *Two Freddies* was in that area, Andrews anchored offshore and took the dinghy to the PT boat headquarters where he asked to speak to the officer in charge. When that officer arrived, Andrews introduced himself and then produced a copy of a chart showing the most prominent coastal features between Cape Nelson and Buna. On that chart, he drew a straight line between Cape Nelson and Oro Bay. The area below that line, he explained, was for Small Ships only. Keep your boats above it, he added.

On 1 January 1943, a more formal meeting was followed by a more formal agreement to prevent such friendly fire incidents from occurring again. Patrick Lang, the Australian COSC Liaison Officer, visited Tufi for discussions to establish a 'protected zone' for Small Ships operations. The PT boats' commanding officer agreed to keep his boats beyond a line drawn from Cape Nelson to Cape Endaiadere unless they were under direct orders from New Guinea Force or if it was a genuine emergency. There were no repeats of the *Eva* incident.

•

By late December, the fighting at Buna had assumed a new and markedly different character. The Japanese entrenchments and strongholds were still as robust and deep as they had been at the start of the campaign, but they were no longer impervious to all Allied attacks. The introduction of tanks and artillery had tilted the balance in favour of the American and, now, Australian troops who confronted them. The Japanese defenders were no less ferocious and fanatical – the first Japanese prisoner was not taken until 30 November, almost two weeks into the attack – but they were now both slowly starving and without any real hope of relief. After the beginning of December, only negligible reinforcements and supplies were brought in to those defenders. The fighting at Guadalcanal drew in more and more Japanese forces, while the Allied air strength was growing as more and more aircraft were brought into the theatre. The Japanese supply line to Buna, never strong, had now all but collapsed.

By contrast, the Allies now had two supply lines. The airfield at Popondetta was fully operational by the beginning of December and, while weather in the rainy season was always an issue, regular supply deliveries were becoming the norm rather than the exception. At sea, the supply line was no longer dependent on a small number of Small Ships. The introduction of new and larger boats, and the introduction of steel barges that could be towed and could carry significant amounts of supplies and equipment, finally tipped the balance in the Allies' favour. Also critical in that supply line was the development of forward bases at Porlock Harbour and Oro Bay.

Those bases provided not just major supply dumps; they supplied a range of secure anchorages and support functions for the sailors of the Small Ships, their vessels and the hundreds of soldiers who were now passing through them. The delivery of the Stuart tanks, followed by the delivery of the Australian soldiers through Operations Hammer and Sledge Hammer, were key factors in the outcome of the fighting at Buna. The introduction of specialised vessels, like the Higgins boats, pointed the way to the future of the Small Ships and also the future of MacArthur's amphibious campaigns. There was a long way to go at Buna and in the South West Pacific Area, but by mid-December, as the end of 1942 approached at a cracking pace, there were some things to both celebrate and to believe in as the basis for bigger and better outcomes in 1943.

12.

BASE B

Base B – Oro Bay – would become the epicentre of the Small Ships Section's activities during the Buna campaign. Nearby locations were also important: Porlock Harbour was a significant supply depot and anchorage, and nearby Harvey Bay, with its inlets and mangrove forests, was a popular lying-up and hiding spot. But Oro Bay was critical to the story of the Small Ships. A large deep-water harbour with a relatively easy approach, it would grow into the most important Allied port between Milne Bay and Lae, a development not lost on the Japanese.

One of the unfortunate elements of Small Ships service was that it could be a lonely existence. They *were*, in the main, small ships and most were crewed by a small number of sailors; the minimum seems to have been two and the norm, at least at this stage of the Pacific War, was probably no more than three or four. Their method of operating didn't lend itself to a wide interaction with others either. For most, the work hours were the hours between dusk and dawn, with daylight a time to hide from the ever-present danger of Japanese aircraft in a sheltered inlet, and rest and recuperate. They did this alone, too, because to congregate meant drawing attention, and that attention could prove fatal.

When they did catch up with one another – at Oro Bay, at the various bases further back, on the *Masaya*, or even on leave in Australia – they swapped stories about what had happened to ships and sailors they all knew or at least knew of. Some were happy and some were sad; some were true and some should have been true. And many were about those ships and sailors and the shuttle run from Oro Bay.

•

As part of transforming Oro Bay into a major operational base for the Small Ships, Jack Gilmore was appointed salvage master there. The title 'salvage master' was something of a misnomer as Gilmore was given far wider responsibilities than just salvage, and worked hard to make the Small Ships Section's operation out of Oro Bay not just successful, but also efficient.

Stories of Gilmore's time at Oro Bay would later become the stuff of legends, but he was most famous for his ability to stock-pile lumber that the small vessels needed for emergency repairs, which would also be used to build better facilities ashore for their sailors. Through an oversight in a bill of lading, Gilmore received a load of bagged cement at Oro Bay; he had no real need for the cement, but stored it in a small shed he had hired some local Papuans to help him build. Nearby was a US Army engineering unit that was working hard to construct port facilities for the large freighters that would soon be coming direct to Oro Bay. They had much more lumber than they could possibly use, and Gilmore noted that it was the kind of quality lumber that he needed.

He approached the Americans and proposed an exchange. For each amount of lumber they gave him, he would give them a bag of cement. It was a deal sealed with a handshake. Over the next few days, Gilmore built up a large stockpile of the lumber while still being able to produce bags of cement to exchange for it.

One of the Small Ships skippers asked Gilmore how he was able to continue such an exchange when the original load of cement bags was hardly enough to cover more than one or two exchanges. At this point, Gilmore swore him to secrecy and then revealed that he paid his Papuans an extra allowance for each bag of cement they were able to steal from the Americans' building supplies dump some distance away. If they were caught, they were instructed to explain that they had been drinking and had heard that the cement had some sort of magical qualities that they wanted to test.

Gilmore got his lumber and no one was ever heard to complain about the exchange.

•

Porlock Harbour had its own stories too. The best known was an incident that occurred there on 29 November. At almost exactly midday, a single Japanese aircraft flew over the harbour at a height of around 5000 metres. Far below, three Small Ships were anchored towards the head of the harbour with a space of perhaps fifty metres between them. The ships were the *Kurimarau*, *Kooraka* and *Muliama*, and they were caught by surprise in the open. The aircraft dropped a single bomb as a sighter and followed up with a string of five bombs.

One bomb fell short of the first ship, the second between the first and second ships in line, the next between the second and third, with the last two landing beyond the third ship. When the water had splashed back down and the smoke had cleared, not one of the three ships had been damaged and no one aboard any of them had been injured. The only obvious result was that a group of Filipino sailors, rudely awakened by the explosions and convinced that a full-scale air raid was on the way, had jumped down into a tethered dinghy, rowed to the nearest shore and taken off into the jungle. It took a lot of convincing to get them back on their boat.

Another early morning at Porlock Harbour, a thick sea mist made vision difficult. At one of the guard posts near the harbour's entrance, a sentry spotted a slow-moving and shadowy boat trying to sneak into the harbour. He armed himself with the post's heaviest weapon, a Boys anti-tank rifle, took careful aim at the shape and fired. As he did so, the mist parted slightly, and the boat revealed itself to be a Small Ships trawler. Fortunately for all involved, the shot missed everything.

Some cases of mistaken identity ended badly – as at Pongani when the *King John* was attacked by an American aircraft, killing Bruce Fahnestock and Barney Darnton, and injuring more than a dozen others – but some didn't. Nerves on all sides were stretched to their limits during the Buna campaign and this sometimes led to snap decisions and snap judgements, often with consequences that could not have been foreseen.

One day, as the *Zoie*, the boat Bert Evans had built on the Crookhaven River, was tied up and hopefully invisible in a mangrove patch along a tidal inlet, one of the crew informed Jack Gardner, the boat's skipper, that he had just spotted three unarmed Japanese walking along a nearby beach. Gardner directed his crew to arm themselves and go down to the beach to capture the Japanese and bring them back to the *Zoie*, which he would be guarding. When asked what to do if the Japanese resisted, the answer was a concise, 'Shoot 'em.'

The crew soon returned with the prisoners under close guard. Gardner attempted to question the men, but it was soon obvious that none of them spoke English. He directed that their hands be tied behind their backs and kept them under guard until he could hand them over to the American garrison at Oro Bay. There he received a reception that was almost the complete opposite to the one he had expected to receive. The American officer to whom the prisoners was brought erupted in a tirade before asking politely, if sarcastically, why Gardner had brought him the Filipino crew of the *Kelton* as hostages. It emerged later that the *Kelton* had run aground on a sandbank and Ireneo Ames had sent three of his crew off to seek assistance.

•

For the captains and crews of the Small Ships, the shuttle runs between Oro Bay and Porlock Harbour at one end, and Hariko and Boreo at the other, melded into a single kind of collective memory, at least for those that didn't end in disaster. All were tests of nerves based on fears of running aground during the night and greater fears of being caught in the open by Japanese aircraft during daylight hours. There was a flurry of activity at the beginning of the run and a flurry of activity at its end. The irregular periods between the runs provided some time – never enough – to grab some rest, catch up with letter reading and letter writing and then prepare for the next turn on the tread-mill that the shuttle runs had become.

Ralph Andrews and the *Two Freddies* had been there from the start. His survival through the dark days of November and December 1942 was due to a combination of good luck, good seamanship and, perhaps, something else. The *Two Freddies* had a resident kitten but it was aboard as a mascot rather than as a talisman. They also had a Papuan boy who knew the local waters well and had a sharp eye; he also had a strong belief in things that could not always be seen. On the morning of 18 November, he told Ralph he had seen a dead fish, and so he was upset. Sensing that there was something more to the story, Ralph asked him to continue. The dead fish, the boy said, meant that someone was about to die. Later that day, the *Two Freddies* was caught in the open by Zeros and barely survived thanks to Ralph running his boat onto a beach. Several of those aboard received injuries during the attack and one man subsequently died.

On another occasion, the boy told Ralph that the previous night he had dreamed of a big aeroplane. Later that day, as the *Two Freddies* was setting off on a run to Hariko, a B-17 Flying Fortress appeared from the west and circled the little boat at a low altitude. It was the first time anyone aboard had ever seen such a large aircraft.

As the Buna campaign ramped up again in early December, Ralph and the other captains were offered US soldiers to man their machine guns – an acknowledgement that the pressure being applied to the supply line would see them operating in daylight as well as darkness. It was an offer he accepted gladly, and the *Two Freddies* was given a sergeant, a corporal and a private as crew for their two .50 calibre machine guns. Unfortunately, one of the first things Ralph learned about his new gun team was that they had not been given any weapons training beforehand. Ralph had, so he decided to pass on some of his knowledge to them, with mixed results. In Ralph's own words, 'The sergeant was useless, so I made him cook', but the other two were both keen to learn and good learners to boot. In quick time, they learned how to strip down and operate the guns.

As one of the more battle-hardened of the Small Ships captains, Ralph could speak of the early days of the shuttle run, when it was just the *Two Freddies* and the *Kelton*, each of them carrying twenty tons of ammunition and supplies per trip; between twelve and fifteen tons in the hold and the remainder as deck cargo. He could tell of the times when the call was for more men urgently needed at the front, and he and Ireneo Ames would somehow squeeze up to 100 soldiers each on their trawlers and how, before the Higgins boats and barges, they would carry planks to put between the canoe and the outrigger on the natives' canoes, creating a platform that could support up to a ton and a half of cargo, and of how they would have to break down all heavy weapons if they hoped to transport them.

He also told the less experienced captains to carry plenty of twist tobacco as it was the universal currency among the Papuans. It could be used to hire deckhands and carriers but, more importantly, it could be traded at the local villages for fruit and vegetables because the rations the Small Ships crews were given were simply not good enough to sustain them in the work they were doing. Without the supplements, they would quickly grow weaker and become more susceptible to all the diseases and ailments prevalent in the area.

•

What would become routine for Ralph Andrews and the other Small Ships sailors, though, was sometimes a major adventure for their passengers. Ely Kahn was a US army sergeant, a soldier of some distinction and a writer of some note. Some time around the middle of December, Kahn, another soldier and an officer were offered a lift aboard one of the trawlers making the shuttle run from Oro Bay to Hariko. The three had been at Embogo, probably visiting Waldron's headquarters there, and were told to wait on the beach and they would be rowed out to meet their transport when it arrived that night.

Shortly before midnight, a dim shape appeared out of the water and the three soldiers were rowed out to it. They climbed up and over the railings of a small trawler and tried to find somewhere comfortable to sit on a deck almost completely covered by boxes of ammunition stacked one on top of another. The three men eventually propped themselves up against a large box of hand grenades and had a look around.

Kahn was initially surprised by how small the boat actually was, and guessed that it could not have been more than thirteen metres from stem to stern. If he was surprised by the size of the ship, he was gobsmacked by the appearance of its crew. He recognised the captain as the man giving all the orders, otherwise he was just 'a scrawny Australian wearing only a pair of shorts and a sleeveless sweater several sizes too big for him'. The captain's assistant, who spoke with what Khan believed was an Italian accent, was wearing nothing but a pair of long pants. The rest of the crew, who Kahn suspected were all Filipinos, were 'a triumph of sartorial inelegance'.

The three American soldiers sat quietly on deck for an hour, waiting for something to happen. Then the engine was started and the boat moved off slowly without a word being spoken. The sea that night was calm and there was a full moon. It would have been idyllic, Kahn thought, except for the blanket ban on smoking on deck. Those and similar thoughts flitted in and out of his mind as they drifted along but were pushed aside when the trawler ran straight onto a sandbank and came to a grinding halt.

This appeared to end their voyage, as the captain offered his opinion to anyone within earshot that they were now stuck fast. After a discussion among the crew, it was decided to move the heavy ammunition from the stacks near the bow to the stacks near the stern, a task they all joined in and one which occupied a sweaty half-hour. Then they tried to fishtail off, but without any success. Eventually, the captain and the three Americans rowed ashore and found, quite fortuitously, an American guard post nearby and organised for the trawler to be unloaded where it was.

After handshakes all around, the captain and his American passengers went their separate ways.

•

The nerves felt by those on the Small Ships were partly a result of the knowledge that they were now working in a war zone, and at the frontlines of that war zone. As 1942 became 1943, the sailors on the Small Ships had been exposed to six weeks of high-intensity warfare, and in many cases it was starting to show. Although they would never talk about it, they all understood that every voyage they took might be their last.

The *Barraconda* was one of the Small Ships rushed forward in the aftermath of the disaster at Hariko on the eve of the offensive. Four Small Ships had been caught in the open by Japanese aircraft and all were destroyed with a considerable loss of life and vital supplies. On a night shuttle run from Oreo Bay to Boreo in mid-December, the *Barraconda* ran aground on an unmarked reef while carrying a cargo that consisted mainly of ration packs. It was a bad grounding and, with the tide falling and daylight just a couple of hours away, the crew abandoned ship and, using the *Barraconda*'s dinghy, transferred as many of the supplies they were carrying as they could to the beach just

500 metres away. Most of the rowing was done by the youngest crewman, an eighteen-year-old junior engineer named Max Hood.

On his last trip back from the *Barraconda*, now in broad daylight and with the dinghy packed full of supplies, Hood heard the sound of an approaching aircraft, which soon proved to be a Zero. Abandoning the dinghy, Hood eventually made it back to the beach after a series of deep dives and underwater swimming. However, both the *Barraconda* and its dinghy were so badly shot up that both were beyond repair.

The crew barely survived the two weeks that followed. There was a large swamp inland from the beach and the men were attacked by mosquitoes night and day. By the time they were eventually found by an American army patrol, all had malaria and a variety of vitamin-deficiency illnesses. As well, most were suffering from open, running sores and had, on average, lost about half their body weight. Most were within just a couple of days of death but they went straight back to their work on the Small Ships when they recovered.

Clarrie Dawes and the *Leprena* also found themselves in the thick of things. Even when they were between runs, anchored somewhere they thought safe in Oro Bay, the war was never far away. Clarrie was one of the many who believed the Japanese had a spotter based somewhere in the foothills of the hinterland. It just seemed too coincidental that every time a large ship arrived at Oro Bay an air raid would inevitably follow. By mid-January, the Allies often had air cover over Oro Bay, usually be a single aircraft, and sometimes a flight of P-39 Airacobras. When the air-raid sirens sounded, the Allied aircraft would disappear, presumably to intercept the Japanese aircraft coming in from Rabaul or Lae.

When the air cover was sent, it would usually remain in the area from early morning until late afternoon. Try as he might, though, Clarrie could never work out how such things as providing air cover were calculated. One day, there were no Airacobras to be seen, but an RAAF Hudson flew overhead. In the blink of an eye, a Zero appeared out of nowhere, shot the Hudson down, and disappeared as quickly as it had arrived.

Clarrie lost count of the number of times the *Leprena* made the Oro Bay to Hariko run from late November 1942 until late January 1943, but it was often enough to give him recurring nightmares. The runs themselves fell into a pattern. Since the *Leprena* was larger than the trawlers – she could carry 100 tons of cargo compared with their twenty to thirty tons – the loading and unloading processes took longer, so she rarely did back-to-back runs. Normally, she would be loaded up with ammunition and rations to take forward, while on the return trip her cargo would be sick and wounded soldiers. The total amount of supplies she carried would have been a figure somewhere in the region of 1500 tons at the least and Clarrie reckoned they would also have carried several hundred soldiers.

Only once were they in real trouble. On a night run back to Oro Bay, the *Leprena* ran onto a reef and the engine's cooling pipe was cut in the process. The grounding had caused little damage apart from that but unless the pipe was fixed, the engine would quickly overheat and seize. Unfortunately, daylight arrived before the repairs were completed. Even more unfortunately, they were spotted by a patrolling Zero, which dived down towards them and circled before flying away again. The conclusion was that he had run out of ammunition, and all aboard believed they owed their lives to that fact.

After the Zero departed, they were able to ease the *Leprena* off the reef on a rising tide and it sailed to Oro Bay with the crew continually topping up the cooling tank with seawater. Back at Oro Bay, a diver went down and cut out the damaged part of the pipe, replacing it with rubber hose. It worked just fine. The *Leprena* was reloaded with supplies and took her place in the shuttle again that night.

•

When not engaged in running supplies up the coast and bringing casualties back down, the Small Ships' vessels were used on a variety of maritime tasks. One of the tasks assigned to the Higgins boats at Oro Bay was greeted with a degree of enthusiasm by the boats' Australian crews.

As American pressure on the Japanese positions at Buna continued to build through December, the Japanese realised that Oro Bay was a key link in the supply chain supporting that American effort, and the bay became a target for Japanese air raids on an almost daily basis. While most were night raids undertaken by multiple bombers, daytime hit-and-run raids by single aircraft were also common. During one of these daylight raids the Dutch KPM freighter, the *Van Heutz*, had her hull split open by a near-miss and sank at her anchorage in almost ten metres of water. When she settled on the bottom all that remained above water were the top deck and the funnel.

Jack Gilmore, in his capacity as salvage master, asked Sheridan Fahnestock, then on a visit to Oro Bay, for permission to use the Higgins boats in the attempt to salvage the *Van Heutz* and its cargo. A number of boats were involved and in relatively quick order had helped to remove everything of value that had been stored on the *Van Heutz*'s top deck. The next day, a salvage diver, identified only as 'Captain Collins', was summoned. Collins collected his diving gear and organised for one of the Higgins boats to tow a steel barge across to the sunken ship. With his support crew and equipment aboard, the barge became Collins' diving platform.

Over the next few hours, Collins and his team of assistants on the barge and in the Higgins boats were able to recover everything of importance that was in the *Van Heutz*'s holds. Collins also somehow managed to bring up a case of beer in the recovery basket on each dive. Even better, it was cool after spending hours in deep water.

•

To all intents and purposes, the 'Battle of the Beachheads' – Buna, Gona and Sanananda – was over by the first week of January 1943. Gona had fallen to the Australians on 9 December, with the surviving Japanese either fleeing north along the coast or falling back onto the prepared positions at Sanananda and Buna; the most significant outer defences at Buna had been overcome or reduced to splinters, entombing the defenders; and Sanananda was being pinched into submission from all sides. The Japanese were unable to bring in any significant reinforcements; and as the supply line that had brought men in had also brought food and medicine, its failure meant that the surviving defenders were very sick and very hungry.

The battle was officially announced as being over on 22 January 1943, when a communiqué from MacArthur's headquarters announced that the last Japanese resistance at Buna had been overcome. It would be some time further before the cost of the battle to both sides could be totalled up. The Allies estimated that there had been around 6000 Japanese troops in the enclave. After the vicious fighting that accompanied Waldron's 5 December offensive was over, Allied aircraft ruled the skies above Buna during daylight hours and on 8 December dropped leaflets instead of bombs across the Japanese positions. Those leaflets pointed out that the Japanese defenders could no longer expect outside support; they had fought well but were now trapped and were slowly starving. They could surrender or they could die. Most chose the latter; at campaign's end, only fifty of those Japanese remained alive.

The Allies' losses were, overall, greater in numbers but lesser in outcome. In two months of fighting the Australians lost 1300 killed and the Americans over a thousand. That was only part of the story, though, as thousands more were incapacitated by wounds and disease, with malaria by far the biggest contributor to that figure. Later US Army assessments showed that of every nine soldiers put out of action, three were battle casualties at a ratio of two wounded for every one killed. The remaining six were victims of illness. The raw figures are just as confronting. The hardest-hit American unit was the 126th Infantry Regiment, part of Hanford MacNider's coastal task force. The 126th went into battle with 131 officers and 3040 enlisted men; it had just thirty-two officers and 579 men fit for duty at the end of the campaign.

For the Americans, the Buna campaign was both an end and a beginning. It was the end of the Japanese drive into the South West Pacific. After Buna fell, all the battles the Japanese fought would be to retain territory captured more than a year earlier; their days of victory after victory were over. Buna and the concomitant battle at Guadalcanal represented the furthest reach of Japanese expansion. It was also the beginning of a new style of warfare: amphibious warfare combined with an island-hopping strategy would now be the norm in the Pacific War. The vast distances involved also dictated that logistics and supply lines would determine outcomes more often than not. That the Americans' supply line worked at Buna was largely due to the skills and courage of a little fleet of fishing boats, coastal yawls and schooners skippered by men who did what they had been doing for years. They might not have been the youngest or the fittest to ever go to war, but for them the war was an extension of their professional lives. Now, though, they were doing it under the eyes and guns of a determined enemy.

•

Just a couple of days later, Clarrie Dawes made his last voyage on the *Leprena*. Right from the moment they cleared Oro Bay, it felt like something was not quite right and Clarrie soon worked out what it was. As was usual, the cargo had been brought aboard during the late afternoon and early evening but this time they waited for daybreak the next morning before setting out. It was a fine morning too, a clear day with no aircraft in the sky to watch out for. Most of the Zeros had been chased away and the Japanese bombers now preferred to operate at night; that didn't stop Clarrie and the other crew from looking up to the sky regularly, though.

At Buna, the crew all went ashore to see the scene of the battle they had worked so long and hard to support. For Clarrie, the battlefield was a landscape unlike anything else he had seen in his life. The damage the American bombers had wrought was almost beyond description. There were enormous craters all along the waterline. The trees in what had once been a coconut palm plantation had all had their foliage blasted away and the area now looked like a forest of sticks.

Clarrie wandered inland a short distance. He found an enormous rabbit warren of pillboxes and bunkers connected by a maze of trenches that both connected and supported the strongpoints. The pillboxes and bunkers appeared to have been built mainly from the trunks of coconut palm trees. They also seemed to have been blasted apart by 25-pound field pieces firing at close range.

When Clarrie returned to the *Leprena*, the cargo had been unloaded and the boat was ready to sail again, this time just a short hop to Sanananda where they were to drop off a team of Australian soldiers. Looking shoreward from the boat as they approached Sanananda, Clarrie thought that everything behind the narrow beach was part of a much larger swamp, but once ashore he found that the Japanese had built a walkway from the beach to the higher dry land behind the swamp.

In one part of that dry land, he found a large number of Japanese graves and was told that the soldiers buried there had been killed by American bombers and local fevers. The grave markers were simply a length of tree trunk that had been split down the centre and buried in the ground. The name of the soldier – at least that was what Clarrie thought it was – had been written in Japanese characters on the flat side of the wooden markers. *You're a long way from home*, he thought, *like me*. He wondered whether he would ever see home again.

As Clarrie was returning to the *Leprena*, he saw an officer and a small squad of Australian soldiers standing guard over a group of Japanese prisoners. There would have been at least thirty, or possibly more, and Clarrie was surprised at how poorly they all looked. The Japanese were thin to the point of starvation and seemed to be suffering from malaria, beri-beri or both. It wasn't something he wanted to dwell on, though, and he walked quickly back to the beach and the *Leprena*.

They sailed directly back to Oro Bay where a surprise was waiting for Clarrie. When he called in to the Small Ships office there, he was informed that there were two things for him. One was a travel warrant authorising him to travel to Sydney aboard a military aircraft. The second was a fourteen-day leave pass. Clarrie would use them both and, when he next returned to sea, neither he nor the Small Ships would be the same.

13.

SETTING SUN

The conclusion of the Buna campaign was also the conclusion of the most intensive operational period in the history of the Small Ships. Sailors and boats – those that had survived anyway – needed a period of quiet for rest and recuperation. For some, the end of the campaign also coincided with the expiration of their six-month employment contracts; they would now have to decide whether or not they wanted to continue and then whether or not they were fit enough to continue. The movement of ships and sailors north was partially replicated three months later. This time, however, they were heading south.

The process had actually begun a little earlier. Alan Reynolds and the crew of the *Eva* had not been given much time to recover from the loss of their ship on the night of 23 December. On Christmas Day, they were ordered to board the *Melinga* for passage from Oro Bay via Porlock Harbour to Milne Bay. The *Melinga* did not depart until 7.30 p.m. on Christmas night and, as if to make up for the disturbance to the traditional day of rest and reflection, the *Melinga*'s cook prepared an especially large and flavourful dinner for the passengers, of whom there were quite a few. As well as the *Eva*'s crew, there were several quite senior US Army officers aboard and one of them approached Alan Reynolds to see whether he and his crew would be prepared to try to salvage the *Hilda Norling*, still sitting on the sand bar onto which she had crashed. After a brief discussion among themselves, they agreed to give it a go.

Reynolds and his crew disembarked at Porlock Harbour at 3 a.m. on Boxing Day, spending the rest of the night trying to go to sleep on the little wharf there. After breakfast in the army mess the next morning, they waited around until early afternoon when they were taken to Sebaga, the village near where the *Hilda Norling* had been abandoned. There, after their recent experiences, they were given what seemed like luxury accommodation: a grass hut, plenty of food and a Papuan boy to cook it. By the time they had eaten and settled in, the day was too far gone to examine the *Hilda Norling* so they settled down in their grass hut for the evening.

The next day, Reynolds and his crew of mate, engineer and deckhand paddled out in canoes to inspect the *Hilda Norling*. They found that her hull was sound although the boat itself had been badly shot up. She was also stuck hard in the sand, with just a metre of water around her at low tide. Reynolds hired some of the Papuan villagers to clean up the general mess and to begin pumping water from the hull. They also tried to pull the boat out of the sand using the winches during the afternoon's high tide, but the *Norling* simply refused to move.

The men repeated the process each evening at high tide, but the tides themselves were never particularly high and the boat still refused to move. On the first day of the new year of 1943, the *Hilda Norling* moved 'just a little'. They finally managed to get her afloat on the high tide during the afternoon of 4 January, but the running seas that lifted her clear of the sand bank almost pushed her onto the beach. Some quick work and some good seamanship saw her float clear of all entanglements before she was steered out beyond the beach breakers and anchored in relatively calm waters.

After several more days' repair work to ensure that she was seaworthy, the *Hilda Norling* set off from Sebaga on 8 January and sailed the short distance back to Porlock Harbour, where carpenters and boat builders repaired most of the damage the bullets and cannon shells had caused to her hull and superstructure. She departed Porlock Harbour two days later and sailed slowly down the north coast, arriving at Milne Bay on 13 January. Two of Reynolds' crew were immediately hospitalised for acute malaria while Reynolds himself was almost as ill. His ailment, though, was partly caused by the amount of paperwork he had to complete over the loss of the *Eva*.

•

Ralph Andrews' war had certainly produced a mixed bag for him in 1942 so he looked forward to 1943 with some trepidation. He had been captain of the *Two Freddies* when she was shot up by Zeros off Embogo on 18 November. In itself, that was a negative, but he had survived the experience and that was certainly a positive. The same day that he escaped death, the trawler that he had built and sailed before the war, the *Willyama II*, had also been attacked and shot up off Mendaropu, probably by the same aircraft that had attacked the *Two Freddies*. Again, a negative, but balanced by the fact that there were relatively few casualties in both attacks and the boats themselves could be salvaged.

The best efforts of the Japanese had failed to leave a mark on him – a positive – but he had seen in the new year of 1943 at the field hospital at Milne Bay, being treated for an array of conditions, including what he suspected was sandy blight in both eyes, a number of tropical ulcers on his legs and recurrent attacks of malaria. One day, between treatments, he was sought out by Laddie Reday who asked him whether he would be interested in sailing a damaged ship back to Townsville for repairs. It had already been suggested to Andrews that it might be best to return to Australia for medical treatment so the suggestion was worth considering. Firstly, though, he asked around about the boat, the *Hilda Norling*, learning little more than that she had run aground on a sandbank and been shot up by Japanese aircraft.

Andrews then went down to the Gili Gili wharf where he cast his professional eye over the former cray boat. He went on board and looked closely above and below decks. The main engine seemed to be sound but most of the auxiliary power suppliers – small engines for specific tasks – were damaged and out of service. Probably the most critical of these was the small diesel donkey engine used to raise and lower the anchor. It had been hit by a bullet that had destroyed its rocker arm but Ralph thought it could be repaired. It was also an essential item, as the *Hilda Norling*'s anchor was unusually heavy and Ralph knew it would be a struggle to raise it manually.

Almost everything aboard seemed to have been hit by at least one bullet. Even the drainpipe from the sink in the captain's cabin had been shot through. There was no stove, most of the deckhouse was wrecked and the mast had been splintered by bullets. Just to finish off the examination, Ralph discovered that literally everything that wasn't bolted down had been removed somewhere in its recent travels.

When Ralph reported back to Laddie Reday he suggested that, in his professional opinion, the best course of action would be for the *Hilda Norling* to be towed back to Townsville for extensive repairs. Reday pushed that suggestion up through the chain of command, and the reply that came back was that Ralph Andrews and another eight medical cases who needed treatment in Australia were to sail the boat back to Australia. When those nine were brought together and had the task explained to them, they immediately set out to scrounge anything they thought might help them survive that voyage.

Their efforts were inspired. The damage below decks meant they would need to be able to sleep on deck. To create an awning to protect that sleeping space, an old and torn sail was cut to the correct dimensions and attached to a boom that could be locked in place. The missing stove was replaced by an empty five-gallon drum with holes punched in it. A brace of .30 calibre machine guns was sourced from who knew where. The other Small Ships also came to their assistance. Ralph organised for one of Jack Savage's mechanics to make a new rocker arm for the donkey engine while one of the other skippers gave Ralph his spare set of charts. Ropes, lamps, dozens of tools, spare clothing and items like crockery and cutlery were given with no thought of their return. The one vital item that was missing was a compass, so Ralph 'borrowed' one from another ship's lifeboat, reasoning that he needed it for survival now rather than a possible survival later. The only item he wasn't able to source was a ship's log.

The *Hilda Norling* and its crew of ambulant medical cases made it safely through to Port Moresby from Milne Bay; it was a slow journey, though, as the best Ralph could coax out of the boat's engine was four knots. Shortly after they dropped anchor there, the air-raid sirens sounded for the first air-raid in several weeks. Fortunately the raid was at the airfields and not the harbour and port facilities this time.

At Port Moresby, common sense seemed to prevail and another vessel was assigned to accompany the *Hilda Norling* back to Townsville just in case the engine failed. The two boats sailed late the next afternoon, the better to avoid prowling Japanese aircraft. Just as it grew dark, Ralph realised that their escort was nowhere to be seen, so they simply resigned themselves to whatever was in store for them.

With only a basic compass and charts, navigation was by dead reckoning and Ralph Andrews was either very good or very lucky as he reached every landfall he set for himself and the boat. When they reached Thursday Island, they had mixed fortunes. The army provided them with rations, including what Ralph would describe as 'beautiful tinned peas'. He was able to purchase a case of gin for just over three shillings a bottle, so he thought things might be looking up. The island's medical authorities had other ideas, though, and wanted to keep most of the crew in hospital to treat their tropical ulcers. After the crew promised to treat themselves with the medications provided by the hospital staff, all but the mate were allowed to leave. He was 'rescued' through a window very late that night.

The sick ship and its equally sick crew never did make it back to Townsville. When they reached Cairns, the port doctor there immediately sent all the crew to Gordonvale Hospital, declaring that none was fit for any kind of service. It was shortly after he was admitted that Ralph learned that 1943 might not turn out to be so bad after all. The newspapers were full of the latest news from MacArthur's headquarters. The battle for Buna was over; the Japanese had been defeated.

•

Bill Priest, the skipper of the *King John* when it was attacked by an American aircraft off Pongani, went on to captain two other Small Ships, the *Brianbarb* and the *Barraconda*, before leaving the Small Ships in April 1943 following a period of hospitalisation for malaria. Bert Evans, Priest's best friend and the chief engineer aboard the *King John* that day at Pongani, had sustained serious injuries to both legs when the American aircraft attacked. He recovered from those wounds and returned to service with the Small Ships in January 1943, firstly as a chief engineer and then as a ship's captain. The *Kurimarau*'s skipper, Bert Cummings, also survived the concentrated attack on his ship but later had a falling-out with US Army authorities and his employment contract was not renewed.

Norm Oddy had so far lived a charmed life in Small Ships service. He survived a rain of Japanese shells aboard the *Minston Brae* at Milne Bay and then survived both bombs and bullets aboard the *Hilda Norling* off Sebaga four months later. That had been a close-run thing, though, and the shrapnel wounds he suffered in the attack were serious enough to see him evacuated back to Australia, to a hospital at Gatton where he slowly recovered. It was a recovery complicated by ongoing bouts of malaria and his health was such that his Small Ships contract was terminated by mutual agreement on 31 January 1943. The reason given was, 'wounded by enemy action in combat zone'.

•

While all those sailors had been setting up Milne Bay as Base A and Oro Bay as Base B, and while the Buna campaign was being planned, fought and won, across the Pacific the industrial capacity of the United States was switching gear and preparing to turn out machines of war in numbers previously considered both incomprehensible and impossible. The waves created by the stirring of the industrial giant made their way across the waters to Australia and, inevitably, to the Small Ships.

The professional transportation men who had been sent to Australia in mid-1942 understood what was coming as they had worked directly in and with the industrial conglomerates that would be making much of that war material, and they also knew just how long the lead times were and how much of that bounty would be directed to the European theatre. So, until some of that output arrived in the South West Pacific Area, the US Army Supply of Services Division (USASOS), the unit responsible for all purchases and supply of materials to the army, looked to local manufacturers for vessels to support the various army operations.

By September 1942, two things had become obvious to the USASOS in Australia when it began the long-term planning for the Small Ships Section. The first was that the supply of vessels the section needed for its operations could not be met by US shipyards until mid-1943 at the earliest. The second was that there were simply not enough Australian vessels currently available to meet the section's needs until the supply of American vessels reached the levels required for warfare in a theatre where at least 80 per cent of the surface was water and not land. That month, the USASOS authorised an Australian ship construction program which, when it was completed, would produce around 1000 vessels of all types.

While the Higgins boats, Liberty ships and armoured vehicle landing craft were preparing to come across the ocean from America, dozens and then hundreds of specialised watercraft were built in Australia to American specifications and with American money. The Small Ships Section would receive significant numbers of these.

Among the first vessels ordered, by the Australian army and navy, as well as by the Small Ships, were large ocean-going steel tugboats of 500 tons' displacement, steam driven and with the capacity to tow vessels of up to 20,000 tons, and numbers of the steel barges the tugs were designed to tow. They were not just ordinary barges either. As well as the normal open steel barges, now standardised to around twenty by five metres, specialised barges were produced, including concrete-lined refrigeration barges, crane barges for heavy lifting, fuel barges, workshops and even barges designed for use as floating dry docks.

A number of Fairmile motor launches were also ordered, built and delivered. Put together from prefabricated components of marine ply construction and over thirty metres in length, they could carry hundreds of litres of fuel, giving them long-range plus endurance. The Fairmiles could be built in several configurations, but those ordered for the Small Ships followed the simple and basic design. In that configuration, they could be used to carry arms and ammunition to coastal landing points and then carry off sick and wounded soldiers before delivering them to hospital ships anchored well offshore. When brought into service with the Small Ships, the Fairmiles would all be given the designation ML and a ship's number.

A new type of vessel was also designed and built specifically for the type of amphibious warfare that would come to characterise the Pacific War. Known as ocean lighters, at almost forty metres in length they were longer than either the Fairmiles or the Higgins boats. Displacing 250 tons and with twin diesel engines, each was built with two holds, which could also be configured for specific purposes. Some were fitted out with refrigerated holds, some were water carriers, most carried normal stores while at least one was fitted out as a fully functioning casualty clearing station. Those delivered to the Small Ships were given the designation OL followed by a ship's number.

Finally, a number of twelve-metre wooden tugboats were also built. These had a large deck area, only needed a three-man crew and were the natural successors to the seine trawlers which had been the basis of the Small Ships' operations.

•

Going into 1943, it was obvious that even without all the new boats that would become available as the year progressed, the Small Ships might struggle to find crews to man the ships they already had on their books. A number of Australians who had signed on for service in July and August had either not signed on again or had indicated their intention to not continue with their employment. Most of those who left did so because the conditions they had experienced, or had heard about, in the New Guinea war zones were not what they believed they had signed up for. Others had been killed or were either wounded or suffering from one or more tropical ailments, with malaria being the most common.

At that time, the Small Ships Section's headquarters in Sydney estimated that a minimum of 150 new crew would be needed just to bring the existing vessels up to their full complement. The section's commanding officer, Colonel Thomas Plant, even went to Washington to ask the Joint Chiefs of Staff for 700 merchant seamen to be sent to Australia to crew his Small Ships. That number, he argued, would both cover the losses they had already sustained and allow them to crew the new vessels being built for them in shipyards all around Australia. Plant received a sympathetic hearing in Washington. However, he was told that the numbers he requested would not be available until late 1943 or early 1944 because of the critical shortage of seamen in the North Atlantic theatre.

A stop-gap solution presented itself when two complementary developments occurred almost simultaneously in early 1943. The first was that the Australian government gave the US Army permission for the Small Ships Section to run a training program for fifteen- and sixteen-year-old Australian boys who wanted to become sailors aboard the Small Ships. The second was that an Australian named Arthur Morgan, a serving member of the Volunteer Coastal Patrol, applied to join the Small Ships.

Part of Arthur Morgan's role within the Coastal Volunteer Patrol had been training the men and boys who volunteered on the basics of seamanship. Because of that experience, Morgan was asked to temporarily postpone a sea-going role and instead write a syllabus and timetable for the apprentice seamen the Small Ships intended to recruit and train for their own sea-going operations. When he agreed to do so, Morgan was appointed Chief Instructor of the Apprentice Seamen's School of the Small Ships Section, effective from 1 April 1943. His stipend would be a very healthy 750 pounds per annum.

Thomas Plant, and Morgan himself, did not believe they would have any trouble in recruiting the 150 apprentice seamen that both believed were necessary to make up the projected short-fall. The Australian government agreed that those who passed a medical examination and were offered a place in the Apprentice Seamen's School could be paid two pounds a week while they were trained. Those who completed the course satisfactorily, including a final examination, would be offered positions as Apprentice Seamen aboard one of the Small Ships at a salary of twenty-six pounds a month. After six months' satisfactory service, they would progress to the rank of Ordinary Seaman and would be paid an additional seven pounds a month. As part of their employment, the apprentices also signed an authority that allowed the Australian Taxation Office to take monthly deductions from that salary.

Arthur Morgan estimated that the needs of those 150 apprentices would best be served by class groups of fifty students with a course of four weeks' duration, meaning he would need to run three such courses. It would be physically impossible for Morgan to run all the program elements by himself, so he approached and appointed three retired ships' captains named May, McCulloch and Wood to assist him with classroom and practical training. Two US Army specialist armourers were also brought in to give instruction in gunnery and gun maintenance.

Classroom lessons were held in one of the storage sheds allocated to the Small Ships on their wharf, Number 10, at Walsh Bay. Not unsurprisingly, both teachers and students found those learning conditions less than ideal. Practical Seamanship and Gunnery, including live firing, were held aboard the *Dover*, a former riverboat from Tasmania, and Arthur Morgan's own yacht. The four-week courses ran from 8.30 a.m. until 5 p.m. each day with a total of six days spent at sea.

The first course, with its fifty trainees, commenced in mid-April 1943, and by the second week it became apparent that many of those trainees were simply not fit enough for some of the more strenuous elements of the syllabus. Because of this, each day began with twenty minutes of physical exercise, a practice that was continued on subsequent courses. Forty-six trainees completed that first course and were then assigned to ships or bases. Some sailed away on Small Ships departing Sydney, while others were flown to New Guinea to take up their assignments on vessels that were already operating there.

The second course commenced on 24 May 1943 and graduated forty-five boy sailors; the other five who had enrolled were rejected during the course as medically unfit. The third program commenced on 23 June with sixty-seven students, a number that would grow to seventy-nine before dropping back to seventy-two because of the extra numbers necessary if the target of 150 was to be reached. The daily hours of instruction were increased while the course itself was extended to five weeks. Again, at its conclusion, all students who passed were despatched to New Guinea by sea or air.

All up, 163 fifteen- and sixteen-year-old boys passed through the Apprentice Seamen's School at Walsh Bay and went on to serve in a very different Small Ships Section from the one established just eighteen months earlier. With the last course completed, Arthur Morgan was given the sea-going post he had desired from the beginning: as Captain Arthur Morgan, he took delivery of the first of the ocean lighters built for the section, OL 1.

•

Returning from his two weeks' leave in February 1943, Clarrie Dawes – part of the old Small Ships Section – became part of a completely new section. From Small Ships' headquarters, Clarrie was sent north to Newcastle to join the crew on a brand-new small steel tugboat, the ST-68.

During the sea trials that followed, Clarrie found the ST-68 a difficult ship, one that had trouble in heavy seas. At such times, he likened it to a submarine as it seemed to spend more time below the waves than it did on the surface. But it was eventually ready for service and was sent off on its first mission, a trip to Cape Melville, a dot on the map some 100 kilometres north of Cooktown on Cape York. There, they were to salvage two large barges that had broken their towlines and run aground.

A king tide was expected shortly after the ST-68 arrived offshore from the beach where the two barges had been beached, and the tug's crew were given shovels and tasked with digging the sand away from the base of the stranded barges. That night, the tugboat moved close inshore and dropped both its anchors. A towline was connected to the nearest barge with another line connecting that barge to the second. Clarrie, as the youngest crewman, was put ashore and given a signal lamp which he was to use to indicate when the tide had risen to the base of the barges.

It was another experience he would remember for the rest of his life. There were noises all around him in the dark, most of them seeming to come from a tidal creek not far from where the barges had been stranded. The worst of them sounded to Clarrie like old, dry sticks being broken but he managed to convince himself that the sounds were actually crocodiles, huge, brutish things that were crushing small trees underfoot as they closed in on him, waiting with his little signal lamp like a tethered goat. The sides of the barges rose three metres above him, a height that would normally necessitate the use of a ladder. Clarrie had no doubt that, if he spotted a crocodile, he would easily leap that distance – even more, if necessary.

Fortunately, the crocodiles held off their attack until the incoming tide reached the barges. When Clarrie felt the first barge begin to move a little, he signalled to the tugboat from the beach. The towline grew taut and the first barge was slowly pulled off the sand. The tether to the second barge also grew taut and it, too, was slowly pulled off the sand and into deeper water. There were rock outcrops and coral reefs off the beach but they were avoided, and soon the ST-68 and its two barges were making a steady eight knots towards the north. The barges would be towed all the way to Milne Bay and handed over to the beach master there.

Clarrie Dawes would go on other missions on other Small Ships – he would eventually serve on a total of eight – and they would take him far beyond northern Australia and New Guinea. Some would be close to the frontlines but most would be a good distance behind those lines, and his lot would be the lot of hundreds of Small Ships' sailors. They and their unit were no longer the thin and fragile supply line to the troops who were fighting to take back the lands captured by the Japanese. That role would be filled by hundreds and thousands of specialised ships and aircraft. They were still part of that supply line, though, just in a different role. One of their founders, Laddie Reday, was given a look at this future just a few weeks and a thousand kilometres from the time and place where Clarrie had waited for the imaginary crocodiles to arrive.

•

The reality of the changes that twelve months of war in the Pacific had wrought was brought home to Laddie Reday in graphic form at the end of June 1943. In the months since the victory at Buna, MacArthur's push along the north coast of New Guinea had become a well-oiled machine. The Japanese held two more strong positions in the old Mandated Territory at Salamaua and Lae and, like the Buna–Gona complex, those positions were interdependent – but increasingly vulnerable. George Kenney's boasts about what his 5th Air Force could do no longer rang hollow. His fighters had all but destroyed the Japanese air forces in the theatre and his bombers, working in concert with the RAAF, made reinforcement and resupply of Lae and Salamaua problematic for the Japanese.

In the lead-up to the campaign to capture the Lae and Salamaua strongholds, smaller Japanese positions further east-wards along the coast were either captured or bombarded into uselessness. Those that were captured were firstly subjected to a heavy bombardment from sea and air before being taken by troops; the Small Ships continued to play a role in landing those troops. One such Japanese position was at Nassau Bay, and its capture would shorten supply lines for the Lae campaign and would also enable that part of the coast to be developed as a supply base, just as Oro Bay and Porlock Harbour had been developed six months earlier.

Thus it was that Laddie Reday and a group of other Small Ships' captains all received the same set of cryptic orders. The men were to board one of the few seine trawlers that had survived the Buna campaign and sail to a set of coordinates some distance off Nassau Bay and back out into the Huon Gulf.

Eight skippers, most of whom had lost their ships in action, were aboard the trawler, which arrived at the designated spot shortly before the specified time of midnight. They waited there in what had become a calm but hazy night. While they waited, the men talked quietly among themselves, reaching a consensus that they were probably there to act as pilots for the landing they all knew was on the way. They thought it would probably take place either later that night or around dawn the following morning.

Suddenly, out of the haze, a large US Navy destroyer appeared, flashed a signal lamp and cruised past. It was soon followed by another. Immediately behind the second destroyer were half a dozen vessels, the likes of which the men on the trawler had not seen before. Those half-dozen were followed by a half-dozen more and then a stream of large and small vessels, loaded with troops and bristling with weapons. The men would come to know those first boats as LCIs – Landing Craft, Infantry – huge vessels compared with the small trawler they were aboard, and armed with both cannon and rockets to boot. The vessels which followed those LCIs were larger again: big, specialised boats with doors and ramps designed to carry and land tanks and self-propelled guns. They were designated LSTs – Landing Ship, Tank.

Laddie Reday and the others silently watched the enormous ships sailing past with a mixture of pride and awe. The landing fleet they were watching was led and protected by US Navy ships equipped with radar and sonar, making much of the Small Ships' skippers' knowledge, and hence the skippers themselves, redundant. Recalling the moment many years later, Reday would write that it was that sight which told him that his time, and the time of the first Small Ships, was over; that 'this new and huge Navy fleet told us eloquently that we ourselves were no longer needed for landing assaults or anything else'.

Almost redundant would have been more accurate, as there was still a lot of work for the Small Ships to do. One of the smaller landing craft approached the little trawler, identified itself and asked whether Lieutenant Reday would like to board the vessel and guide it to their landing point. It was an invitation he accepted with real pleasure.

14.

HOME FROM THE SEA

By mid-1943, the Small Ships Section had been absorbed, operationally at least, into its parent unit, the US Army's Transportation Service (ATS). It was a logical move. When the Small Ships first moved to New Guinea, they were seen as a tactical component of the armed services, used to support tactical operations and directed in their deployment and actions by the senior local US Army commander. After Buna, the larger operational movements involved anything from dozens to hundreds of vessels, many of them purpose-built. They were undertaken in deeper waters where the Small Ships' unique features and local knowledge were no longer as relevant as they had once been. Instead of being a vital part of a relatively small machine, the Small Ships became an important cog in a much larger machine.

In practical terms for the Small Ships' Australian soldiers, this re-emphasis rather than reorganisation provided a number of opportunities. When new sailors signed on, or when experienced sailors opted to renew their contracts, they were given the option of serving on the larger ATS vessels rather than with the traditional old and new, and certainly smaller, Small Ships. It was an opportunity that many of them took up.

By mid-1944, all the major Japanese positions along the north coast of New Guinea between Milne Bay and the old Dutch colonial capital of Hollandia had either been destroyed or simply bypassed. While the larger Japanese positions were reduced and captured, the Small Ships had been heavily involved in small unit actions, such as infiltrating and exfiltrating commando units and carrying supplies to remote outposts, like the American PT boat bases. Such missions were beginning to lose their allure and many of the Small Ships' sailors, both Australian and American, already had their hearts and sights set elsewhere, over the seas to the north-west where the Philippines awaited. General MacArthur had promised to return and was preparing to do so at the head of an enormous armada, a giant machine made for amphibious warfare. Again, the Small Ships Section would be a cog in that machine.

It almost didn't happen though. In late 1944, a series of newspaper reports suggested that US Army Headquarters (read Douglas MacArthur) did not want anyone but Americans directly involved in the liberation of the Philippines and had therefore instructed that Australian Small Ships sailors would not be permitted to work north of the Equator. There were also claims that the Australians likely to be involved – and it was a relatively small number – had been informed of this and were preparing to return to areas south of the Equator. When reporters pressed Australian politicians up to ministerial level, the issue was soon resolved. It was all a misunderstanding and the Australians would serve alongside their American brethren in the action north of the Equator.

On 10 October 1944, a Small Ships convoy comprising thirteen tugboats towing forty barges departed Hollandia under the command of US Army Major Leon Lancaster, who had served with the section from its early days in Sydney. Their destination was Tacloban on the Philippine island of Leyte, and they arrived there soon after the first American troops splashed ashore on 20 October. A second convoy of fourteen tugboats and another forty barges departed Hollandia on the day the Americans landed and arrived at Tacloban on 3 November. Both convoys, and the several others that would follow, remained off Leyte where they supported the Americans now fighting ashore. As well as carrying and offloading supplies, the tugboats, barges and accompanying ocean lighters were vital to the process of taking off the sick and wounded.

Those were the types of roles that would occupy the Small Ships for the remainder of the war. They supported further landings at Lingayen, Cebu and Dagupan in the Philippines, carrying troops, equipment and supplies in, and taking off the sick and wounded to be delivered to the hospital ships offshore. On more than one occasion they would also bring back the bodies of those who had been killed in the fighting. A lesser number of Small Ships were involved in supporting the guerrilla groups that continued to harass the retreating Japanese. Laddie Reday, for example, was given a new boat and spent the last months of the war contacting and supplying the guerrilla groups operating in remote corners of the Philippines.

The roles they had filled during the Buna campaign were not completely lost to them, although most had been taken over by larger, purpose-built vessels. The original Small Ships, those that had survived, were usually relegated to rear echelon areas with roles like carrying freight to and from established bases. While some of the original sailors transferred across to new roles in the larger boats of the ATS, a surprising number seemed perfectly content with their roles.

•

In early 1945, Sheridan Fahnestock was promoted to colonel and named Chief of Overseas Operations, Transport Command, for the remainder of the South West Pacific Area campaigns and the proposed invasion of Japan itself. As amphibious operations carried both army and marine forces ever closer to Japan's home islands, those islands were themselves being mercilessly pounded by waves of American aircraft operating from aircraft carriers and captured land bases. Any plans Sheridan had became moot, however, when atomic weapons were unleashed on two Japanese cities, Hiroshima and Nagasaki.

The devastating attacks were followed by a Japanese surrender. The surrender instrument was signed aboard the USS *Missouri* in Tokyo Bay, with Douglas MacArthur signing on behalf of the United States. The decks and gun turrets of the giant battleship were crowded with sailors all eager to witness history being made. There were also a number of official observers representing services that had contributed to the defeat of the Japanese. One of them was a full colonel in the uniform of the US Army Transportation Service. His name was Sheridan Fahnestock and he was representing all the Small Ships sailors, those who died in the service and those who never heard a shot fired in anger. His presence that day was a salute from the man at the top to all those unknown Australian sailors who had chosen to serve at sea and contribute to the war effort. They would all have been proud of the recognition.

•

The Small Ships Section outlived many of its vessels and at least thirty-two of its sailors. Long after the surrender document was signed in Tokyo Bay, the Small Ships continued moving men, machinery and supplies around the thousands of islands and tens of thousands of square kilometres of ocean that made up the South West Pacific Area.

Manila became the centre for US Army operations in that immediate post-war period. It was a clearing house for both American and Allied troops returning home from the far-flung battlefields of the Pacific. It was also a halfway house for the thousands of Allied prisoners of war who had survived imprisonment in Japan and elsewhere in North Asia. In the camps scattered around Clark Field, they were fattened up before being sent home, lest their appearance frighten friends and relatives and lead to calls for vengeance on a defeated enemy.

Manila was also the collection point for the materials of war that continued to have some value in peace time. The Allies, and the Americans in particular, had produced hitherto unbelievable amounts of hardware to support their fighting men – machines of all kinds and the prefabricated structures and supplies to support those machines. Mess kits and helmet liners could be left behind when hostilities ended but the larger objects – the boats, aircraft and heavy weapons – had an intrinsic as well as a quantifiable value, and because of this, huge amounts of such objects were brought to Manila to be catalogued and stored before a decision on what to do with them was made.

The Small Ships were an important part of this process. Their sea-going tugboats and the enormous, purpose-built barges they towed had carried men and machines across thousands of kilometres of ocean, sometimes under enemy attack, in wartime. It was a task they could undertake with equal efficiency now that peace had come.

•

As well as being the clear winner in the second world war in twenty-five years, the United States was determined to champion the cause of world peace, and threw its considerable weight behind the fledgling guardian of that peace, the United Nations. The Small Ships also had a role to play in this.

Now completely integrated into the US Army Transportation Service, a number of the Small Ships and a number of Australian soldiers in that service were involved in humanitarian projects under the auspices of the United Nations Relief and Rehabilitation Administration (UNRRA). These projects were primarily in China, where millions remained homeless and destitute and where the smaller boats of the Small Ships Section could navigate rivers to the interior of that vast country.

In addition to the food and clothing they carried as part of the relief effort, the Small Ships themselves were sometimes part of the aid offered, most notably those gifted or sold cheaply to the Nationalist Chinese leader, Chiang Kai-shek. While they were ostensibly part of a larger aid package, no one was in any doubt that they would find a use in the looming war between the Nationalists and Mao Zedong's Communist forces.

A number of Small Ships sailors were involved in this relief effort, including one of the first to join the section, Neil Sandery. After captaining the *Timoshenko* with distinction at Pongani and on the Oro Bay shuttle run, Sandery was promoted to the captain's position on other, larger ships. Recognising his potential, the US Army Transport Service encouraged him to transfer across into their ranks in late 1944 and he served the remainder of the war as a captain of Liberty ships. As captain of one of these, the USS *Sam Houston*, Sandery sailed up the Whampoa River in January 1946 to deliver relief supplies before handing over his ship to the Nationalists.

Shortly after the *Sam Houston* arrived in Shanghai, Neil Sandery contracted smallpox and, despite the best treatment then available at a US hospital, he died there at just twenty-eight years of age. Back in Sydney, Sandery left behind a widow, Isabel, and a daughter named Julie who had been born in October 1944. Isabel was also pregnant and in early May 1945 gave birth to a son she named Neil Lyndon King Sandery.

Neil Sandery's death was another tragedy for the Small Ships, coming on top of years of mass tragedy, and there was still a little more to come. In April 1946, an RAAF B-24 Liberator crashed into the sea off the southern Philippine island of Mindanao while en route from Manila to Australia. The crew and most of the passengers survived the crash, although most of those survivors suffered injuries. Among the passengers were two Australian sailors returning home from the Philippines after service there with the Small Ships Section. One of the two was posted as missing, believed killed, and the other was listed as slightly injured; no names were released.

Those two were the last casualties in the Small Ships Section's long war, one that was now over.

•

By then, the Small Ships' operations were all but wound up in the South West Pacific Area. In Australia, the Walsh Bay and Grace Building bases were among the last to be closed.

Cliff Callen was possibly the last Australian employee to end his Small Ships service and, although Callen was not a sailor, he had been part of the section and at the heart of its operations since it moved to Sydney in 1942. His first job had been issuing uniforms to the newly minted sailors and in the years since he had undertaken almost every administrative job in the section. When the Pacific War ended, Callen was involved with returning the vessels that had been acquired two or three years earlier to their owners or otherwise disposing of them. He was involved, too, with the discharge of the section's personnel, who were paid off and then farewelled into a world that had changed immensely in the time they had been away.

In January 1946, the last American serviceman on the books of the Small Ships Section in Sydney signed himself on as a crew member of a US Army freighter headed back to the United States. Cliff Callen then saw the offices in the Grace Building and the sheds at Number 10, Walsh Bay handed back to their owners before he, too, walked away into a world without war.

•

In January 1947, in Washington DC, the Small Ships Section of the US Army Transport Service was officially disbanded.

•

Many of the Small Ships that had saved the day at Buna, and performed with distinction elsewhere in the Pacific theatre, did not survive to see the end of the war. Several of the fishing trawlers, well past their use-by date in amphibious warfare, were sent back to Australia at the end of 1944 and others were sent south during the early months of 1945, either individually or in small groups. Any that survived until the end of the war were then sailed back to the Small Ships base at Townsville.

Among those sent back in early 1945 was the *Two Freddies*, the trawler that Ralph Andrews sailed so steadfastly through the darkest days of the Oro Bay to Hariko shuttle, and which had twice survived attacks by Japanese aircraft. The damage sustained in those attacks, on top of general wear and tear, made the long voyage to Townsville problematic and so, instead of attempting it under her own power, the *Two Freddies* commenced the return trip under tow. In rough seas towards the end of her trip, the towline parted and the *Two Freddies* sank off Hawkins Point on Magnetic Island on 12 February 1945. The wreck was subsequently sold by tender; the *Two Freddies* was refloated, repaired and renamed the *Monty*. It spent its remaining days doing what it had been built to do: seine trawling in the waters to the east of Australia.

The first of the Small Ships to face the Japanese, albeit accidentally, was the *Minston Brae*, caught up in the Japanese attempt to capture Milne Bay in August 1942. The *Minston Brae* survived that encounter and went on to survive the war before returning to work as a fishing boat. While on a fishing trip in 1950, the gallant little *Minston Brae* sank off Portland Roads near Hamilton Island.

During the build-up to the Buna Campaign, the first two Small Ships into action in October were Bill Priest's *King John* and Neil Sandery's *Timoshenko*. Sandery moved on, leaving the *Timoshenko* to other skippers. She remained in and around New Guinea, and in 1944 moved her base of operations to Manus Island, where she remained for the rest of the war. The *Timoshenko* returned to Australia in August 1945 and was sold by tender at Townsville. The *King John* was another of the original seine trawlers that was towed back to Australia at the end of the Pacific War. The tow was lost in heavy seas and the *King John* sank off Cape Byron.

The *Kelton*, another of the first Small Ships to go into action at Buna with her all-Filipino crew under Ireneo Ames, did not survive the war. Overworked beyond her capacity – for a short period the *Kelton* was the only boat on the Oro Bay to Hariko run – and damaged by near-misses and groundings in the waters around the beachheads, she was examined and condemned at Oro Bay on 20 November 1943. The next day she was stripped, splashed with petrol and burned.

It was a fate she shared – although at some distance – with her workmate from those early days at Buna, Clarrie Dawes' first billet, the *Leprena*. The *Leprena* survived the war despite her problems in heavy seas, and after the war she was sailed back to her home harbour of Port Adelaide. Some months later, she underwent conversion into an ocean-going cray fishing boat. In that role, she ran aground and could not be salvaged so everything useful was removed before she, too, was splashed with petrol and burned; a sad end for a grand lady.

Two of the more storied Small Ships survived both the war and many years of peace afterwards. The *Melanesia* was at the centre of many adventures involving her skipper, Alan Reynolds, and her chief engineer, Ray Parer. Despite coming close to complete destruction on several occasions, she overcame all obstacles, Japanese and natural, and at the end of hostilities she was handed back to her original owners, the Seventh Day Adventist Church. She remained in New Guinea waters thereafter, continuing to support the church's missionary work there.

The *Shangri-La*, the luxury motor yacht that was Ralph Andrews' command for a few short weeks in late 1942, went on to serve out the war as a kind of first-class floating lounge for senior American commanders in and around New Guinea waters. She saw lots of action but it was of a less dangerous nature than actual combat, and she sailed back to Australia at war's end. After several other roles, including a long stint as a charter boat cruising the Great Barrier Reef, she found her way down to Victoria where, restored to her original condition, she is now part of a maritime museum at Westernport Bay.

•

Like most fleets, the many boats that made up the Small Ships Section included a number of vessels that sailors regarded as lucky ships and others they believed to be unlucky ships; it also included the *Hilda Norling* which at times seemed to need a category of her own.

The pride of Victoria's cray fishing fleet was in trouble from almost the moment she was acquired by the section. A tortuous voyage to Milne Bay was followed by a horrific beating in New Guinea, almost shot to pieces by a Japanese aircraft off Sebaga. After being brought to Milne Bay for assessment by Alan Reynolds, she was nursed back to Australia by Ralph Andrews and his crew of invalids to be repaired at the Small Ships base at Townsville. When that process was complete, the *Hilda Norling* returned to service with a new captain and crew in October 1943, travelling directly to the supply runs along the northern coastline of New Guinea.

The *Hilda Norling* anchored off Tufi on 23 December, loaded with supplies for Allied troops further along the coast and with a deck cargo that comprised dozens of drums of fuel to be unloaded the next day for the US Navy PT boat base there. The next morning, when her captain tried to start the main engine, the electric starter motor threw out a spark. Fumes from all the fuel she was carrying had settled in the bilges overnight and were ignited by the spark. Within seconds, the *Hilda Norling* blew herself apart and disappeared in a massive fireball. Miraculously, no one was killed or seriously injured in the explosion and, predictably, there was nothing left of the *Hilda Norling* when the flames and smoke dissipated.

The *Argosy Lemal* – Laddie Reday's *Agony Remorse* – survived a very interesting war. Converted into a sophisticated communic-ations vessel, she was firstly stationed off Port Moresby before being relocated to the Lae/Salamaua area in mid-1943 to support Allied operations along New Guinea's north coast. After the war moved into the Philippines, the *Argosy Lemal* was transferred again and spent the remainder of the war in the Arafura and Timor Seas, supporting the Allied mopping-up operations among the surrounding islands.

Through a combination of good luck and a good disguise, the *Argosy Lemal* survived the war without being attacked by either Japanese aircraft or Japanese surface craft, but her luck did not extend much beyond that. The war in the Pacific was a multinational war that at times required communications in several languages, and so the *Argosy Lemal* always carried a crew of mixed nationalities, not all of whom saw eye to eye. As well, and somewhat strangely, the *Argosy Lemal* was an army ship that was required to operate to US Navy regulations and this restricted her ability to operate sensitive communications equipment on a twenty-four-hour, seven-day basis.

Finally, she was a bit unfortunate with the captains posted to her during her war service. Not all were particularly happy with the posting or particularly competent as ship's captains. In fact, two of them were replaced for gross incompetence; the second of these miscalculated the ship's position by over 100 kilometres and, despite being advised that he was wrong, continued on a course that led them straight onto a known reef. Happily for all but the captain, the boat was eventually rescued and towed to Port Moresby for repairs and a replacement captain.

The *Argosy Lemal* survived that incident and the rest of the war, and even a later grounding in Far North Queensland, to return to her pre-war role in carrying cargo across and through Bass Strait. She was subsequently bought and sold several times, and was eventually purchased by the Mornington Island Fishing Company, which renamed her *Booya*. As the *Booya*, she was used as a fuel-supply and mothership to the northern waters prawn fleet.

Sold for the last time in 1968, the *Booya* was employed in carrying cargo between Darwin and Dili in East Timor, then a Portuguese colony. On 24 December 1974, the *Booya* was moored in Darwin Harbour when all vessels there were ordered to sea to try to avoid the oncoming Cyclone Tracy. When the storm passed, there was no sign of her.

Almost thirty years later, on 22 October 2003, divers found the wreck of the *Booya* on the bottom of Darwin Harbour, some nine kilometres from shore and not all that far away from her last known sighting. She was in around twenty metres of water and was in almost pristine condition. There was no trace of her four crewmen and the one visitor she had aboard when she made her run for the safety of the open sea. In 2005, the wreck of the *Booya/Argosy Lemal* and its surrounds were declared a heritage site.

•

The Small Ships' captains and crews also tried to return to their pre-war lives after the cessation of hostilities, including some of those who had been invalided out of service well before the last shots had been fired.

Bill Priest had left the Small Ships in April 1943 following a period of hospitalisation for recurring attacks of malaria. Priest returned home to his family at Greenwell Point and, after the war was over, moved to Queensland where he returned to professional fishing. He also earned his Master Mariner's Certificate, retired from fishing and ended his working life employed on a number of mining projects in the Gulf of Carpentaria.

Bert Evans, Bill Priest's best friend, had been badly wounded when working as chief engineer aboard Priest's *King John*. He recovered from his wounds and rejoined the *King John* at Milne Bay in January 1943. Later in the war, he was appointed chief engineer aboard the *Joe Ellen* before being promoted to captain of the *Mary Ellen*. Retiring from sea-going duties in 1944, Bert was made an inspector in the Small Ships' construction section, a position he held until the war ended. He returned to the Crookhaven River and lighthouse duties after being offered a position there by the New South Wales Maritime Services Board. Bert also continued to build his own boats and inspect others for the board until his retirement in 1973.

Ralph Andrews' war was nothing if not interesting. After captaining the *Shangri-La*, *Two Freddies* and *Hilda Norling*, he was hospitalised in Cairns for several weeks to recover from a range of ailments, including malaria and sandy blight. When he was fit enough to be discharged, Ralph travelled by train all the way down the east coast to Sydney. It was a trip he would remember for a long time. On the first leg, the train was full of armed soldiers who would shoot out the windows at ducks, or anything that resembled a duck, whenever they passed a river or lake. Any settlement they passed through also became a compulsory stop if there was a pub within its environs.

Ralph's health was such that his Small Ships' contract was not renewed. As a civilian, he was now required to report to the Manpower Planning authorities who directed him to Victoria Barracks in Paddington for assessment. There, he was rejected for military service. He was, in fact, given the lowest possible medical grading.

Back at the Small Ships headquarters, Major George Bradford, one of the transportation specialists sent out from America, and who was subsequently given command of the Section, learned of Ralph's health issues and followed up on them, arguing that Ralph was too valuable an asset to the section to simply let him go. Bradford arranged for Ralph to be treated at an American military hospital and, when he had made a complete recovery, arranged for him to then be re-signed onto a Small Ships contract. Ralph was placed in charge of outfitting all new vessels acquired by the section. He finished the war with the official title of Executive, Maintenance and Supply.

Ralph returned to Eden after the war, fishing for sharks aboard the *Willyama III* with his brothers John and Frank. They could not make a go of it and, after trying prawn fishing out of Yamba, Ralph returned to Sydney and to one of his pre-war jobs as a salesman. He married Isabel in 1953 and built a house for them to live in on a block at North Curl Curl, later building them a houseboat in the backyard. Ralph and Isabel moved to Drummoyne when he retired; the houseboat, *Willyama IV*, moved with them and sat in a little bay opposite their unit. Ralph Edmund Andrews died in 2011, aged ninety-three years. The locals in Drummoyne still call the little bay where he moored his houseboat 'Willyama Cove'.

Alan Reynolds survived the adventures he had aboard the *Eva* and the *Melanesia* and remained with the Small Ships for the rest of the war. After sailing the *Hilda Norling* to Milne Bay, he served as chief officer aboard the *Lorinna* before progressing to the newer vessels – the steel tugboats and the ocean lighters. During the reconquest of the Philippines, he was involved primarily in the evacuation of sick and wounded American soldiers. He was nominated for a decoration for his work during the New Guinea Campaign, but was never awarded it. After the war, Alan Reynolds sailed with the Burns Philp company before owning and running Sydney's Oatley Bay Boatshed for over a decade. He retired to Ballina in the early 1970s and died there in 1991, aged eighty-seven years.

Ray Parer left the Small Ships before the war ended, but his service with them became legendary. His pre-war life had been a succession of adventures and the pattern continued while he served as chief engineer aboard the *Melanesia*. The adventures included the *Melanesia* being bombed and strafed by Japanese aircraft, a number of close-run encounters when infiltrating and exfiltrating US Army reconnaissance patrols behind the lines, and numerous run-ins with authority. His most famous adventure, though, occurred when he and his boat were doing nothing.

One evening, as those aboard the *Melanesia* were waiting for nightfall under cover in a tidal creek, just passing time until it was dark enough to be safe from Japanese aircraft, Ray Parer was sitting on deck with one of his shipmates, smoking and generally enjoying life. Unknown to Parer, his companion had quietly slipped below decks and he was now alone. Although partially deaf in one ear, Parer thought he heard a splash near the side of the boat.

He half-turned and asked, 'Are you all right?'

As he stood to see if his companion had fallen overboard, he spotted a Japanese swimming towards the *Melanesia*, a knife clasped firmly between his teeth. Parer moved back from the railings and crouched down. As the Japanese man began to climb aboard, Parer grabbed him and killed him with his bare hands. He threw the body overboard but kept the knife as a memento mori. When he left the Small Ships, he was still carrying the sheath knife he had taken from the Japanese soldier and telling anyone who cared to listen the story of how it came to be in his possession – a story that sometimes grew with the telling.

After Parer left the Small Ships, he bought a grocery business at Edgecliff in Sydney, but that was never going to hold him. After the war his restless spirit kicked in again and he moved on. He tried pearling in the Torres Strait, attempted to establish a business shipping plywood from north Queensland to Melbourne, skippered a barge in Papua New Guinea and eventually retired to southern Queensland where he managed two farms at Mount Nebo outside Brisbane – and continued to tinker with engines – until his death on 4 July 1967.

Jack Gilmore was the English-born former proprietor of the Rabaul Hotel who escaped with his wife in a small boat after the Japanese invaded New Britain. Jack could obviously sail, but it was his work on dry land as beach master or salvage master at a number of the Small Ships bases along the north coast of New Guinea that would best be remembered by his colleagues. His efforts were recognised by the American government who awarded Jack their nation's highest civilian award, the Legion of

Merit, for his work with the Small Ships. Apparently, they never did discover the secret of his seemingly endless supply of cement.

The skipper of the *Kurimarau* during the Buna campaign, Bert Cummings, left the Small Ships after an acrimonious exchange with US Army authorities. He continued serving at sea for the remainder of the war; however, that service was on Australian merchant vessels. After forty years at sea, Cummings returned to a job on land as a publican. He spent his spare time writing a book about his life at sea which he called *Confessions of a Mud Skipper.*

Norm Oddy was discharged from the Small Ships because of the wounds he sustained when captain of the *Hilda Norling.* He somehow managed to return to England aboard the *Queen Mary,* possibly as a supernumerary. He then wangled his way out to India where he was employed in a ship repair and maintenance facility in Mumbai. He was there in 1944 when the ammunition freighter *Fort Stikine* exploded, killing between 800 and 1500 people and devastating much of the port area.

That tragic accident may have prompted Oddy to return to the sea and he signed on as crew on another freighter, the *Nellore.* Halfway through a voyage from Mumbai to Australia in 1944, the *Nellore* was torpedoed and sunk by a Japanese submarine. Oddy and the other survivors spent more than a week crowded into lifeboats drifting in the Indian Ocean before being rescued. Oddy returned to his native Bradford at war's end but didn't exactly settle down. His musical, and perhaps nautical, background saw him gain work with P&O Lines, playing bass fiddle in the orchestra on their trans-Atlantic liners.

In July 1946, Norm Oddy married his childhood sweetheart, Margie (Hilda Marjory Whitehead), and announced that he planned to sail a former RAF crash boat to Australia on his honeymoon. That plan fell through but the couple eventually made it to Australia as assisted migrants in March 1948. Even that arrival was tinged with excitement when Customs officers found a sub-machine gun – a war souvenir – in Norm's luggage. For this he was charged with attempting to import a prohibited weapon. After being described by his barrister as 'an army veteran with a brilliant record', Oddy was found guilty and handed a one-month suspended sentence and a twelve-month good behaviour bond.

Norm and Margie Oddy settled down to life in Sydney, raising their only child, a little girl they called Jenny. Norm found employment as an engineer and continued to also work as a professional musician. Big adventures no longer came his way but he dabbled a bit, including at one time trying to organise a syndicate to buy HMAS *Melbourne*, the decommissioned RAN aircraft carrier. The plan was to moor it permanently in Sydney Harbour as a floating entertainment centre, but that idea slowly faded from view. Norm Oddy passed away in Sydney on 10 August 2000 at the age of eighty-six and after a life well lived.

In December 1942, Norm Oddy had buried two of his shipmates from the *Hilda Norling* – George Smith and George Brooks – in the coconut grove at Sebaga. For some reason, the remains of those two men were not reinterred in the main Allied war cemetery at Lae when the war was over. Another former shipmate of Norm Oddy's, this one from the *Minston Brae*, was the New Zealand–born Singapore Docks policeman Norm Byrne, who had been awarded the Military Medal in World War I. Norm Byrne did not survive the war either. Struck down by illness – most probably malaria – he died on 25 February 1945 while still serving with the Small Ships in New Guinea. Aged forty-nine years when he died, Norm Byrne is buried in the Lae Military Cemetery.

Others from the Small Ships Section were just glimpsed briefly before they left the stage of war to resume their real lives among family and friends.

Jim Alsop sailed the *Ulladulla* from Gladstone to New Guinea after the death of Tom Prestnol and he later succeeded Bill Priest as skipper of the *King John*. Alsop survived the war to return to fishing, but the *Ulladulla* did not; surveyed and condemned, she was burned at Milne Bay in April 1945. Jack Gardner of the *Zoie* did not renew his contract and left the Small Ships Section in October 1943, returning to Eden where he resumed his work as a professional fisherman. Jack Simcock also returned to the sea after the war, both in a professional capacity and as a sportsman. His yacht, *Rani*, won the inaugural Sydney–Hobart Ocean Race.

•

When the war ended, Clarrie Dawes was operating out of Manila, working on one of the large ocean-going tugboats, the only Australian in an otherwise all-American crew. Clarrie had spent the last few months of the war aboard that boat, the eighth Small Ship on which he had served, and a large part of that time had been spent towing ships that had survived kamikaze aircraft strikes to shipyards for repair. Clarrie continued working after the surrender as there was more than enough work for his tug and many others. It was February 1946 before he was paid off in Sydney.

There, Clarrie drifted for a while, feeling sorry for himself, drinking and generally going downhill. After a stern talking-to from his landlady, who pointed out that he was the only one who could help himself, Clarrie wrote to his father in Western

Australia and then joined him in a fishing venture there. That didn't work out, nor did another solo fishing venture at Esperance or mining near Kalgoorlie. He did, though, meet his future wife Mary at a telephone exchange and, through Mary's relatives, learned of regular work available for those who were prepared to live isolated lives in the bush.

Clarrie remained with the National Railways for several years, spending most of his time at the remote settlement of Naretha, firstly as a fettler and then as a ganger, moving from worker to boss. Mary and their newborn son, Norman, joined Clarrie there and the three lived a sometimes idyllic life until it was time for Norman to go to school. The Dawes then moved to Kalgoorlie where Clarrie was employed in the mines for several years. When Norman finished school, the family relocated again, this time to Ceduna, where they settled in Clarrie's old neighbourhood of Thevenard.

Joined by Norman, Clarrie returned to the sea as a shark fisherman until, aged sixty, he was diagnosed with cancer and retired to fight the disease. He did so successfully, and became involved in a number of community organisations. In 2016, after seventeen years as president of the Ceduna RSL and many years of contributing to the community, Melville Clarence 'Clarrie' Dawes was named Ceduna's Citizen of the Year.

•

Geoffrey Reading, the war correspondent who so graphically described the disaster at Hariko on 16 November, returned to newspaper journalism after the war, working for, among others, the Sydney *Truth*. He also wrote a book about his wartime experiences entitled *Papuan Story*, which was ublished by Angus and Robertson in 1946. Reading later left journalism to become Press

Secretary to the New South Wales Premier, Sir Robin Askin. Geoffrey Reading died in 2005.

•

The first Australian to be employed in what would become the Small Ships Section was Jack Savage, and he would remain with the section until the war was won, never once asking for or being offered an employment contract. When the war was over, he returned to the family business – Savage Boats – and helped turn it into an internationally recognised business. Jack returned initially to the business at its base in Melbourne and that was where, in January 1951, he married Margaret Garnsworthy. Jack subsequently moved with his family to Sydney where he hoped to grow the business, and they settled in Narrabeen.

The Savage Boat business grew and prospered from the 1950s onwards while Jack and his family made a real home for themselves in Sydney. In December 1975, their youngest daughter, Jenny, married Richard Cutler, son of the-then Governor of New South Wales, Sir Roden Cutler. There was a side story to the wedding, which tied it into events of more than thirty years earlier on the north coast of New Guinea in the midst of a world war.

Laddie Reday had been keeping a diary during the war but lost it in late 1943 when it was left in a suitcase aboard his Higgins boat, which was abandoned in the Morobe River after being shot full of holes by marauding Zeros near an army base that Reday was supplying. Some time later, an Australian soldier named Mick Morris, a member of the Australian Army's Water Transport Unit, was reconnoitring the Morobe River in a small launch when he spotted the abandoned boat. He tied up alongside it and went aboard to see whether he could find anything worth salvaging. He found just the one item, a suitcase containing a diary and a pewter mug engraved with the name 'Ladislaw Reday'. He took the suitcase with him, brought it home at the end of the war, put it in a shed and promptly forgot about it.

In 1975, Mick Morris was living in Sydney. Reading a newspaper one day, he discovered that a Mr and Mrs Reday were visiting Sydney, as house guests at the Savage home for the forthcoming wedding of Mr Jack Savage's daughter. Morris had sailed with Jack Savage before the war, so he phoned him and confirmed that the Mr Reday was the Ladislaw/Laddie Reday who had served with the Small Ships in New Guinea during the war.

Mick Morris made an appointment to meet Laddie Reday at a hotel in William Street in the city and there, over a few drinks and reminiscences from thirty years earlier, handed back the diary and pewter mug he had found all those years earlier.

Jack Savage cut back his involvement in the family business during the 1970s and eased into retirement during the 1980s. Even in retirement, though, he was never far from the sea, both physically and emotionally. He was Australia's representative on the Measurement Panel when Alan Bond's *Australia II* won the America's Cup off Newport, Rhode Island, in 1983, a venue not all that far from where the Fahnestock boys had grown up. John Blennerhassett (Jack) Savage died on 6 March 2015 after a long and very successful life.

•

After his war service, which saw him promoted to full colonel, Sheridan Fahnestock had a stint in public relations with Transworld Airlines for five years. He subsequently became the owner and publisher of the weekly *St. Mary's Enterprise* in southern Maryland. Sheridan controlled and operated the paper until his health began to fail in 1963. Like his father, John Sheridan Fahnestock died young, passing away in 1965 at the age of fifty-two.

After the war, Bruce Fahnestock's remains were taken from the Bomana War Cemetery outside Port Moresby and reinterred in the Arlington National Cemetery just outside Washington, DC.

The Fahnestocks' South Seas and East Indies recordings are now lodged in the Library of Congress and were released in 1994 as a music CD entitled, *Music for the Gods: The Fahnestock South Seas Expedition: Indonesia.*

•

Barney Darnton's remains were also removed from Bomana and reinterred in the Darnton family plot at the Oakwood Cemetery in Adrian, Michigan, on 24 June 1948. The Liberty ship that was named after him was launched at Baltimore on 16 March 1943 by his widow, Tootie, accompanied by her two young sons. Sent across the Atlantic to Britain, it operated on the Murmansk run for the remainder of the war, surviving all the perils of the northern seas. However, it did not survive the peace, running aground on the Scottish island of Sanda in 1946 and subsequently breaking in two. When a hotel was built on the island, it was named the Byron Darnton Inn.

Barney Darnton left behind two sons, both too young to ever remember him. The younger son, John Darnton, followed his father's footsteps into journalism in New York. In an article he wrote, published in the *New York Times* on 16 October 2005, John Darnton wrote how, several years earlier and the week before he went abroad as a foreign correspondent, a mysterious package arrived for him from a newspaper in Chicago. The package contained his father's notebook, which had been retrieved from Barney Darnton's body by another reporter at Pongani, who was now returning it to the Darnton family.

On the last page of the notebook was a question Barney had jotted down about an aircraft that had just been spotted heading towards the little trawler he was on. 'Jap or ours?' said the jotting but, in the end, it didn't really matter.

•

Among the other young Americans from the *Director II*'s explorations across the Pacific, George Folster was the only one not to join the armed services. Shortly after Pearl Harbor, he started with the NBC network as a war correspondent, covering the fighting in the Pacific. In 1945, as NBC's Far East Director, he reached Tokyo to cover the surrender ceremony the day before General MacArthur. Folster remained with NBC, based in Tokyo, until 1957, when he resigned to take up a position as president of a Japanese music publishing company. He died in Tokyo in April 1964 aged fifty-seven years.

Dawson 'Gubby' Glover appears to have settled down after the excitement of the war years, and his post-war career is difficult to chart beyond the fact that he died in 1975 aged fifty-seven years.

Shortly after the war ended, Laddie Reday married an Australian girl named Marjorie Gladys Sullivan. She was from the Melbourne bayside suburb of Carrum and during the war she had worked as a secretary to MacArthur's Chief of Transportation. Laddie and Peg – her preferred name – began their married life in the Philippines where Laddie had accepted a position with the Everett Steamship Company under his old boss, the former Major George Bradford. From Manila, the Redays relocated to Kobe in Japan, still with Everett's, and after many years in Japan

Laddie finally returned to the United States where he and Peg settled at Newport Beach in southern California.

While working for Everett's, Laddie and Peg also nurtured a growing interest in the arts. Laddie's interest was mainly in writing, beginning in 1946 when he wrote an article for the January edition of *Esquire* magazine called 'Remembering Combat Cheer'. He would also become a travel writer for, among others, *The Rotarian* magazine and the *Los Angeles Times*. Peg was more interested in music and the theatre, as she had a background in both from her younger days in Carrum. One high point for both of them came in 1957 when they were given roles in the Warner Brothers film, *Sayonara*, starring Marlon Brando and shot on location in Japan. Laddie was cast in the role of a US consul with Peg playing the role of a lady vice-consul. Laddie Reday died on 25 August 1987, aged seventy-four years.

Laddie had worked on the diary that had been returned to him by Mick Morris, hoping to turn it into a book that reflected his experiences within the Small Ships Section, from the original idea through to the end of the war. Unfortunately, Laddie died before anything concrete could be put in place, but Peg was determined that, if possible, her late husband's story would be told. Several years after Laddie's death, Peg was contacted by another former Small Ships sailor named Ern Flint and the two were able to work together on the project. Laddie Reday's book appeared in 2004 with a title that he would have loved, *The Raggle Taggle Fleet*.

In Laddie's honour, Peg established the Ladislaw Reday Memorial Scholarship at the University of California, Irvine. The scholarship is awarded annually to one incoming or continuing undergraduate major in music. Peg Reday died at her home in Newport Beach on 9 July 2009 after a long battle with cancer.

With the death of the 95-year-old Phil Farley in New York in July 2015, the last of the young men who had sailed the South Seas and formed the nucleus of the Small Ships Section had gone. Like his shipmates, Farley was an immensely popular figure and his obituary in the *New York Times* read, 'The world will be a less entertaining place without him in it.' It is a beautiful epitaph, all that one could wish for, and those words should serve as an epitaph for all those young men who sailed the *Director II* off into adventures that others can only dream about.

The world is a less interesting place without the Gubby Glovers and Phil Farleys and, particularly, without the sheer joy of living that the Fahnestock boys, Bruce and Sheridan, carried with them to the far corners of the Pacific in peacetime and in war.

EPILOGUE
THE SMALL SHIPS OF BUNA

The contribution made by the US Army's Small Ships Section to the Allies' victory at Buna was just fleetingly noted at the time and subsequently almost completely ignored. The reasons for this underestimation at the time are obvious with the benefit of hindsight. After a series of setbacks against the Japanese in Malaya and the Netherlands East Indies, the success of Australians on the Kokoda Track and at Gona deservedly grabbed all the headlines in Australia. The Australian involvement at Buna was both noted and praised, but that notation and praise were for the Australian infantry, artillery and armoured vehicles that were put in after the failure of the 5 December offensive. Apart from the eyewitness accounts of the Hariko disaster by Geoffrey Reading and Frank Bagnall, there was next to nothing in print about the Small Ships.

The lack of recognition on the American side is also understandable. General Douglas MacArthur was obsessed with controlling what was reported about his command. MacArthur was almost as obsessive about Australian criticisms of the combat readiness of his troops. So identifying the decisive contribution of a US Army unit composed almost entirely of Australian civilians unsuitable for Australia's armed forces, and sailing in a motley variety of small Australian boats, was simply never going to happen. The situation was also complicated by the internal politics of MacArthur's headquarters. George Kenney was part of the in-group and MacArthur accepted his assurances on just what his 5th Air Force could deliver. When it failed to do so in several critical instances, that failure was firstly downplayed and then attributed to a number of external factors – the weather and the like.

Some recognition was given to the Small Ships at the time. In his Order of the Day on 22 January 1943, Lieutenant General Edmund Herring, Commander in Chief of New Guinea Forces, thanked all involved in bringing the Buna campaign to a successful end. He singled out the Small Ships for special attention: 'I want to thank all those in the service who kept supplies going to the forward troops, and also . . . the small boat section that has braved hazardous waters and enemy action in getting supplies up the coast.' That was about it for wartime, as bigger victories in other theatres increasingly captured the public's imagination.

Later in the war and in the immediate post-war period, the trend to ignore the Small Ships' contribution continued for a short time at least. The first official American account noted that, 'Our victory at Buna was the fruit of cooperation between ground and air forces. The Australian and American units of the US 5th Air Force, under Lieutenant General George C. Kenney, met all demands, strategic, tactical and logistic.' It was an untruth perpetuated by Robert Eichelberger in his post-war account of the Buna campaign, where he pretty much gives Kenney's air forces credit for everything while pointing out that it was all done at his direction, of course.

Later military histories and memoirs provided a more balanced assessment of the Small Ships at Buna. The official US Army history memoirs of the war in the Pacific, written by Samuel Milner and published in 1957, noted, 'The luggers and freighters . . . brought in by sea more than three times the tonnage that had come in by air. By the end of December, the freighters had brought forward more than 3000 tons of cargo, exclusive of vehicles and tanks. That figure reached 8650 tons by 22 January without addition of tanks, vehicles and road-building equipment.'

The Australian John O'Brien wrote the history of the 2/5th Field Regiment, the unit he commanded for much of World War II. It was his guns and gunners that the Small Ships carried to the Buna battlefield, and he was in no doubt as to their value: 'These little ships were the lifelines of the Allied fighting men. Their number and capacity controlled the scope of military operations. On these vessels . . . dangers from the sea or the enemy were to be expected on every voyage.'

George Kenney made the proud claim on the eve of the Buna campaign that 'the artillery in this theatre flies', and the role of the air force in the Buna victory has never really been examined.

Day after day of aerial bombardment impacted on the morale of those Japanese defenders, and caused both casualties and disruptions, but it didn't stop them from fighting. Wearing gas masks and handkerchiefs to blot out the stench of their dead comrades around them, thousands of Japanese soldiers fought on until their bunkers were blasted apart by point-blank rounds from Australian 25-pound field guns or until they were overrun by the infantry whose approach had been covered and masked by Australian tanks. Kenney was wrong. The artillery in the theatre didn't fly; it floated on barges brought to the front by small

Australian fishing boats and schooners, captained and crewed in the main by Australian sailors.

That is the true story of the victory at Buna.

•

Somewhat ironically, the only time the broader general public learned anything about the role of the Small Ships Section in the Pacific War was when Hollywood made a movie about it. In 1960, some of the more unusual aspects of the section's wartime exploits – both real and imagined – were celebrated in the movie, *The Wackiest Ship in the Army*, starring Jack Lemmon and Chips Rafferty. A modest hit, the movie was followed by a television series of the same name in 1965.

•

On 23 August 1945, less than ten days after the Emperor Hirohito asked the Japanese people to bear the unbearable when announcing an unconditional surrender, a former Small Ships sailor who identified himself only as ATS 7868, wrote a letter to his local paper in Adelaide. ATS 7868 wrote that, 'I was too old to join the Navy or Army so I joined up with our Allies in the Small Ships Section of the US Army, taking food and munition supplies to New Guinea and the Philippines through submarine-infested waters and often bombed by the Japanese. Yet with all the praise we have received, we are not eligible to join the RSL because we fought under the American flag.' The letter was an opening shot in a campaign that would last far, far longer than the war that preceded it.

•

In 1986, along with Australian merchant marine veterans of World War II, the Small Ships veterans became eligible for benefits under the Veterans' Affairs system but, unlike merchant mariners, not for any Australian service awards. The nub of the issue first identified by ATS 7868 forty-one years earlier – that Australian Small Ships sailors somehow had nothing to do with Australia's war effort – still interfered with efforts to tell the truth about that contribution. Many of those Small Ships veterans felt that the situation slighted their service and the service of those who were no longer around to argue the case. Over the next few years, a number of those veterans emerged to tell their story and gain Australian recognition for the war service of Australians who sailed and died in the same way as other Australian servicemen. One of them was a hard worker and dedicated Small Ships sailor named Ern Flint.

Ernest A. Flint (junior) joined the Small Ships in 1944, possibly at the same time as his father, Ernest A. Flint (senior). On 23 October 1944, sixteen-year-old Ern set sail for New Guinea.

While Ern senior spent most of his Small Ships service aboard the first vessel he joined, young Ern was posted to different ships several times as the fighting, and the front, moved from New Guinea to the Philippines and beyond. Young Ern had no doubt that he and his father would catch up with each other somewhere in their travels, and bought a case of bottled beer to share with his father when they did.

When Ern junior arrived in Manila in mid-1945 he heard that his father's ship was there too, so he went looking for it. Unable to find either his father or his father's ship, Ern junior returned to his own vessel. There, his crewmates convinced him that Manila was the largest port in Asia with ships coming and going all the time. His chances of finding his father were slim at best and it would be a shame to let good, cold beer go to waste.

Young Ern and his mates started on the case of beer and had finished all but one bottle when they were hailed from the dock by Ern senior and his ship's captain. That last bottle was sipped very, very slowly.

At war's end both Ern Flints were still with the Small Ships, working on different vessels operating in and around the Philippines. Both stayed on for a considerable length of time, Ern senior working with the UNRRA on the Shanghai run and Ern junior on more general towing and salvage work. The younger Flint was the first to be discharged, leaving the Small Ships Section on 7 November 1946, returning to the family home in Sydney's Surry Hills. His father returned soon afterwards. Young Ern later returned to the armed services, the Australian Army this time, and as Captain Ernest Alfred Flint of the Royal Australian Ordnance Corps was awarded the Order of the British Empire on 31 December 1976.

When he left the army and looked to continue to make a contribution, Ern Flint – like ATS 7868 in Adelaide – discovered that his wartime service with the Small Ships carried far less weight than his peacetime service with the Ordnance Corps. Ern decided to fight for recognition of the service he and his fellow sailors had rendered to the Australian and Allied cause during the Pacific War. He soon learned that the Defence Department's Honours and Awards Tribunal could be as tenacious as any other foe he had confronted in his years of service.

On behalf of all those who had served, Flint argued that the Small Ships veterans should be treated in the same way as Australian merchant seamen who sailed on foreign vessels during the war. Those sailors received Australian and Imperial campaign medals in addition to service medals from the country on whose ships they served. In Flint's early attempts to gain that recognition, he was rebuffed several times by officials. The Australian Small Ships sailors, they said, had chosen to serve in a foreign armed service rather than their own. That service was not in support of Australians. They wore American Army uniforms, served on American vessels and had, moreover, been given American medals for their service.

In October 2004, Ern Flint met with the Director of Honours and Awards and comprehensively debunked all the excuses that had been used to justify rejecting the Small Ships sailors' claims. He provided the director with a number of documents, including written evidence that they did not enlist in the US Army but had been hired as civilians on civilian contracts, and offered up photographic evidence that the Small Ships supported Australian forces in the South West Pacific Area.

Flint also made a number of supporting points at this meeting. He pointed out that the Australians involved were, without exception, too young, too old or medically unfit for service with the Australian military forces. They all paid income tax to the Australian government for the term of their contracts. They were each issued with US Army working dress consisting of two pairs of trousers, two shirts and underwear and a pair of boots; it was working gear and not a uniform. Finally, while their vessels flew an American flag, they remained British-registered.

It was a waste of time. The arguments Ern Flint put forward were formally rejected by the Director of Honours and Awards in 2004 and then again when they were presented in 2005, 2006, 2007 and 2008. But their time was coming.

Earlier, on 15 May 2001, the US Small Ships Association, founded in the United States in 1985, through the American

Consul-General in Sydney, presented a commemorative plaque to the Grace Hotel, noting its role in the history of the Small Ships Section. Perhaps inspired by this, Ern Flint helped to establish an Australian US Army Small Ships Section Association, serving as its inaugural president.

There had also been growing interest in the Small Ships following the publication of two books on the section in the 1990s. The first was simply called *Forgotten Fleet*, and was a compilation of stories, biographies of boats and sailors, and photographs, brought together and published by Bill Lunney and Frank Finch. The second was Laddie Reday's *The Raggle Taggle Fleet*. The Lunney and Finch book was revised and updated in 2004 by Bill Lunney and his wife, the academic Ruth Lunney. Together with the Small Ships Association, this provided a focus for those prepared to gain recognition of the veterans' war service.

There were other positive developments. In 2008, Australia's Minister for Veterans' Affairs unveiled a Sydney harbourside memorial to the boys who graduated as apprentice seamen from the Walsh Bay training school near the site of the original classrooms. The following year, the Australian Small Ships veterans received notice that the US Congress had approved the award of the US Army's Sea Duty Ribbon to all Australian Small Ships crew.

And then, on Monday 9 November 2009, the Honourable Dr Mike Kelly, ex-soldier and the then Minister for Defence Support, issued a press release headed, 'Defence Honours and Awards Tribunal Report – Inquiry into Recognition for Service with the United States Small Ships Section'. It was a relatively short press release, and went straight to the point. The report recommended that:

1. Australian civilian personnel who served in ships operated by the United States Army Small Ships Section between 1942 and 1945 be recognised as eligible for Australian and Imperial recognition for that service on the same basis as members of the Merchant Navy; and,
2. There should be no requirement for those persons to relinquish any US awards that they may have received in respect of their service in the United States Small Ships prior to receiving Australian recognition for that service.

The long wait was over.

A NOTE ON SOURCES

One of the reasons so little has been written about the Small Ships Section, and in particular its contribution to the victory at Buna, is that the section was neither fish nor fowl in terms of where it sat in the order of battle. It was a US Army unit, but part of larger, better-known units – the Combined Operations Service Command and the US Army Transportation Service. While its members saw themselves as a unique part of a much bigger machine, those at the levers of the machine saw them as a tool to be used where appropriate. A second reason was the politics of war in the South West Pacific Area, where there were Australian Army and US Army imperatives that did not always align. As a US Army unit staffed almost entirely by Australians, there were always going to be tensions in recognising their contributions as well as their status. Their leaders – most of whom had come from the business world – were intent on achieving results rather than recognition.

The literature on the Small Ships is patchy and spread across a range of sources. Most of the official material generated by the section is simply not available. Hints and suggestions found elsewhere indicate that all the official documentation was divided at war's end; the original documents were shipped back to America and the duplicates remained behind in the Grace Building. More than one recollection is that those duplicates were used to fire up the boilers that provided the building's heat and hot water until they were all gone. The documents taken to America, if they exist, are not in the usual place, the National Archives and Records Administration, while the US Army Transportation Corps and the Transport Museum do not list them on their sites and are too short-staffed to provide any form of research service.

Thankfully, there are documents and primary material available. The Australian US Army Small Ships Association, and its ever-helpful secretary, Dan O'Brien, hold a number of recordings, diaries and reminiscences which were invaluable. They also put me in touch with several members who either served or were related to those who served with the section. Clarrie Dawes, Ruth Lunney, Neil Lyndon King Sandery, the son that Neil Sandery never met, Ross Andrews and Isabel Andrews provided a wealth of material and were both gracious and generous with their time and recollections. Several others contributed elements to the wider story.

A number of books also help fill out the picture. John Darnton's recollections of trying to find out just who his father was, published as *Almost a Family*, are a wonderfully written story of a journey of discovery. A companion piece is Geoffrey Reading's *Papuan Story*, a well-written first-hand account of the first year of fighting in New Guinea which contains stirring description of the disaster at Hariko. Many of the other books listed in the Bibliography also contributed parts of the story, albeit from different perspectives. The two priceless books I used constantly were Laddie Reday's *The Raggle Taggle Fleet* and Bill and Ruth Lunney's *Forgotten Fleet 2*. Between them, they cover the story of the Small Ships Section through the recollections of those who were part of it.

Parts of the whole story can also be gleaned from contemporary newspapers, and from the columns of newspapers in more recent times where the careers of local citizens are recalled upon their deaths.

Finally, the Australian and American Official War Histories offer glimpses of the story, usually as seen from above, while the memoirs of senior soldiers and unit histories also offer other, sometimes contradictory, stories. Some of the American accounts are simply wrong in attributing accolades for the men behind the fighting men at Buna. Buna was a battle that the Allies were always going to win just as the Japanese were always going to lose. The work of the men and boats of the Small Ships Section wasn't the difference between victory and defeat but it was the difference between victory in mid-January and victory several weeks later when Kenney's air force would have been able to do the job that he had promised it would. The weather, the strength of the Japanese defences and the resolve of the Japanese defenders were factors that Kenney's planners had missed. Given that Allied casualties were between 150 and 250 a day for the duration of the campaign, there were at least two thousand soldiers alive on 22 January 1943 who would not have been alive without the Small Ships. That alone is why the story is worth telling.

ENDNOTES

Prologue: Sailing the Southern Seas, 1934–41

p. xiv   . . . *he simply stopped filming* . . . Fahnestock & Fahnestock, *Stars to Windward*, p. 292

p. xv   . . . *extremely fond of her young cousins* . . . Helen Hubbard was one of the leading dowagers in the American colony in Paris as well as a prominent member of New York society. She had two major loves: music and travel. The first led her to found the Manhattan School of Music and dedicate its auditorium to the memory of her late husband. The second led her to sail across the Atlantic eighty-seven times. She had also visited the South Seas before either Bruce or Sheridan had been born.

p. xv   . . . *promptly named Director II* . . . Originally named *Sachem*, the schooner had been built in Lunenburg, Nova Scotia, for the Nova Scotia–Portugal salt fish trade. She had also acted as a rum runner during America's Prohibition period and had subsequently been converted into a luxury diesel auxiliary yacht. She was lying idle at Gloucester, Massachusetts, before being purchased for the Fahnestocks.

p. xvi   . . . *in the Oval Office* . . . *see* www.fdrlibrary.marist.edu. No minutes or notes from the meeting exist in publicly available material but Sheridan Fahnestock's partial and unpublished memoirs give enough hints to make an educated guess about what was said.

p. xvi   . . . *family and social connections* . . . Mary Fahnestock may have been Maid of Honour at one of Teddy Roosevelt's two marriages, and the Fahnestocks were friends with the major branches of the Roosevelt family.

p. xvii   . . . *a number of department stores* . . . *New York Times*, 26 April 1964.

p. xvii   . . . *other crewmen and friends* . . . Like most of the others, Phil Farley was well connected. His father, James Farley, was US Postmaster

General between 1933 and 1940. A consummate political operator, Farley was more responsible than almost anyone else for Franklin Roosevelt's success at both the state and national levels.

p. xx   ... *keeping diaries of their voyage* ... The most comprehensive, and most effusive, report was that published in the *Sydney Morning Herald* on 15 October 1940.

p. xxi   ... *mass of raw material* ... *Townsville Daily Bulletin*, 8 December 1941.

p. xxii   ... *painting the portraits* ... Ned Dair was still in Sydney when the Pacific War commenced; he returned to the United States and promptly enlisted in the US Navy.

p. xxiii ... *the British colonies of* ... Although no formal record of either official meeting between the Fahnestock brothers and President Roosevelt exists in the public forum, the intelligence role of the Fahnestocks seems to have been quite widely known. See, for instance, Darnton, *Almost a Family*, p. 305.

p. xxiii ... *Singapore and Biliton* ... US Archives, Document 16618974.

1. Mission X

p. 4   ... *the name of the operation* ... Sheridan Fahnestock's unpublished memoirs, pp. 16–29.

p. 6   ... *take any actions necessary* ... The presence of any US military personnel was kept from the Australian public well into 1942.

p. 6   ... *the lease or purchase* ... Williford, *Racing the Sunrise*, p. 230

p. 6   ... *to prolong the defence* ... ibid., p. 231

p. 12   ... *white-haired, red-cheeked and jolly* ... Reday, *The Raggle Taggle Fleet*, p. 32.

p. 12   ... *also known as Jack* ... Jack junior's full name was John Blennerhassett Savage. He was born on 16 April 1917.

p. 14   ... *could not countenance* ... Babcock, *MacArthur's Small Ships*, p. 27.

p. 16   ... *was up and running* ... An April 1942 report indicated that Plant's team included 'a staff of approximately nine experienced Water Transportation men with an additional seven to come'. By the end of the year, Plant's section had expanded to fifty officers, twenty enlisted men and forty-four civilians. Babcock, pp. 32/33.

p. 17   ... *maintain their small boat fleet* ... ibid., p. 33.

p. 18   ... *own freight storage area* ... Reday, p. 25.

2. Forming a Fleet

p. 23   ... *assist with the process* ... Babcock, p. 33.

p. 25   ... *run up the flagpole* ... Despite this, the US Army never formally registered the vessels acquired in this process. Years later, some of the Australians who would sign on for service aboard them would argue that, technically, they did not serve on foreign vessels during the war.

p. 25   ... *and arming the ships* ... Reday, p. 32.

p. 26   ... *his orders were obeyed* ... Richards, *North Coast Run*, p. 142.

p. 26   ... *and an easy grin* ... Reday, p. 26.

p. 27   ... *the Bonwin* ... Owned by the Sydney firm, Cranwin Fisheries, the *Bonwin* had an interesting pedigree. Around seventeen metres long, she had been launched at Lavender Bay in March 1939, and was designed partly to be used in the shark-netting operations off Sydney's main beaches. This was not a long-term prospect, though, and she soon reverted to normal fishing operations off the South Coast under Bill Priest's command.

p. 29   ... *perhaps at another time* ... Ralph Andrews, interview.

p. 34   ... *become a key part* ... Milner, *Victory in Papua*, p. 26

p. 36   ... *her name was the Leprena* ... Clarrie was quite familiar with the *Leprena*, a two-masted schooner that operated out of Port Adelaide. Like the *Coorabie*, pre-war she was used to carry wheat from shallow water ports, and could carry up to 100 tons.

p. 38   ... *all before he turned twenty-one* ... Sandery's reports on these voyages were published in several capital city newspapers between 1937 and 1939.

p. 38   ... *Parer promptly resigned* ... Ray Parer's cousin, Damien Parer, would find fame as Australia's finest war cameraman, a skill that won him numerous awards but would ultimately cost him his life.

p. 38   ... *bums and ne'er-do-wells* ... Reday, p. 25

p. 39   ... *he made his way to Sydney* ... Hardy, *Uncle Sam's Australians*, p. 34

p. 40   ... *the final days of that conflict* ... Although both his parents were Australian, Byrne was born in New Zealand, at Nelson on the South Island. After his mother left to return to Australia, Byrne remained with his father at Gisborne on the North Island, joining the army from there as a twenty-one-year-old in 1917.

3. North

p. 44   ... *the key to its defence* ... Milner, p. 24.

p. 44   ... *given the codename 'Boston'* ... In mid-1941, the US Army adopted a code word system to designate overseas locations. Hawaii became 'Copper', Alaska was 'Bronze' and Panama was 'Mercury', while the Philippines were given the codename 'Plum'.

p. 45   ... *despatched by sea* ... Mayo, *Bloody Buna*, p. 11.

p. 46   ... *without the risks* ... A number of maps used by Japanese planners apparently showed a road linking Buna and Port Moresby. See Edgerton, *Warriors of the Rising Sun*, p. 282.

p. 47   ... *especially sea transport* ... Milner, p. 72.

p. 48   ... *a young man named Cliff* ... Cliff Callen came from a well-known family of shipbuilders, Callen Brothers, of Stockton near Newcastle.

p. 51   ... *several coats of grey paint* ... *Townsville Daily Bulletin*, 20 September 1945.

p. 53   ... *one of the first boats* ... Launched in 1940, the *Minston Brae* had actually started its working life as a pearling boat.

p. 54   ... *tubby and balding* ... Lunney, *Forgotten Fleet 2*, p. 336 The 45-year-old Slight had a wonderful past. Attached to a Canadian army unit, the ship on which he was serving assisted the Allied forces that landed at Narvik in Norway. That ship was torpedoed and sunk just off the Norwegian coast. Later, at Dunkirk during the evacuation of British forces, his ship was dive-bombed and sunk. Slight had served

with the British Army during World War I and in India. Adelaide
News, 25 September 1942.

p. 55 ... *sailed the* Minston Brae *to the Gili Gili wharf* ... The original wharf
at Gili Gili, located at the head of Milne Bay and connected to the
Lever Brothers' palm plantation there, consisted of two barges side
by side, leading to a small dilapidated jetty. Large new docks were
under construction when the *Minston Brae* arrived.

p. 56 ... *Then they waited.* The description of the action is based on several
sources including Lunney, Reday and an interview the *Minston Brae*
crew had with Australian war correspondent George Johnston,
published in the Melbourne *Age* on 16 October 1942.

p. 57 ... *They slowed down* ... Ralph Andrews, interview.

p. 63 ... *COSC was given direct* ... AWM 577/7/29, p. 2.

p. 63 ... *control and movement* ... Ibid., see also Milner, p. 103.

p. 63 ... *some distance to the west* ... The *Shangri-La* would not be the first
Small Ship in that area. A few weeks earlier, the trawler *Barraconda*
had been caught in a storm in the Gulf of Papua, ending up in the
Fly River delta.

4. The Smell of Land, the Bark of a Dog

p. 66 ... *bring an entire division* ... The 32nd Division was a former National
Guard division composed of volunteers primarily from the states of
Michigan and Wisconsin. It had sailed into Adelaide in May 1942
and had just settled in there when it was on the move again, relo-
cating to Brisbane in August.

p. 68 ... *audacious and uncertain* ... Wolk, *George C. Kenney*, in Leary, *We
Shall Return.*

p. 68 ... *had been detached* ... A highly decorated officer with battlefield
experience during World War I, MacNider had been an ardent isol-
ationist afterwards and was an active member of the America First
movement. He resigned from it three days before Pearl Harbor and
requested a return to active service.

p. 68 ... *apparently dried off* ... General Robert Eichelberger, then in charge
of all American troops in and around Brisbane, where they were
undergoing training, organised for a Brisbane cleaning company to
dye the men's fatigues a mottled brown, green and yellow pattern for
jungle warfare. However, in the rain and extreme humidity of New
Guinea, the dye ran and clogged the cloth, causing men to develop
skin ulcers. See both Gailey, *MacArthur Strikes Back*, pp. 104, and
Campbell, *The Ghost Mountain Boys*, p. xv.

p. 70 ... *a regular supply* ... Reday, p. 49.

p. 73 ... *the presence of breakers* ... Reday, p. 67.

p. 73 ... *land to be cleared* ... Wanigela Mission had been run by the Church
of England before the war. When the Japanese landed at Buna, all
those living at the mission – some forty people in total – walked out
to safety, abandoning the mission.

p. 75 ... *Lieutenant Colonel Laurence McKenny* ... Pre-war, McKenny had
been a school principal in Detroit. Like the overwhelming majority
of the division, he was not a professional soldier but part of the

National Guard who had been transferred across to the regular army for the duration.

p. 75   . . . *from that point* . . . Milner, p. 105.

p. 75   . . . *The reef was spotted by* . . . Feldt, *The Coast Watchers*, p. 189. The reef retains the name to this day and is now a popular spot for recreational divers.

p. 78   . . . *an all-Filipino crew* . . . Ames and his crew were rapidly becoming favourites among the Small Ships sailors. Ames was a professional hairdresser, while his second in command, Melchior Bernal, was a natural comedian who was proud of saying that he served with the 'Small Sheeps'.

p. 79   . . . *the stretch of coastline* . . . The Americans would eventually christen Pongani 'Fever Ridge' and describe it as 'a sweltering, sun-beaten hellhole infested with sand-fleas, flies and mosquitoes': Campbell, p. 163.

5. Friendly Fire

p. 84   . . . *the 'Coastal Task Force'* . . . It was designated the Coastal Task Force to distinguish it from the elements that would launch their opening attack from the interior. It would also be called Warren Force with the inland component known as Urbana Force.

p. 86   . . . *inside his Army manual* . . . Darnton, p. 11.

p. 86   . . . *a swell guy* . . . Milner, p. 108.

p. 87   . . . *how to preserve peace* . . . Adelaide *Advertiser*, 23 October 1942.

p. 86   . . . *two pirate ships* . . . Darnton, p. 16.

p. 88   . . . *The move's so secret* . . . Milner, p. 93.

p. 91   . . . *Jap or ours?* . . . Darnton, p. 13.

p. 91   . . . *hated wearing helmets* . . . ibid., p. 303.

p. 94   . . . *had also been hit* . . . Beecher lost part of his nose and one eye when struck, but would survive the wounds.

p. 98   . . . *side by side in the cemetery* . . . Forrest Harding wrote to Richard Sutherland, MacArthur's aide, about the incident, saying, 'He [Darnton] was hot to be on the spot for the first contact of American Army ground troops with the Japs. I told him that this would probably be it and gave him permission to go.' Milner, p. 108.

p. 98   . . . *keep it as a souvenir* . . . Reading, *Papuan Story*, p. 110.

p. 99   . . . *were to be considered* . . . Reday, p. 45.

6. The Red Arrow Line

p. 102   . . . *night-vision marker buoys* . . . Moremon, *Battle of the Beachheads*, p. 3.

p. 102   . . . *off the main route* . . . Official Sailing Instructions, p. 2.

p. 102   . . . *in a 'favourable' position* . . . ibid., p. 7.

p. 102   . . . *roll off production lines* . . . One of the first Liberty ships to reach Australia, the *Rufus King* did not have an auspicious arrival, being wrecked in the South Passage below Moreton Island in July 1942. The wreck was not a total write-off, however. The forward section of the ship was salvaged and fitted out as a floating workshop and fuel store. Taken over by the Small Ships, she was given a designation – S 217 – and a new name, the *Half-Rufus.*

p. 106 ... *seemed to stop them* ... These were the aircraft that so concerned Ralph Andrews on his Fly River reconnaissance aboard the *Shangri-La.*

p. 106 ... *a range of problems* ... The *Leprena* was so notoriously unstable in high seas that those who served aboard her usually referred to her as the 'Leaping Lena', claiming she would simply bounce from wave to wave.

p. 107 ... *were frequently detached* ... On 26 October, for example, the *Bonwin* carried seventeen young Papuans from Abau to Port Moresby, where they were to join the Papuan Infantry Battalion.

p. 107 ... *somewhat exotic background* ... Born in India in 1904 while his father was stationed there with the British Army, Reynolds learned his trade as a sailor aboard a training ship on the Thames. After several years at sea, he started a business in Sydney to eradicate prickly pear. When that failed, he returned to sailing as a merchant seaman until joining the Small Ships.

p. 108 ... *getting his clothes dirty* ... Reday, p. 131.

p. 109 ... *was used to bring in* ... The waters to the north and north-west of the Japanese positions between Buna and Gona were considerably deeper than those the Allies had to navigate, and allowed both supplies and reinforcements to be brought in by surface vessels and submarines.

p. 112 ... *still remained confident* ... AWM 423/4/99.

p. 112 ... *Not quickly but faintly.* AWM PR91/040. Many of the Japanese manning the defences had arrived back from the Kokoda Track wearing a combination of rice bags and blankets because their uniforms had literally rotted away.

p. 113 ... *the rest died slowly* ... Eames, *The Searchers*, pp. 156–80.

p. 113 ... *and their gun crews* ... The Battery's Right Section, with two 3.7 inch mountain howitzers and under the command of Major Martin O'Hare, was flown into Wanigela on 12 November and was collected there by the Japanese barge.

p. 115 ... *and then returning* ... Because it had a shallow draught and front-opening door, the barge was an ideal vessel to carry artillery pieces.

p. 116 ... *one of the American officers* ... Melvin McCreary would be awarded the Distinguished Service Cross on 24 December for bravery when directing mortar fire from a position so exposed that he was wounded while doing so.

p. 118 ... *planners had estimated* ... US Army: Papua Campaign.

7. In Harm's Way

p. 119 ... *also be focused on* ... MacArthur had moved his own advanced headquarters to Port Moresby on 6 November to be closer to the centre of action. That was as close as he would come to the fighting. Kenney supported his commander by having one of his aircraft fly the first flushing toilet seen in New Guinea to Government House where MacArthur was staying. Edgerton, p. 216.

p. 122   ... *the security of the hospital* ... The 22nd Portable Hospital – a forerunner to the Mobile Army Surgical Hospital (MASH) – had only
recently arrived in New Guinea after being formed in Australia. It
was flown into Wanigela on 12 November and had moved from
there to Oro Bay aboard a Small Ship. Early that morning, the
hospital's men and equipment had been loaded aboard the *Alacrity*
and its barge at Oro Bay.

p. 123   ... *the forthcoming attack* ... Geoffrey Reading would describe Laux as
'Colonel A.B. Laux of Washington ... Laux was an artillery officer
going forward to make observations. He had a hard-bitten, wise-
cracking sense of humour that caught my fancy.' Reading, p. 144.

p. 124   ... *a lean young man* ... ibid., p. 147.

p. 128   ... *let your thoughts wander* ... Reading devotes Chapter 9 of *Papuan
Story* to describing this incident.

p. 134   ... *he simply dived over* ... Pre-war, Bagnall had swum competitively for
Sydney's Rose Bay Swimming Club.

8.   Hariko

p. 139   ... *jumped into the barge* ... Milner, p. 169.

p. 140   ... *several other actions* ... The Distinguished Service Cross is the second
highest American military decoration behind the Congressional Medal
of Honour.

p. 140   ... *continued to fire* ... Robinson, *Fight for New Guinea*, p. 153.

p. 142   ... *machine-gun fire* ... See Milner, p. 168.

p. 148   ... *an empty fuel drum* ... *Army News*, 29 November 1942 For his
actions, Gunner Tommy Hale would be Mentioned in Despatches.

p. 151   ... *the only loss* ... Allen and Cutts, *As It Seemed to Us*, p. 45.

p. 154   ... *a copybook attack* ... Michael Claringbould, author of *Eagles of the
Southern Sky*, conversation with author. The ebullient Claringbould
is Australia's recognised expert on the air war in the South West
Pacific.

p. 155   ... *The only supplies* ... As well as John Harbert, ten other American
servicemen would be awarded the Distinguished Service Cross for
their actions that day.

p. 156   ... *just how deadly* ... AWM 581/7/20.

p. 157   ... *back at Embogo* ... O'Brien, p. 172 Frank Bagnall would return to
Australia on 27 November.

9.   Into the Maelstrom

p. 161   ... *drove as hard for the beach* ... Some of the soldiers aboard
subsequently claimed to have shot down one of those aircraft, saying
it crashed into the sea further out.

p. 163   ... *operate forward of Porlock* ... AWM 581/7/11.

p. 165   ... *heavy rain at Port Moresby* ... See McAulay, *To the Bitter End*, p. 31.

p. 168   ... *even the natives feared* ... Robinson, p. 144.

p. 169   ... *brought in by air* ... O'Brien, p. 169.

p. 169   ... *suited their capabilities* ... The mountain howitzers would be used
continuously in the battle for Buna until 26 December when they ran

out of ammunition. As further ammunition was not available, they took no further part in the battle.

p. 170 ... *were all brought ashore* ... AWM 581/6/11B.

p. 173 ... *rammed at high speed* ... Cummings, *Confessions of a Mud Skipper*, p. 22.

10. The Return of the Red Arrow Line

p. 183 ... *briefings for selected newsmen* ... From almost the time he arrived at Government House, lower-level officers and the rank and file soldiers began to refer to it as the Ivory Tower.

p. 184 ... *only one vessel available* ... Gailey, p. 135.

p. 185 ... *act as a floating reserve* ... AWM 557/7/29.

p. 185 ... *would later relocate* ... The senior COSC Liaison Officer was Captain Patrick Lang, formerly of the 2/5th Independent Company. Lang had arrived at Wanigela on 14 October and moved to Porlock Harbour from there.

p. 186 ... *suddenly very obvious* ... As an example of what this meant on the ground, Patrick Lang reported that the shore holdings at Porlock Harbour, the smaller of the two sites, on 7 December included 500,000 rations, 200 tons of ammunition and hundreds of drums of POL. Lang, p. 7.

p. 186 ... *surrendered to the Japanese* ... Sinclair, who won the DSO as a naval officer serving at Gallipoli in 1915, later became a Singapore harbour pilot and who, as captain of HMS *Kedah*, led one of the last convoys to leave Singapore, sailing on the night of 11/12 February 1942. Following his arrival in Australia, Sinclair was seconded to the RAN. Gill *Royal Australian Navy, 1942–45*, p. 240.

p. 186 ... *to be no movements* ... Lang, p. 9

p. 187 ... *member of a well-known* ... Both Horace and his younger brother Harris Horder were Australian champions and internationally recognised cyclists. Harris Horder moved to the United States in the mid-1930s and became an American citizen to help progress his professional cycling career. In Australia, when the Pacific War broke out, he immediately volunteered to serve in the US Army. After training in the United States, Harris was posted as a nose gunner in a B-24 Liberator bomber. He was killed when his aircraft crashed in New Guinea in 1943.

p. 193 ... *evacuated back to Australia* ... The wound would cost MacNider the sight of his left eye. He would later return to a combat command, but not until the Buna campaign was well and truly over.

p. 195 ... *during daylight hours* ... Veale was aboard as a kind of armed guard in case there was any need for protection when, as part of its role, *Paluma* landed or took off coastwatchers from enemy territory.

p. 196 ... *after just one bombing run* ... www.australiansatwar.gov.au.

11. Waiting for the Cavalry

p. 206 . . . *on the north coast* . . . AWM 44/1/5.

p. 207 . . . *returning to Port Moresby* . . . Before the Buna–Gona campaign was over, the 2/6th Armoured Regiment would send twenty-seven of its tanks to the battlefront there.

p. 208 . . . *waiting with their crews* . . . *Karsik's* first trip to Oro Bay with the tanks was designated 'Operation Karsik'; some wag at COSC named the second tank delivery, 'Operation Tramsik'. Gill, *Royal Australian Navy, 1939–42*, p. 243.

p. 213 . . . *the tracks they left* . . . Handel, *History of the 2/6th Armoured Regiment*, p. 3.

p. 214 . . . *when a Japanese shell* . . . Harry Hopperton was a twenty-one-year-old sapper from Perth. He was also a very good Australian Rules footballer, playing pre-war for both the Perth and East Perth clubs, while he also represented the AIF.

p. 218 . . . *some scared Yank* . . . AWM PR 91/061.

p. 219 . . . *also partly right* . . . US War Department, *Papuan Campaign: The Buna–Sanananda Operation*.

p. 219 . . . *for Small Ships only* . . . Ralph Andrews, interview.

p. 220 . . . *There were no repeats* . . . AWM 577/7/29, p. 11.

12. Base B

p. 225 . . . *a lot of convincing* . . . Both Gailey, p. 135, and Lang, p. 5, relate this incident.

p. 230 . . . *After handshakes all around* . . . Kahn, *G.I. Jungle*, pp. 92/3.

p. 231 . . . *went straight back* . . . Max Hood was sent to hospital in Townsville and when he recovered was sent further south to the Small Ships Section's main base at Walsh Bay. There he became part of the team carrying out sea trials on the new craft being produced for the Small Ships by Halvorsen's and other boat builders.

p. 235 . . . *only fifty of those* . . . Moremon, p. 1 and Chan, *War on Our Doorstep*, p. 269.

p. 235 . . . *victims of illness* . . . US War Department, p. 85.

p. 235 . . . *fit for duty* . . . Red Arrow/Wisconsin.

13. Setting Sun

p. 249 . . . *a serving member* . . . The Volunteer Coastal Patrol had been formed in 1937 to complement the work of the military and police services. By the end of 1942, it was operating several boats in Sydney Harbour each night. From 6 p.m. until 6 a.m., those boats – often with a police officer on board – patrolled around the harbour's vital installations. These sites included the various wharves, fuel depots, the flying boat base at Rose Bay and the ammunition depot at Bantry Bay. Their duty completed, the crews would then return to their day jobs.

p. 251 . . . *he took delivery of* . . . Morgan served with the Small Ships until 5 July 1944, when he chose not to renew his employment contract.

p. 254 ... *and back out into* ... I have not been able to identify just which
trawler this was.

p. 255 ... *were no longer needed* ... Reday, p. 164.

14. Home from the Sea

p. 270 ... *He finished the war* ... One of Ralph Andrews' fondest memories
from this period was when he was approached by some US Army
engineers who had developed a bulletproof shield for the wheel-
houses of smaller vessels. He had one fitted to a small boat, which he
sailed around to Long Bay for a series of tests. The shield shattered
when struck by the first burst of machine-gun fire. Ralph then
explained to the engineers that he had himself built a protective
shield around the *Two Freddies'* wheelhouse using tins of army-issue
biscuits. They were more effective as they would also stop armour-
piercing bullets.

p. 271 ... *sitting on deck* ... Godwin, *Battling Parer*, p. 174.

p. 272 ... *kept the knife* ... Parer had a particular dislike of the Japanese, an
antipathy that might have dated back to the early days of the war
when his younger brother, Kevin, was killed by Japanese aircraft
during an air raid on the airfield at Salamaua.

p. 273 ... *a former RAF crash boat* ... *Northern Miner*, 29 July 1946.

p. 274 ... *was found guilty* ... Adelaide *Advertiser*, 14 April 1948.

p. 277 ... *In December 1975* ... The event was given some prominence in the
Australian Women's Weekly of 17 December 1975.

p. 281 ... *died at her home* ... *Los Angeles Times*, 14 July 2009.

Epilogue: The Small Ships of Buna

p. 284 ... *The first official American account* ... US War Department.

p. 284 ... *it was all done at his direction* ... See Eichelberger's *My Jungle Road
to Tokyo* for a somewhat self-serving account of Buna and other
battles Eichelberger directed.

p. 285 ... *The official US Army history* ... Milner, p. 375.

p. 285 ... *'These little ships were ...'* O'Brien, p. 169.

p. 286 ... *ATS 7868 wrote that* ... Adelaide *Advertiser*, 23 August 1945.

p. 289 ... *Earlier, on 15 May 2001* ... There is a replica plaque at the US
Army's Transportation Museum at Fort Eustis in Virginia.

p. 290 ... *The first was simply called* ... Bill Lunney was one of the apprentice seamen from Arthur Morgan's Walsh Bay school. He was fifteen
years old when he joined in 1943, and went on to serve aboard the
Mactan, Hilda Norling, Kurimarau and the *Bingarra.*

p. 290 ... *the US Congress had approved* ... More good news would come
the following year when, on 9 July 2010, the US Army Corps of
Transportation inducted the Small Ships Section into its Hall of
Fame, 'for demonstrating exceptionally distinguished service to the
Corps in World War Two'.

p. 290 ... *issued a press release* ... Minister for Defence Support, Press
Release 73/09.

BIBLIOGRAPHY

Books

Allan, Jack & Cutts, Chris (Eds.), *As it Seemed to Us*, Aebis Publishing, Brisbane, 1994

Balfe, J.D., *War Without Glory,* Macmillan, Melbourne, 1984

Blakeley, H.W., *32nd Infantry Division, World War II,* State of Wisconsin, Madison, WI, 1955

Bolger, W.P. & Littlewood, J.G., *The Fiery Phoenix*, 2/7th Battalion Association, Parkdale, n.d.

Brune, Peter, *The Spell Broken,* Allen & Unwin, Sydney, 1997

——*A Bastard of a Place,* Allen & Unwin, Sydney, 2004

Campbell, James, *The Ghost Mountain Boys,* Crown, New York, 2007

Carty, William, *Flickers of History, a Newsreel Cameraman's Story*, HarperCollins, Sydney, 1999

Chan, Gabrielle (ed.), *War on Our Doorstep,* Hardie Grant, Melbourne, 2003

Chwialkowski, Paul, *In Caesar's Shadow*, Greenwood Press, Westport, CT, 1993

Collie, C. & Hajimi, M., *Path of Infinite Sorrow*, Allen & Unwin, Sydney, 2009

Cummings, H.W., *Confessions of a Mud Skipper*, Self-published, Cooktown, 1980

Darnton, John, *Almost a Family,* A.A. Knopf, New York, 2011

Dennis, Peter, et al., *The Oxford Companion to Australian Military History*, Oxford University Press, Melbourne, 1995

Eames, Jim, *The Searchers*, University of Queensland Press, Brisbane, 1999

Edgerton, Robert, *Warriors of the Rising Sun*, Westview Press, Boulder, CO, 1997

Eichelberger, Robert, *Our Jungle Road to Tokyo*, Viking Press, New York, 1950

Fahnestock, Bruce & Sheridan, *Stars to Windward*, Harcourt, Brace & Co., New York, 1938

Fahnestock, Mary, *I Ran Away to Sea at 50*, Harcourt, Brace & Co., New York, 1939

Feldt, Eric, *The Coast Watchers*, Penguin, Melbourne, 1991

Flint, Ernest, *Formation and Operation of the US Army Small Ships in World War II*, Self-Published, Sydney, N.D.

Gailey, Harry, *MacArthur Strikes Back: Decision at Buna, New Guinea, 1942–3*, Presidio Press, Novato, 2000

Gill, G. Hermon, *Royal Australian Navy, 1939–42*, Australian War Memorial, Canberra, 1957

——*Royal Australian Navy, 1942–45*, Australian War Memorial, Canberra, 1968

Godwin, John, *Battling Parer*, Rigby, Adelaide, 1968

Handel, Paul, *History of the 2/6th Armoured Regiment*, Self-published, Sydney, 1945

Harries, Meirion & Susan, *Soldiers of the Sun*, Random House, New York, 1991

Hopkins, R.N.L., *Australian Armour*, Australian War Memorial, Canberra, 1978

The Jap was Thrashed, Public Relations Directorate, Melbourne, 1944

Kahn, Ely, *G.I. Jungle*, Simon & Schuster, New York, 1943

Kelly, C. Brian, *Best Little Stories from World War II*, Cumberland House, Nashville, 2010

Keogh, E.G., *The South West Pacific, 1941–45*, Grayflower, Melbourne, 1965

Laws, John & Stewart, Christopher, *It Doesn't End There*, Macmillan, Sydney, 2006

Leary, William (ed.), *We Shall Return: MacArthur's Commanders and the Defeat of Japan, 1942–45*, University Press of Kentucky, Lexington, KY, 1988

Lunney, Bill and Ruth, *Forgotten Fleet 2*, Forfleet Publishing, Medowie, 2004

Luvaas, Jay (ed.), *Dear Miss Em: General Eichelberger's War in the Pacific*, Greenwood Press, Westport, KT, 1972

Mayo, Lyda, *Bloody Buna*, David & Charles, London, 1975

McAulay, Lex, *To the Bitter End*, Random House, Sydney, 1992

Milner, Samuel, *Victory in Papua*, Army Department, Washington, 1957

Moremon, John, *Battle of the Beachheads: 1942–3*, Department of Veterans Affairs, Canberra, 2002

O'Brien, John, *Guns and Gunners*, Angus & Robertson, Sydney, 1950

Ohl, John, *Supplying the Troops: General Somervell and American Logistics in World War II*, Northern Illinois University Press, De Kalb, IL, 1994

Paull, Raymond, *Retreat from Kokoda*, Heinemann, Melbourne, 1982

Phillips, W.H.J., *Buna–Gona Campaign, 1942/43*, Self-published, Coffs Harbour, n.d.

Ralph, Barry, *They Passed This Way*, Kangaroo Press, Sydney, 2000

Reading, Geoffrey, *Papuan Story*, Angus & Robertson, Sydney, 1949

Reday, Ladislaw, *The Raggle Taggle Fleet*, Ligare P/L, Riverwood, n.d.

Richards, Mike, *North Coast Run*, Turton & Armstrong, Killara, 1997

Robinson, Pat, *Fight for New Guinea: General Douglas MacArthur's First Offensive*, Random House, New York, 1943

Ruffato, Luca & Claringbould, Michael, *Eagles of the Southern Sky*, Tainan Publishing, New York, 2012

Tapert, Annette, *Lines of Battle: Letters from American Servicemen, 1941–45*, Pocket Books, Washington, DC, 1989

Thompson, Peter, *Pacific Fury*, Heinemann, Sydney, 2008

US War Department, *Papuan Campaign: The Buna–Sanananda Operation*, Military Intelligence Division, Washington, DC, 1944

Williford, Glen, *Racing the Sunrise: Reinforcing America's Pacific Outposts, 1941–42*, Naval Institute Press, Annapolis, MD, 2010

Wurth, Bob, *1942*, Pan Macmillan, Sydney, 2008

Articles and monographs

Babcock, Kenneth, 'MacArthur's Small Ships', *Army History*, Winter 2014

Brien, James, 'The Bloody Beachheads: The Battles of Gona, Buna and Sanananda, November 1942 – January 1943', www.awm.gov.au, accessed 14.5.16

Cahill, Rowan, 'Anthropologists, Spooks and the Boys who went to War', *Radical History*, 30 July 2012

Fahnestock, Bruce & Sheridan, 'South Seas War Baby', *Harper's Magazine*, 182, May 2014

Frick, Erin, 'On this Day: The Ragtag Fleet is Born', *Australian Geographic*, 21 March 2014

Grahamslaw, Tom, 'Recollections of ANGAU', *Pacific Islands Monthly*, May 1971

Hardy, Owen, 'Uncle Sam's Australians', *Motor Boating*, June 1945

Heath, Lenore, 'Australian Yanks Wartime', 59, Winter 2012

Lack, Clem, 'Australia's Merchant Navy', Queensland Historical Society, Proceedings, 24 October 1957

Murray, Leonard, 'Courses and Anchorages: Milne Bay to Buna Coast', Allied Geographic Section, SWPA, 22 October 1942

Price, Arthur, 'Forgotten Fleet Review United Service', 64, March 2013

Reday, Ladislaw, 'The Raggle Taggle Fleet', *Oceans*, November/December 1982

Shindo, Hiroyuki, 'Japanese Air Operations in New Guinea during the Second World War', *AWM Journal*, 34, June 2001

Stephens, Harold, 'Saving the Endangered Music of Bali and the South Pacific', *Frugal Fun*, 30 December 2015

'History of the 2/6th Australian Armoured Regiment', privately published, 1945

Australian War Memorial Records

PR 91/040 Hiseda Akiyoshi

PR 91/061 Shaw Brown

3 DRL/5048   Carfax-Foster Papers

AWM 54 Series

44/1/5   2/6th Armoured Regiment

419/017/012   Carfax-Foster Papers

423/4/99   Captured Japanese diary

577/7/29   Report on Operations in New Guinea No. 14: Report by COSC

581/3/6   COSC G3 to General Chamberlain re immediate action required in Milne Bay/Buna area

581/6/8   History of the Buna Campaign, 1.12.42–25.1.43

581/6/11B 2/5th Field Regiment, Operations, November 1942–February 1943

581/7/2   South-East coast of New Guinea: Supply by sea before, during and after operations at Buna. Prepared at Port Moresby, 10.8.43

581/7/11   Messages between 32nd Division and New Guinea Force, October 1942–January 1943

581/7/20   War Diary of the 107th Quartermaster Company
581/7/34   Operations, 32nd Division, Buna–Sanananda, 19.11.42–22.1.43
917/3/12   Notes on supply operations, Owen Stanleys – Buna 1942
963/22/7   Milne Bay Mutiny

Newspapers/Magazines

Army News	Darwin
Barrier Miner	Broken Hill
Centralian Advocate	Alice Springs
Central Queensland Herald	Rockhampton
Courier-Mail	Brisbane
Daily News	Adelaide
Glen Innes Examiner	New South Wales
Harper's Magazine	New York
Los Angeles Times	California
Milwaukee Journal	Wisconsin
Montreal Gazette	Canada
Muswellbrook Chronicle	New South Wales
Northern Miner	Charters Towers
Northern Territory News	Darwin
Sydney Morning Herald	Sydney
The Advertiser	Adelaide
The Age	Melbourne
The Australian Women's Weekly	National
The Sun	Newcastle
Townsville Daily Bulletin	Townsville
Weekly Times	Melbourne
Williamstown Chronicle	Melbourne

Websites

www.battleforaustralia.org
www.fdrlibrary.marist.edu
www.FrugalFun.com
www.history.army.mil
www.marinebusiness.com.au
www.nautical.asn.au
www.oceannavigator.com
www.pioneerbooks.wordpress.com
www.10thfieldambulance.com
www.32nd-division.org

ACKNOWLEDGEMENTS

While the author's name always appears on the cover of a book, the contents are rarely the result of a single person's efforts and *The Rag Tag Fleet* is not an exception to the rule. I would like to recognise and thank a number of people who helped me bring this story to life. At Hachette Australia, Matthew Kelly first raised the possibility of a story about the US Army's Small Ships Section and has been encouraging and supportive since that initial conversation in 2015. Hachette's Tom Bailey-Smith has been a keen director of the final stages of the book's publication. The editor I was fortunate to work with, Deonie Fiford, has done a wonderful and professional job with what she was given.

My agent, Sarah McKenzie of Hindsight Literary Agency, has been a strong and positive support since I first approached her about helping me further develop a career in the literary world, and I thank both Sarah and Michael Cortis for their forbearance and encouragement.

The Australian US Army Small Ships Association, and its secretary, Dan O'Brien, have been equally supportive over the months of the project, and Dan provided an entrée into the lives of a number of Small Ships' veterans and their families. To all those who gave me a little part of their own, or their loved one's experiences, I offer a heartfelt thank you. In particular, I would like to thank three people and, through them, many others who did not want to be named as they thought they had little or nothing to contribute; they did, and the book is better for that contribution.

Neil Sandery was generous in his sharing of materials about the life, and untimely death, of the father he never knew. Ross Andrews shared a collection of photographs, interviews and personal reminiscences about his uncle, Ralph Andrews, all of it fascinating. Finally, Melville Clarence 'Clarrie' Dawes spoke and wrote at length of his life from the early years at Thevenard through to the present. It has been a life lived well, with due recognition of all he has done only coming in recent years. Clarrie continually reminds me that the designation of his contemporaries, male and female alike, as 'The Greatest Generation' is a worthy accolade.

As always, the Research Centre at the Australian War Memorial, the National Library of Australia and the National Archives provided much valuable material for the book and their staffs continue to make research a pleasure to undertake. The Gladstone Maritime Museum and its helpful and energetic president Lindsay Wassell contributed photographs from their Sheridan Collection to help make the story that little bit more accessible. Thank you to all four institutions.

Finally, to Pamela, our children and our grandchildren, it is your love and support that make it a pleasure to be able to research and write the way I do. May all your dreams come true.

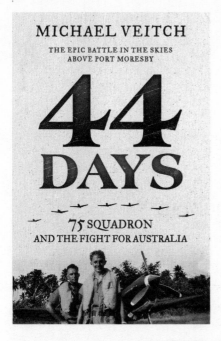

MICHAEL VEITCH

THE EPIC BATTLE IN THE SKIES
ABOVE PORT MORESBY

44
DAYS

75 SQUADRON
AND THE FIGHT FOR AUSTRALIA

MARCH 1942, THE JAPANESE
ARE BOMBING DARWIN
AND ADVANCING TOWARDS
AUSTRALIA THROUGH
NEW GUINEA.

In the midst of this dire military situation, RAAF 75 Squadron was born – and for 44 days these fearless but barely trained pilots fought a desperate battle at Australia's edge. In March and April 1942, the squadron bravely defended Port Moresby when Australia truly stood alone against the Japanese. This group of raw young recruits scrambled ceaselessly in their Kittyhawk fighters to an extraordinary and heroic battle, the story of which has been largely left untold – until now.

The recruits had almost nothing going for them against the Japanese war machine, except for one extraordinary leader named John Jackson, a big laconic Queenslander who said little, led from the front, and who had absolutely no sense of physical fear. Time and time again this brave group were hurled into battle, against all odds and logic, and succeeded in mauling a far superior enemy – whilst also fighting against the air force hierarchy. After a relentless Japanese onslaught, the squadron was almost wiped out by the time relief came . . .

'should be part of Australian military folklore. ★★★★'
—*Adelaide Advertiser*

'Brilliantly researched and sympathetically told, *44 Days* is more than just a fitting tribute to brave but overlooked heroes. It's also a top read.'
—*Daily Telegraph*

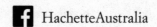
AUSTRALIA

If you would like to find out more about Hachette Australia,
our authors, upcoming events and new releases you can visit
our website or our social media channels:

hachette.com.au

 HachetteAustralia

HachetteAus